I0796808

Wellington's Light Division and the Invasion of Spain

Wellington's Light Division and the Invasion of Spain

The Sieges of 1812

Robert Burnham
and
Ron McGuigan

Frontline Books

First published in Great Britain in 2025 by
Frontline Books
An imprint of Pen & Sword Books Limited
Yorkshire – Philadelphia

ISBN 978 1 39903 688 7

A CIP catalogue record for this book is available from the British Library.

Typeset by Mac Style
Printed in the UK by CPI Group (UK) Ltd, Croydon, CR0 4YY.

The Publisher's authorised representative in the EU for product safety is Authorised Rep Compliance Ltd., Ground Floor, 71 Lower Baggot Street, Dublin D02 P593, Ireland.
www.arccompliance.com

For a complete list of Pen & Sword titles please contact:

PEN & SWORD BOOKS LIMITED
47 Church Street, Barnsley, South Yorkshire, S70 2AS, England
E-mail: enquiries@pen-and-sword.co.uk
Website: www.pen-and-sword.co.uk
or
PEN AND SWORD BOOKS
1950 Lawrence Road, Havertown, PA 19083, USA
E-mail: uspen-and-sword@casematepublishers.com
Website: www.penandswordbooks.com

Contents

Acknowledgments		vi
List of Abbreviations		viii
List of Maps		x
Map Legends		xi
List of Tables		xii
Introduction		xv
Chapter 1	The State of the Light Division in Early January 1812	1
Chapter 2	Trench Warfare January 1812	18
Chapter 3	The Assault on Ciudad Rodrigo	40
Chapter 4	The Sack of Ciudad Rodrigo	58
Chapter 5	Light Division Casualties During the Siege of Ciudad Rodrigo	69
Chapter 6	Winter Quarters 21 January–25 February 1812	80
Chapter 7	The Road to Badajoz	90
Chapter 8	The Siege of Badajoz 17 March–5 April 1812	99
Chapter 9	The Taking of Badajoz 5 April–7 April 1812	123
Chapter 10	The Aftermath of the Assault 7 April–9 April 1812	146
Chapter 11	Light Division Casualties at Badajoz	161
Chapter 12	The Return to Ciudad Rodrigo 9 April–30 April 1812	182
Chapter 13	What Happened to Them	196
Appendix I: Strength of the Light Division's British Units January–April 1812		204
Appendix II: Strength of the 1st and 3rd Caçadores January–April 1812		209
Appendix III: Major General Craufurd's Funeral		213
Bibliography		216
Index		220

Acknowledgments

One of the pleasures of writing this book is the support I receive from my fellow historians with my research. Without their help this book would have been much more difficult to write. In alphabetical order there are: Steve Brown, my friend from down under, who has provided much of the biographical data on the soldiers in this book. Dr Michael Crumplin, whose insights into the military medicine of the Napoleonic Wars were instrumental to my understanding of how casualties were treated during the two sieges. Jonas De Neef and Daniel Studer, whose knowledge of French databases was essential to me being able to find the names of French officers. Moisés Gaudêncio, whose knowledge of the Portuguese Army Archives enabled me to provide the Portuguese perspective of the sieges, which is often missing in similar works on the sieges. John Gill, who helped me by finding and translating accounts by the Germans who helped defend Badajoz. Gareth Glover, who has discovered and edited the many new Light Division primary sources that are essential to this book. Mark Thompson, the leading expert on the British Royal Engineers and sieges during the Napoleonic Wars. He patiently answered my many questions and shared with me unpublished diaries of the sieges, photos of the walls and the cities, and once again designed all the maps used in this book. Zack White, of the Napoleonic Wars Podcast, was also there to answer my numerous questions on the legal system of the British Army of the time. Then there are the members of the Napoleonic Wars Forum who never failed to help me when I hit a roadblock in my research. Foremost among them was Tom Holmberg. Thank you all for your help! I must also thank noted military artist, Christa Hook, for her permission to use her evocative painting 'In Hell before Daylight, Badajoz' that captures so well the chaos of the assault. Finally, I must thank the State Library of South Australia, the State Library of New South Wales, the Anne S.K. Brown Military Collection, and the King's Own Royal Regiment Museum Trust for the use of images from their collections. I must of course thank my wife Denah, who has patiently sat through my recounting of the tales of the soldiers who feature so prominently in this book!

Robert Burnham

I thank Bob for asking me to again join him in writing Volume 3. I am honoured. I second our thank you to all those who generously gave of their time and research. It is appreciated. As always, I thank my wife Debbie for her support and understanding.

Ron McGuigan

List of Abbreviations

AAG: Assistant Adjutant General
ACG: Assistant Commissary General
ADC: Aide-de-Camp
Adj: Adjutant
Adj Sgt : Adjutant Sergeant
AGC: Army Gold Cross
AGM: Army Gold Medal
AS: Assistant Surgeon
AWOL: Absent Without Leave
BD: Bandmaster
BH: Sick but With the Battalion
BM: Bugle Major
Bn: Battalion
Bu: Bugler
Bvt LTC: Brevet Lieutenant Colonel
Bvt Maj: Brevet Major
Caç: Caçadores
CB: Companion of the Most Honourable Order of the Bath
CH: Chaplain
Cor: Coronheiro: An Artificer Who Worked on Maintaining the Musket's Wooden Parts
Cpt: Captain
DAAG: Deputy Assistant Adjutant General
DAQMG: Deputy Assistant Quartermaster General
Det: Detached
DoW: Died of Wounds
Dr: Drummer
Ens: Ensign
Esp: Espingadeiro: An Artificer Who Worked on Maintaining the Musket's Metal Parts
Fur: Furriel: A Junior Sergeant. This Rank Did Not Exist in the British Army

GCB:	Grand Cross of the Most Honourable Order of the Bath
GO:	General Order
Hos:	Sick in Army Hospital
HQ:	Headquarters
KCB:	Knight Commander of the Most Honourable Order of the Bath
KGL:	The King's German Legion
KIA:	Killed in Action
km:	Kilometre (s)
Leave:	Authorised Absence
LT:	Lieutenant
LTC:	Lieutenant Colonel
LW:	Left Wing
Maj:	Major
Maj Gen:	Major General
MGSM:	Military General Service Medal
MIA:	Missing in Action
MUS:	Musician: Who Formed the Battalion's Band
NA:	Not Available
NCO:	Non-Commissioned Officer
OR:	Other Ranks
Pay:	Paymaster
PFD:	Present for Duty
QM:	Quartermaster
QMG:	Quartermaster General
QMS:	Quartermaster Sergeant
RW:	Right Wing
Sgt:	Sergeant
Sur:	Surgeon
WIA:	Wounded in Action
2Cpt:	Second Captain
1LT:	First Lieutenant
2LT:	Second Lieutenant
£:	Pounds

List of Maps

Light Division During the Siege of Ciudad Rodrigo January 1812 25
Assault on Ciudad Rodrigo 19 January 1812 39
Wall Profile at Ciudad Rodrigo 47
The March to and From Badajoz 1812 89
Badajoz: Picurina Fort Profile 112
Assault of Badajoz 6 April 1812 122

Map Legends

Light (XX)	Light Division
1 (X)	1st Brigade Light Division
2 (X)	2nd Brigade Light Division
1 (II) 43	1st Battalion 43rd Foot
1 (II) 52	1st Battalion 52nd Foot
2 (II) 52	2nd Battalion 52nd Foot
LW 1 (II) 95	Left Wing 1st Bn 95th Rifles
RW 1 (II) 95	Right Wing 1st Bn 95th Rifles
RW 3 (II) 95	Right Wing 3rd Bn 95th Rifles
1 (II) Caç	1st Caçadores Battalion
3 (II) Caç	3rd Caçadores Battalion

List of Tables

Table 1.1	Number of Officers Serving on the Staff on 31 December 1811	5
Table 1.2	Number of Officers on Home Leave on 31 December 1811	5
Table 1.3	Number of Officers Present for Duty in the Light Division's Battalions in December 1811	6
Table 1.4	Light Division Casualties February 1810–December 1811	7
Table 1.5	Total Number of Other Ranks Sick Per Unit on 25 December 1811	7
Table 1.6	Total of All Ranks With the Colours	10
Table 1.7	Attrition of Officers in the 1st Battalion 95th Rifles From January 1810–December 1811	13
Table 2.1	Organisation 1 January 1812	19
Table 2.2	Number of Other Ranks on Command 24 December 1811	20
Table 2.3	Price Paid for Each Item Made	20
Table 2.4	Amount of Engineer Material Needed	20
Table 2.5	Work Schedule for the Building of the Siege Works	24
Table 2.6	Location of the Light Division Cantonments During the Siege of Ciudad Rodrigo	24
Table 2.7	The Light Division Assault Force on the Renaud Redoubt 8 January 1812	28
Table 2.8	Light Division Casualties at the Assault on the Renaud Redoubt 8 January 1812	32
Table 2.9	The 3rd Caçadores Casualties 8 January–18 January 1812	39
Table 5.1	The 3rd Caçadores Casualties During the Assault on Ciudad Rodrigo 19 January–20 January 1812	71
Table 5.2	Light Division Casualties From 8 January–20 January 1812	72
Table 6.1	Organisation 21 January 1812	80
Table 6.2	Location of the Light Division 31 January 1812	83
Table 7.1	Number of Light Division Officers as Shown in the February 1812 Theatre Returns	91

Table 7.2	Number of Officers That Are Named as With the Battalion in February 1812 Theatre Returns	91
Table 7.3	Light Division Strength 1 March 1812	92
Table 7.4	Organisation of the Light Division 1 March 1812	92
Table 8.1	French Garrison of Badajoz 16 March 1812	100
Table 8.2	Light Division Work Schedule During the Siege of Badajoz 17 March–5 April 1812	104
Table 9.1	Light Division Troops Available for the Assault on 6 April 1812	129
Table 11.1	Light Division Casualties During the Siege of Badajoz 17 March–6 April 1812	161
Table 11.2	Light Division Officer Casualties During the Siege of Badajoz 17 March–6 April 1812	162
Table 11.3	Status of the Light Division's Severely Wounded Officers in the British Battalions	162
Table 11.4	British Regiments Officers Killed or Severely Wounded and Returned to England (RTE)	163
Table 11.5	The 43rd Foot Casualties 17 March–6 April 1812	164
Table 11.6	The 43rd Foot Officer Casualties 17 March–6 April 1812	164
Table 11.7	The 52nd Foot Casualties 17 March–5 April 1812	169
Table 11.8	The 52nd Foot Casualties 6 April 1812	169
Table 11.9	The 52nd Foot Casualties 17 March–6 April 1812	169
Table 11.10	The 52nd Foot Officer Casualties 17 March–6 April 1812	169
Table 11.11	The 1st Battalion 95th Rifles Officer Casualties 17 March–6 April 1812	174
Table 11.12	The 2nd Battalion 95th Rifles Casualties 17 March–6 April 1812	177
Table 11.13	The 3rd Battalion 95th Rifles Casualties 17 March–6 April 1812	177
Table 11.14	The 3rd Battalion 95th Rifles Officer Casualties 17 March–6 April 1812	177
Table 11.15	The 1st and 3rd Caçadores Casualties During the Siege of Badajoz 17 March–5 April 1812	179
Table 11.16	The 1st and 3rd Caçadores Casualties During the Assault on Badajoz 6 April 1812	179
Table 11.17	Total Casualties the 1st and 3rd Caçadores Casualties at Badajoz 17 March–6 April 1812	179
Table 12.1	The March North 11 April–26 April 1812	183
Table 12.2	Organisation of the Light Division 30 April 1812	184

Table 12.3	Strength of the Light Division 25 April 1812 Based on Theatre Returns	185
Table 12.4	Strength of the Light Division 25 April 1812 Based on Payrolls and Officer Casualties	187
Table 12.5	Number of Officers Authorised Versus Number Present for Duty (PFD) 25 April 1812	189
Table 12.6	Officer Experience in the 43rd Foot 25 April 1812	190
Table 12.7	Officer Experience in the 52nd Foot 25 April 1812	190
Table 12.8	Officer Experience in the 1st Battalion 95th Rifles 25 April 1812	191
Table 12.9	Officer Experience in the 3rd Battalion 95th Rifles 25 April 1812	191
Table 12.10	Officer Experience in the 1st and 3rd Caçadores 25 April 1812	192
Table 12.11	Officer Losses From 1 January 1812–25 April 1812	194
Table AI.1	1st Battalion 43rd Foot January–April 1812	206
Table AI.2	1st Battalion 52nd Foot January–April 1812	206
Table AI.3	2nd Battalion 52nd Foot January–February 1812	207
Table AI.4	1st Battalion 95th Rifles January–April 1812	207
Table AI.5	2nd Battalion 95th Rifles January–April 1812	208
Table AI.6	Right Wing 3rd Battalion 95th Rifles January–April 1812	208
Table AII.1	1st Caçadores January–April 1812	211
Table AII.2	3rd Caçadores January–April 1812	212

Introduction

This is the third volume in a planned five-volume history of the Light Division during the Peninsular War.[1] Like the first two volumes, Volume 3 is based on eight volumes of previously unpublished or rare primary sources, that were published in the past five years.[2] As importantly, we have drawn extensively on the Portuguese Army Archives for never published before material on the Portuguese Army. This information, including strength and casualty reports, sheds light on the key role the 1st and 3rd Caçadores played in the successes of the division.

Our goal was to devote each volume to one of the five years that the Light Division was in existence. This would allow us to provide an in-depth chronology of the division's activities instead of just covering its major battles. We started writing Volume 3 with the intention of following the same format. After researching the first four months of 1812, when the Light Division was heavily involved in the sieges of Ciudad Rodrigo and Badajoz, we realised how much we did not know. So, we spent several months looking for answers. We wanted to know more than just what the division did during the assault, but such things as how the days in the siege lines affected the men. What was their work schedule? Was the whole division employed every day? What was it like to ford a chest deep river in the middle of winter and then have to work twelve hours in the trenches without a chance to dry your clothes? What was it like to climb a breach? How did the French and their allies defend the breaches? Was the Light Division involved in the sack of both cities? What steps did the division's officers take to stop it? What were the division's casualties during the sieges? How did they affect the leadership, morale, and discipline of the division? How did it affect the ability of the division in the upcoming campaigns of 1812?

The questions seemed endless. We not only scoured hundreds of letters, diaries, and memoirs, written by the division's officers and soldiers, we also accessed

1. Volume 1: *Wellington's Light Division in the Peninsular War: The Formation, Campaigns & Battles of Wellington's Famous Fighting Force, 1810*. Volume 2: *Wellington's Light Division and the Defence of Portugal: The Battles of 1811*. Frontline Books published both volumes.
2. These were found and transcribed by Robert Burnham and Gareth Glover. They include many diaries and hundreds of pages of letters. Four volumes were published by Frontline Books and four by Ken Trotman. These books are listed in the bibliography at the end of this book.

unpublished British Royal Engineers primary sources, as well as French and German ones. We had so much new information we decided to end the book after the Siege of Badajoz and move the campaigns of 1812 to Volume 4.

As in our previous volumes, we do not censor the material we find in our primary sources. While showing how the Light Division earned its well-deserved reputation of courage and innovation that made it the elite of Wellington's Army, we also write about things that are too often ignored in other histories. The first four months of 1812 was a crucial time for the Light Division. Its discipline began to break down and for the first time the primary sources openly wrote of desertion, flogging, and even execution of its soldiers. We could have chosen to ignore it, but as ugly as these stories are, they are as much of its history as the tales of its valour.

Chapter 1

The State of the Light Division in Early January 1812

The Light Division was formed in February 1810 with the mission of screening Wellington's Army along an 85-km long front in vicinity of the Spanish fortress city of Ciudad Rodrigo. To accomplish this, it initially had five infantry battalions, a light cavalry regiment, and a troop of Royal Horse Artillery. Its performance over the next five months earned it the reputation of being one of the premier fighting forces of the Napoleonic Wars. Its reputation was cemented in history by its actions throughout 1811. In the first twenty-two months of its existence, the Light Division fought in three major battles,[1] five minor battles,[2] two actions,[3] and innumerable skirmishes. It was part of the rear guard during an epic 360km retreat from the Spanish border to the vicinity of Lisbon in the autumn of 1810 and in the advance guard five months later when they pursued the French army as it retreated to Spain. If that was not enough, two other times the division was poised to fight against unknown odds, before Wellington intervened and stopped it.[4]

As impressive as this list is, it only tells part of their story. Since February 1810, the division spent eighteen of those months either on outpost duty or part of the rear / advance guard. While on the outpost duty, they were on call twenty-four hours a day seven days a week. To prevent being surprised well before dawn, the soldiers who were not manning the outposts broke down their billets, packed up everything they owned, and stood to in case the enemy decided to attack. A few hours later they were either released from the ranks or were marched off to a new location. In October 1810, after serving in the rear guard, they entered the Lines of Torres Vedras, just north of Lisbon. There in the relative security of the fortifications, they were allowed to rest. For some it was the first time they had removed their uniforms in over a year. Their respite lasted five weeks, but then word reached Wellington that the French

1. Bussaco, Sabugal, and Fuentes de Oñoro.
2. Côa River, Pombal, Redinha, Casal Novo, and Foz de Arouce.
3. Barba del Puerco and Villa de Puerco.
4. Mortágua and Cartaxo.

had retreated 50km northeast to Santarem. The Light Division was ordered to follow them and once again they were manning outposts.

The division's new area of responsibility was a few kilometres south of Santarem and the conditions were harsh. It was wintertime and it rained every day. The villages and farms that they would normally be billeted in, had been devastated by French foragers. There was little fuel for their fires to dry their wet uniforms and cook their food. Furthermore, many of the buildings were missing their doors, shutters, and furniture that had been used to feed fires. On 6 March, the division's outposts notified their chain of command that the French had left. Wellington was quick to order a pursuit and over the next four weeks they hounded the French out of Portugal. The Light Division was in the advance guard and occasionally the French would stop to fight. At one point, the Light Division fought in four minor battles in six days. It was not long before the pursuit turned into a series of advances and halts. Not because the division was not willing to follow the French, but it had moved so quickly, its supply train could not keep up. Several times they were forced to halt for a day because they had run out of food and were short of ammunition.

In early April, Wellington had caught the French rear guard at Sabugal and the Light Division was in the thick of the fighting. There the French were forced to retreat after taking heavy casualties. Having stopped briefly in the vicinity of Ciudad Rodrigo, the bulk of the French army then moved on to Salamanca. After the French departed, the Light Division resumed its outpost duties just to the east of Fuentes de Oñoro. It was there in early May, the division fought in a battle to prevent the French from supplying its garrison in Almeida. On the third day of the battle, the division added to its laurels by conducting a fighting withdrawal over 5km while threatened by 2,000 French cavalry.

After the battle, there was no rest for the weary. The Light Division once again resumed the outposts until mid-June when it received orders to march 300km south to assist with the Siege of Badajoz. The route took them through the mountains of eastern Portugal. Shortly after their arrival, the siege was called off, but the Light Division stayed in the south for two months. It bivouacked in the open under horrible conditions. The weather was extremely hot, and water was scarce. Compounding their misery, Guadiana fever, a form of tertian malaria, was endemic to the area. By mid-July, 17 per cent of the British troops in the division were hospitalised with an unknown fever. Although the disease was usually not fatal, those who caught it would have recurrent bouts of it for months afterwards. Adding to its problems, the supply system set up to feed them in the north was not able to adjust to their sudden movement to the south and by July the division was on short rations again.

In late July, the Light Division was ordered north and by mid-August were within 25km of Ciudad Rodrigo. There they set up a loose line of outposts. The next three months were spent responding to French foraging parties from the city and four times it was called out to intercept the monthly convoy sent to resupply the fortress.[5]

In late November the division was relieved of its outpost duties and went into winter quarters. Moving from the south to the healthier northern region should have seen a drop in the sick rate, but by October, 26 per cent of the division's corporals and privates were hospitalised. By the end of the year the number had dropped slightly, but one soldier in five was still in the hospital. During this time preparations were being made to besiege Ciudad Rodrigo early in the coming year. Thousands of tonnes of supplies had to be moved from depots far in the rear to locations close to the city. To do this, carts and waggons were requisition from their normal duties of moving food to feed the forward deployed divisions, including the ones for the Light Division. Before long, the division was on short rations again, which did not help the sick to recover nor the soldiers to regain their strength. Twenty-two months of being on the sharp end had taken its toll.

The Senior Leadership

The senior officers were not immune to the hardships and danger. By the end of 1810, the division's commander, Major General Robert Craufurd, was physically and mentally exhausted. He went on home leave in January and only returned to the division on 4 May. He arrived just in time to lead the division on the final day of the Battle of Fuentes de Oñoro but missed the pursuit of the French from Portugal. Its brigade commanders also fell to wounds and disease. In early August 1810, Lieutenant Colonel Thomas Beckwith of the 1st Battalion 95th Rifles was appointed the commander of the newly formed 1st Brigade, and Lieutenant Colonel Robert Barclay, of the 1st Battalion 52nd Foot, took command of the newly formed 2nd Brigade. Lieutenant Colonel Barclay arrived in the Peninsula with his battalion in early July 1809, part of Craufurd's Light Brigade that would form the nucleus of the Light Division. He commanded his battalion until he was appointed the commander of the 2nd Brigade. He was wounded at Bussaco on 27 September 1810. His wound would not heal, and he returned to England in October 1810 and died of his wounds on 3 May 1811. He was replaced by Brevet Colonel James Wynch, the commander of the 4th Foot, on 4 November 1810. Wynch died of typhus

5. They never caught one.

on 6 January 1811, two months after taking command. Wynch was replaced by Brevet Colonel George Drummond of the 24th Foot on 7 February 1811. Drummond commanded the 2nd Brigade throughout the campaigns of 1811, but died of a severely inflamed throat, often caused by strep throat or diphtheria, on 8 September 1811. On 30 September, Major General John Ormsby Vandeleur was assigned to the division and took command of the 2nd Brigade. He was not a logical choice to command a light infantry brigade, because he was a light cavalry officer and had not served in the infantry since 1792.

The 1st Brigade had one commander in its first year. Lieutenant Colonel Beckwith of the 1st Battalion 95th Rifles had been with the Light Brigade when it landed in Lisbon in July 1809 and with the Light Division since it was formed. He fought in all the battles and campaigns of 1810 and 1811, but by August 1811 he was exhausted after twenty-five months of active service. He requested a medical board to determine his fitness, so he could go home to rest. Instead, Wellington sent him to England on leave, knowing that if a medical board found Beckwith unfit, he would have to permanently replace him with a general. If he placed him on temporary leave, Wellington could hold the position open until Beckwith returned. This pretense allowed him to appoint Lieutenant Colonel Andrew Barnard, of the 3rd Battalion 95th Rifles, the temporary commander of the 1st Brigade. Barnard, a very junior lieutenant colonel, had less than three years' time in grade. He had been part of the British force at Cádiz and was seriously wounded at Barossa on 5 March 1811. He was the senior lieutenant colonel in the division, but other than the one battle five months before, he had not been on campaign in twelve years.

The Battalions

The British Army of the Napoleonic Wars had no permanent division or brigade structure. When the government decided to send an army overseas it would create the army from scratch and decide the subordinate structure it would have, usually by setting up divisions and brigades. Commanders of each unit would be named and then the army would decide what battalions would be in each brigade. Once the war or expedition was over, the divisions and brigades would be disbanded, and the battalions would return to their barracks.

Unlike twenty-first-century armies, the British Army of the early 1800s had very few permanent staff officers to fill the necessary staff at the newly formed army headquarters or on the division or brigade staffs. Instead, these positions would be manned by officers drawn from the infantry battalions and cavalry regiments. Army regulations prohibited more than two captains and two subalterns from a regiment from serving in a staff position outside of the regiment. These regulations also prohibited an officer from serving on the staff before he had at least four years of service.[6] These restrictions were usually followed, but a regimental colonel could give permission for additional officers to be drawn from the regiment for staff duty. This was supposed to keep the higher headquarters from weakening the command structure of its subordinate units by taking officers from the battalions to fill their staffs. In theory this should have worked. The reality was much different.

By the end of 1811, the Light Division's four British battalions had twenty-three (17 per cent) of its officers[7] serving outside of their battalions on the staff.

Table 1.1: Number of Officers Serving on the Staff on 31 December 1811

Unit	LTC	Maj	Cpt	LT	Ens/2LT	Total
1st Bn 43rd Foot	-	-	1	4	2	7
1st Bn 52nd Foot	-	-	2	2	-	4
2nd Bn 52nd Foot	-	1	1	3	-	5
1st Bn 95th Foot (8 Companies)	1	-	2	4	-	7
Total	**1**	**1**	**6**	**13**	**2**	**23**

The need to fill staff billets was not the only cause of officer shortages at the battalion level. After going into winter quarters in November 1811, home leave was granted for some officers.

Table 1.2: Number of Officers on Home Leave on 31 December 1811

Unit	LTC	Maj	Cpt	LT	Ens/2LT	Total
1st Bn 43rd Foot	-	-	4	2	1	7
1st Bn 52nd Foot	1	1	1	2	3	8
2nd Bn 52nd Foot	-	-	-	1	-	1
1st Bn 95th Foot (8 Companies)	-	1	-	2	-	3
Total	**1**	**2**	**5**	**7**	**4**	**19**

Officers were also sick or on duty away from the battalion. When combined with those on home leave and on the staff, the division was missing a quarter of its officers in the battalions. Notably absent were the senior officers. Half of the lieutenant colonels and four of the eleven majors were elsewhere. All of this

6. *General Regulations and Orders for the Army*, London: Adjutant General's Office, 1811, p.29.
7. These numbers do not include the battalion's staff officers, such as the adjutant, quartermaster and surgeon.

had a trickle-down effect. A battalion that did not have a lieutenant colonel would be commanded by its senior major. Since every British battalion was short one major, when the senior major took command, the two senior captains would assume the duties of the majors. The senior lieutenants would replace them. It did not matter when the battalion was in cantonments, however for the upcoming campaign season, a lieutenant would command fifteen of the fifty-seven companies.

Table 1.3: Number of Officers Present for Duty in the Light Division's Battalions in December 1811[8]

Unit	LTC	Maj	Cpt	LT	Ens	Total	Number Short	Per Cent of Authorised Strength
1st Bn 43rd Foot	1	1	6	13	3	24	19	56%
1st Bn 52nd Foot	0	1	9	17	9	36	7	84%
2nd Bn 52nd Foot	1	1	7	16	1	26	17	60%
1st Bn 95th Foot (8 Companies)	0	1	7	16	6	30	6	83%
2nd Bn 95th Foot (2 Companies)	NA	NA	2	4	1	7	1	88%
3rd Bn 95th Foot (5 Companies)	NA	1	6	11	4	22	0	100%
1st Caç Bn	0	2	4	5	5	16	10	62%
3rd Caç Bn	1	1	5	6	4	17	9	65%
Total	3	8	46	88	33	178	69	72%

The Strength of the Battalions

By the end of 1811, the Light Division's battalions were badly understrength.

Almost two years of fighting and marching had taken its toll. Its losses in battle were just under 900 men.

However, these numbers only represent combat losses. What devastated the ranks was not combat, but disease exacerbated by exhaustion, living rough, and often going hungry. The Light Division saw no combat since early May 1811, so by December the men who died or were hospitalised were mostly from disease. Among the other ranks, for every two soldiers who were killed in action or died from his wounds three died from disease or sickness. In October, the numbers of hospitalised soldiers peaked at 1,337, which was 26 per cent of the

8. The number does not include staff officers such as the adjutant and quartermaster. It includes agregado officers.

Table 1.4: Light Division Casualties February 1810–December 1811

	Officers				Enlisted				
Unit	KIA/ DoW	WIA	MIA	Total	KIA/ DoW	WIA	MIA	Total	Total
1st Bn 43rd Foot	4	18	-	**22**	30	160	13	**203**	**225**
1st Bn 52nd Foot	1	14	-	**15**	20	141	4	**165**	**180**
2nd Bn 52nd Foot	-	-	-	**-**	-	7	-	**7**	**7**
1st Bn 95th Rifles (8 Companies)	7	14	1	**22**	29	108	53	**190**	**212**
2nd Bn 95th Rifles (2 Companies)	-	1	-	**1**	4	4	-	**8**	**9**
1st Caç	-	2	-	**2**	5	72	7	**84**	**86**
3rd Caç	-	7	-	**7**	40	121	4	**165**	**172**
Total	**12**	**56**	**1**	**69**	**128**	**613**	**81**	**822**	**891**

other ranks! By the end of 1811, after being in winter quarters for almost two months, where they rested in comfortable billets away from the disease ridden south, 20 per cent of the other ranks were still hospitalised.

Table 1.5: Total Number of Other Ranks Sick Per Unit on 25 December 1811

Unit	Total Other Rank Strength	In Hospital	Per Cent of Strength	Dead in Last Month	Dead in Past 6 Months
1st Bn 43rd Foot	1,176	208	18%	16	54
1st Bn 52nd Foot	850	166	20%	7	37
2nd Bn 52nd Foot	555	223	40%	20	64
1st Bn 95th Rifles (8 Companies)	702	113	16%	5	26
2nd Bn 95th Rifles (2 Companies)	185	36	19%	2	5
3rd Bn 95th Rifles (5 Companies)	375	109	29%	13	29[9]
1st Caç	550	78	14%	2	5[10]
3rd Caç	538	49	9%	4	10[11]
Total	**4,931**	**982**	**20%**	**69**	**230**[12]

9. Figures are only for August–December 1811.
10. Figures were only available for the last three months in 1811.
11. Figures were only available for the last three months in 1811.
12. This is 5 per cent of the total other rank strength.

How the Battalions Received Replacements

At the beginning of the nineteenth century many British infantry regiments were authorised two battalions. In theory the 1st Battalion would be sent on active service, and the 2nd Battalion stayed in the garrison, recruited new soldiers, and trained them in preparation of joining the 1st Battalion. When the 2nd Battalion was notified that the 1st Battalion needed replacements, it would take the best trained and physically fit soldiers from its ranks and send them out to the 1st Battalion. They would then start the recruiting and training cycle again to be ready when the next call for replacements was received. As the war progressed there was a greater need for battalions to go on active service. By 1808, the 2nd Battalions were often deployed, and the replacement system began to break down.

After 1809, the three British regiments in the Light Division each had a different system for supplying replacements. The 43rd Foot kept to the old method. Its 2nd Battalion took part in the Walcheren expedition of 1809, but upon its return to England in October, it stayed at home and served as the recruiting and training battalion to keep the 1st Battalion up to strength. The 52nd Foot took a different approach. It was authorised to have a recruiting company in each of its two battalions and these companies were responsible for recruiting and training replacements.

The 95th Rifles was a three-battalion regiment by the summer of 1809. Each battalion was responsible for recruiting and training its own men. Unlike the other two regiments, the 95th Rifles rarely deployed in battalion strength. They were mostly sent out in groups of two or three companies and would occasionally join up with other companies already in the theatre of operations. The deployment of all ten companies of the 1st Battalion as part of Craufurd's Light Brigade in the spring of 1809 was the only time during the Napoleonic Wars the 95th Rifles deployed a ten-company battalion. By the spring of 1810, the 1st Battalion had lost so many men to disease and combat it had trouble maintaining its strength. With no replacements in sight, the battalion commander reduced the battalion to eight companies and brought the remaining companies up to strength by taking the necessary officers, sergeants, musicians, and other ranks from the two companies going home and sending the excess officers and sergeants back to England to recruit replacements. The 1st Battalion would never again have more than eight companies in the Peninsula.

Some replacements were sent out in 1811. The 43rd Foot was the only British unit in the Light Division to receive a large number of replacements in two years. In July 1811, 14 officers and 343 enlisted soldiers arrived to fill its ranks. They included 1 major, 3 captains, 8 lieutenants, 2 ensigns, 6 sergeants, a drummer, and 336 other ranks. It was the strongest battalion in the Light Division.

At the formation of the Light Division in February 1810, the 1st Battalion 52nd Foot had 1,047 other ranks; by the end of 1811 it was down to 850. It had received no replacements for the other ranks who were killed, died, or sent home broken in health. Instead, the 2nd Battalion 52nd Foot was sent to the division in March 1811. It came with 562 other ranks and received 58 replacements over the next 9 months. However, it had participated in the Walcheren campaign, where many of its men had been exposed to a deadly mix of typhus and malaria. Their weakened constitutions could not stand up to the rigours of campaigning in the Peninsula and by the end of 1811, 40 per cent of the other ranks were hospitalised.

The 1st Battalion 95th Rifles received no replacements since it deployed to the Peninsula in July 1809. It kept its companies up to strength by sending home the officers and NCOs from two companies in April 1810 and drafting the other ranks into the remaining eight companies. Attrition continued to mount and in 1811 the battalion had fifty-five men die from combat, disease, or exhaustion and another forty-eight sent home broken in health. Each company was authorised 101 other ranks (6 corporals and 95 riflemen), but by December 1811, the battalion was down to 702 other ranks or 88 men per company. However, due to hospitalisations and soldiers on command, the battalion could only field 578 other ranks, or 72 soldiers per company.

The 2 companies of the 2nd Battalion 95th Rifles were authorised 113 officers and men: 1 captain, 2 lieutenants, 1 second lieutenant, 6 sergeants, 6 corporals, 2 buglers, and 95 riflemen each. One company joined the division in September 1810, and the other joined in September 1810. They were at 92 per cent of authorised strength, but due to hospitalisations they would be only able to field 75 per cent of its officers and men.

The 3rd Battalion 95th Rifles started 1811 with only one company in the division but in August Lieutenant Colonel Andrew Barnard arrived from Cádiz with four additional companies. The four companies had fought in the Barrosa campaign in March 1811 but remained in the garrison at Cádiz until ordered to join the Light Division in July. The battalion had trouble adjusting to the rigours of life along the Portuguese–Spanish border and by October had 173 (43 per cent) of its other ranks in the hospital. By the end of the year the health of the battalion had slightly improved, with only 109 men hospitalised, but in the same period 20 men of its men had died. The five companies could only field fifty men each.

The situation with the division's two caçadore battalions was a bit different. Conscription was the main source of replacements. The 1st Caçadores received conscripts from Beira, and the 3rd Caçadores from Trás-os-Montes. Finding replacements was not difficult, despite the fact they were competing with infantry and cavalry regiments who also recruited in the same provinces. Conscription was unpopular and since the two battalions were relatively close to the conscripts' homes it led to a higher rate of desertion than the British. By the end of 1811, the two battalions were each at 98 per cent of their authorised strength. The 1st Caçadores had 600 other ranks, but sickness and desertion kept them from fielding full strength companies. At the end of 1811, the battalion reported seventy-eight men in the hospital and sixty deserters in the past two months. The battalion could only muster 387 other ranks leaving the companies at 65 per cent strength. The companies were authorised a captain, a lieutenant, and two ensigns. All the companies were short of officers. Four of the companies had three officers, but two had only two officers. A captain commanded five of its six companies, and all had a lieutenant, but none had more than one ensign. The battalion was short of four sergeants, but every company had at least five of the six it was authorised and two had the six.

The 3rd Caçadores was healthier and had very few deserters compared to the 1st Caçadores. At the end of the year, they reported only forty-eight men in the hospital and four deserters. It had 468 other ranks fit for duty or 78 per cent of its authorised total. Like the 1st Caçadores, it too was short officers at the company level, with five of its six companies being commanded by a captain, with each having a lieutenant, but none had more than one ensign. It was also short four sergeants. Based solely on per cent of authorised strength, the 3rd Caçadores had the second highest per cent of its men with the colours of any unit in the Light Division.

Table 1.6: Total of All Ranks With the Colours

Unit	With the Colours	Per Cent of Authorised Strength
1st Bn 43rd Foot	1,043	91%
1st Bn 52nd Foot	768	67%
2nd Bn 52nd Foot	415	44%
1st Bn 95th Rifles (8 Companies)	675	73%
2nd Bn 95th Rifles (2 Companies)	167	75%
3rd Bn 95th Rifles (5 Companies)	327	69%
1st Caç	465	67%
3rd Caç	550	79%
Total	**4,410**	**71%**

Experience of the Battalions

Although the number of men with the colours is very important, equally so is the experience of the officers and enlisted soldiers. Were they combat veterans? How many skirmishes and battles had they fought in? Were they hardened campaigners who knew how to take care of themselves or would the shortage of food and water, the miserable living conditions, and the exposure to disease and illness, kill them or wear them out?

The 43rd Foot was the strongest battalion in the division, however about 25 per cent of its strength were replacements that had arrived in July. These replacements were a combination of new recruits and men who survived the diseases of the Walcheren campaign two years previous. The replacements had about six months to acclimatise themselves to life in the Light Division before the 1812 campaign began. The rest of the battalion were seasoned campaigners and veterans of numerous battles and skirmishes. The past two years, however, had taken a toll on its officers. All had at least six months campaign experience, but only fifteen of the officers who came to Portugal with the battalion in 1809 were still with it. Its commander, Lieutenant Colonel Charles McLeod was with the battalion when it arrived in Portugal in July 1809 and he took command of it after its commander was killed at the Côa River on 24 July 1810. McLeod went on home leave in December 1810 and did not return until mid-May 1811, having missed all the battles of 1811. Major Joseph Wells was the only major in the battalion. He had been with the battalion since its arrival in Portugal. He was a very junior major, having been promoted in October 1811. The battalion had only six captains to command its companies. Three of them had been with the battalion since July 1809, and another joined it in July 1810. All four of them were experienced campaigners and had fought in numerous battles. The other two captains arrived in July 1811. Both had fought during the 1809 retreat to Corunna but had not been back to the Peninsula since. The battalion had twenty-nine of the thirty lieutenants and ensigns it was authorised; however, only eight of them had been in Portugal since 1809. Unlike the enlisted soldiers, of whom 75 per cent were combat veterans, only twenty of the officers had seen combat.

On paper the 1st Battalion 52nd Foot also looked very strong. It had not received any replacements since it arrived in Portugal in July 1809. Although not as heavily engaged as the 43rd Foot, it still lost 198 soldiers due to combat, disease, or exhaustion; 139 had died and the rest were sent home broken in health. After peaking at 225 soldiers in the hospital in October, the number had been reduced to 166 by December. Between those in the hospital and those on detached duty elsewhere, the battalion could only field 650 other ranks. Although this was only two thirds of what the 43rd Foot could field, these soldiers were all survivors of thirty months of campaigning – experienced in both combat and enduring the hardships of life in the field. Of its forty-three officers, all but three ensigns were combat veterans; 50 per cent of the officers had been with the battalion since July 1809, another three had joined in September 1810, and 40 per cent of the officers had arrived in March 1811. By December, the 52nd Foot's two battalions had exchanged many of its officers. The 1st Battalion received one major, two captains, seven lieutenants, and five ensigns from the 2nd Battalion and sent the 2nd Battalion one major, three captains, and four lieutenants. Six of the officers that the 2nd Battalion received had been in the country since 1809 and two for about a year. The real weakness among the 1st Battalion's officers was its senior leadership. The battalion had been commanded by Lieutenant Colonel Hugh Arbuthnott, who went on home leave in November 1811. The battalion had two majors, John Hunt and George Napier. Hunt went on home leave in December and Napier was still recovering from his wounds received the previous March. Major Edward Gibbs transferred to the 1st Battalion in December and took command of it. Gibbs had fought at Sabugal and Fuentes de Oñoro but missed the battles prior to Sabugal. The shortage of senior officers was offset by its nine company commanders. All were veterans of the 1809 Corunna campaign, while six had been with the battalion since it arrived in Portugal in 1809.

The 2nd Battalion 52nd Foot was the weakest and the least experienced of all the battalions in the Light Division. It was a sickly battalion. Despite only being in the Peninsula for nine months, the rigours of life on campaign were too much for many of the soldiers. At its peak strength in April, it had 588 other ranks. By the end of the year, seventy-one (12 per cent) of them had died, only one in combat; 40 per cent of its other ranks were still hospitalised at the end of the year. The battalion had three very experienced senior officers, Lieutenant Colonel John Colborne, Major George Napier, who came from the 1st Battalion, and Captain William Jones. All three were bullet magnets and had been seriously wounded in the past nine months. The transfers from the 1st Battalion provided them with additional officers who had combat experience and were used to campaigning. Among its officers, the biggest issue was numbers. It was short one major, three company commanders, and thirteen lieutenants and ensigns.

The eight-company strong 1st Battalion 95th Rifles was able to field 578 other ranks or 72 per company at the end of 1811. These men were hardened soldiers, veterans of many skirmishes and battles, and thirty months of living in the field. It was similar for the officers. Of the forty-two officers who were with the battalion in January 1810, only sixteen, or 38 per cent, were still with the battalion at the end of 1811. Nine of the officers had been killed, died of wounds, or died of disease. Another eight had been pulled from the battalion to serve on the staff elsewhere, seconded to the Portuguese Army, or had returned to England.

Table 1.7: Attrition of Officers in the 1st Battalion 95th Rifles From January 1810–December 1811

Rank	With the Battalion 1 January 1810	Still With the Battalion 1 January 1812
LTC	1	0
Maj	2	0
Cpt	10	6
LT/2LT	29	10
Total	**42**	**16**[13]

Despite losing so many officers, the battalion had thirty officers, including one major, seven company commanders, fourteen lieutenants, and four ensigns, as well as four staff officers. The major, the captains, and eight of the lieutenants were with the battalion when it arrived in Portugal in July 1809. All of them, plus five other lieutenants and ensigns, were combat veterans. The only weakness among the officers was the battalion was missing two of its senior officers. Its commander was Major Peter O'Hare, a very junior major, having held the rank for only eight months. The 1st Battalion 95th Rifles was the most experienced battalion in the Light Division. Its main weakness was the lack of a system to bring in replacements. It could not afford to take heavy casualties in the next campaign.

The two companies of the 2nd Battalion 95th Rifles were a mixed bag. Captain Samuel Mitchell's company was the more experienced of the two companies, having been with the division since September 1810 and fought in all the battles of 1811. Captain John Hart's company was part of the British garrison in Cádiz and joined the 1st Brigade in September 1811, having missed the battles of 1811. Unfortunately, the returns for both companies are compiled together so it is difficult to determine the strength of either company. Thirty-six other ranks in the two companies were hospitalised at the end of 1811, about 20 per cent of the other ranks. It is likely that 60 per cent of the sick were from Captain Hart's company, which was not as experienced on campaign as Captain Mitchell's company. The two companies had an average of 100 total troops, or 88 per cent of its authorised strength, at the end of the year. It had two captains, four first lieutenants, and one second lieutenant. Captain Hart's company was short one second lieutenant. All but one first lieutenant had seen combat.

13. This is 38 per cent of the total officers who were with the battalion on 1 January 1810.

The five companies of the Right Wing of the 3rd Battalion 95th Rifles joined the Light Division in August 1811. It had taken part in the Barrosa campaign, in March 1811, but spent the next six months as part of the garrison in Cádiz. Almost all the other ranks were combat veterans but prior to coming to Portugal had spent little time on campaign and were not prepared for the hardship of being in the field. Within two months of its arrival 43 per cent of the troops were hospitalised and nine had died. By the end of the year the number of troops in the hospital had dropped to 103 but the total dead for the past 4 months was 29 other ranks or 7 per cent of their other ranks; all died without firing a shot. Between the sick and dead, the 3rd Battalion had lost a third of its strength and could only field 258 other ranks. Unlike the other units in the Light Division, the Right Wing of the 3rd Battalion was overstrength in officers. Lieutenant Colonel Andrew Barnard commanded them, but soon he was appointed the temporary commander of the 1st Brigade. It had no major assigned to it, so it was commanded by Captain William Percival. All the companies were commanded by a captain, and each company had three subalterns. Of its twenty-two officers, all but two first lieutenants and two second lieutenants were combat veterans. Its only major weakness was its lack of experience living on campaign. It must develop the necessary skills required to survive living under rigorous field conditions, otherwise the battalion would be reduced to skeleton strength.

At the end of December 1811, the 1st Caçadores reported that they had 600 corporals and privates or 100 per cent of what they were authorised. However, fifty of the privates were new recruits and still at the recruit training depot, while seventy-eight were hospitalised. Another eighty-five were on duty away from the battalion. This left only 387 corporals and privates present for duty. The battalion also reported that forty men had deserted. It is unclear whether that number reflects all the men who had deserted, regardless of when they ran, or new deserters since the previous report. It is likely a total of all men who deserted. These forty deserters were 7 per cent of the battalion's authorised strength. The battalion received thirty-nine replacements in the last three months of the year, of which thirty-five were conscripts (90 per cent). The number of new men was about equal to the number of men who deserted. The battalion had thirty-two of thirty-six of its authorised sergeants. It was short two captains, a lieutenant, and eight ensigns at the company level, a total of eleven out of twenty-four officers. Not all the shortages were due to casualties and disease. The battalion was tasked in July 1811 to provide some experienced officers to the newly formed caçadore battalions. One ensign was promoted and transferred to the 9th Caçadores, and one lieutenant and an ensign were promoted and transferred to the 11th Caçadores.

The 1st Caçadores was temporarily commanded by Major John Algeo, a British officer who joined the battalion in 1810. He had been in the Peninsula since July 1809. The previous commander, Lieutenant Colonel Jorge de Avilez Juzarte de Sousa Tavares, who had been in command since January 1809, went on leave in October 1811 and never returned. Captain Charles Maclean, 79th Foot, was appointed a major agregado[14] in the battalion in late October. Most of the company commanders were very experienced. The senior commander was Captain Manuel Jorge Rodrigues, who had commanded since January 1809. Two others, Captains José da Rosa e Sousa and Dom João de Abreu Silva Lobo had commanded since May 1809. The fourth commander, Joaquim António da Cunha e Meneses had taken command in December 1810. Captain Manuel Inácio Sécio, the commander of the 6th Company had been sent to the recruit training depot. He was relieved of his duties for negligence and dismissed from the army soon after. Lieutenant Manuel António Sobral replaced him. Sobral had been a lieutenant for nineteen months. The last company was commanded by Lieutenant Joaquim Accioli da Fonseca, who also had been a lieutenant for nineteen months. The battalion had three other lieutenants and four ensigns with the colours. The three lieutenants had at least eighteen months of experience, and the four ensigns had at least a year's experience. The 1st Caçadores was an experienced battalion, but the health of its men and the number of deserters prevented it from fielding its full strength. Missing 45 per cent of its company officers could have a detrimental effect on its ability to control its skirmishers in combat.[15]

The rifle armed 3rd Caçadores reported at the end of December 1811 that they were at 100 per cent authorised strength with 600 corporals and privates. They had only forty-nine soldiers in the hospital and with only fourteen

14. An officer with an agregado rank, could mean one of two things. Under Marshal Beresford it was used to appoint a British officer to a unit who did not have a vacancy in that rank but to which Beresford wanted to have a British presence, mostly to improve training and discipline. Beresford was anticipating Lieutenant Colonel de Avilez's promotion to colonel and appointment to command an infantry regiment. Once this happened Major Algeo would be promoted to lieutenant colonel in his place and given command of the battalion. Maclean's status would be changed from agregado to efetivo in May 1812, which meant he became the effective major of the battalion. Beresford also use it also as a form of punishment. An officer could be court martialed and instead of being reduced in rank, he could be made agregado. As an agregado he became the junior officer of the rank he held prior to being court martialed, in the unit. He could not be promoted and his pay was reduced. He continued serve in the unit, so there was no loss of officers. It was hoped that by humiliating the officer he would learn his lesson. The agregado officer who demonstrated through his actions that he had learned from his mistakes could be restored to his efetivo status.

15. Much of the information on the officers of the 1st and 3rd Caçadores is drawn from the research of Moisés Gaudêncio, who gave us permission to use it.

soldiers on command, it somehow had avoided having to send many men on duty elsewhere. Its morale may have been better than the 1st Caçadores, for it only reported four deserters. It was also successful in obtaining new recruits, with sixty-two volunteers at the recruit training depot. It reported that it had 468 men present for duty which was 78 per cent of its authorised strength. Its 8 per cent sick rate was half that of any other unit in the Light Division. Like the 1st Caçadores, it too was short four sergeants. The battalion was also not up to strength with officers. Two of its company commanders, Captains Luís Evaristo de Figueiredo and José de Sousa Pereira, were court martialed for not returning to the battalion after being released from the hospital. They were found guilty but not removed from command. Instead, they were placed in agregado status making them the junior captains in the battalion and having their pay reduced. By the end of the year the battalion was short eight ensigns. The battalion was also tasked to send experienced officers to the newly formed caçadore battalions. Captain Robert Haddock and Lieutenant Anthony de Bruenig, British officers serving in the battalion, were transferred to the 12th and 8th Caçadores respectively. Ensign Damião Cândido Botelho was promoted to lieutenant in the 9th Caçadores, while Ensign Miguel Correia de Mesquita was promoted and sent to the 10th Caçadores. Lieutenant Vicente Correia de Mesquita was promoted to captain and Ensign Pedro de Magalhães Peixoto was promoted to lieutenant, both in the 11th Caçadores. This left the battalion only seventeen officers in the companies. Its commander, Lieutenant Colonel George Elder, another British officer, had commanded the battalion since June 1809, and was the most experienced battalion commander in the Light Division. Its major, Manuel Pinto da Silveira, was with the battalion when it was first formed in July 1808 as the Trás-os-Montes' Caçadores except for six months in early 1810. Five of its captains[16] had been in command since the battalion was formed in July 1809 and four of its lieutenants had been with it since the beginning. They were a tight knit group. Two of the other companies were commanded by British officers, Captains William Dobbin and Powell Morphew. Dobbin took command in May 1811 but had been in the Peninsula since November 1808. Morphew had no combat experience and had been in country less than two months. Lieutenant Afonso Botelho commanded the 2nd Company. He had been promoted to lieutenant in November and was one of the original officers. The 3rd Caçadores was one of the best battalions in the Light Division, however its lack of junior officers could be problematic.

16. Including the two captains who were captain agregado, and two captains who were on detached duty.

Conclusion

By the end of 1811 the Light Division was Wellington's most battle-hardened division, filled with experienced campaigners, and a cadre of officers and NCOs who led from the front. Yet it had several weaknesses that needed to be fixed. The biggest was institutional. The system to send replacements to the British battalions had failed, except for the 43rd Foot. If it was not fixed the battalions would have to find another solution to replace those who became casualties. The second problem was the heavy casualties among its senior officers. In less than two years, the division had to find suitable brigade commanders six times, plus a temporary commander for the division. Four times the division appointed battalion commanders to fill the vacancies, which then created shortfalls in the senior officers in the battalions. The majors would replace the lieutenant colonels, which created gaps in the senior leadership of the battalions. These were filled by their senior captains. The division was already short eleven captains, which was 19 per cent of the number authorised; and that does not include the seven that would be taken from their companies to fill in for the missing majors! When they went into combat 30 per cent of the companies would be missing their captains.

The Light Division was the best Wellington had. However, it was fragile. It could not take heavy casualties and continue to operate at the same level as it had for the previous two years.

Chapter 2

Trench Warfare January 1812

> You may conceive me not at all glad, for the nights are now amazingly cold, hard hoar frosty nights, obliged to our pipes, tobacco & spirits for what warmth we can get, no wood near the place.[1]
>
> Lieutenant Charles Dawson, 2nd Battalion 52nd Foot,
> at the Siege of Ciudad Rodrigo

The 4,400 men of the Light Division knew that the Siege of Ciudad Rodrigo would begin soon, but none of them knew when. Primarily because Wellington had not made a final decision. The planning for the siege had begun months before when the order was given to move thousands of tonnes of equipment, heavy guns, and ammunition from Lisbon and other ports to the area. By mid-November thousands of carts and mules were requisition to bring this matériel forward, and the Light Division had to give up much of its transport to support the effort. This had a trickledown effect since these conveyances were used by the division to feed its troop. The shortage of food did not help the sick and wounded recover. However, once the matériel had been brought forward, the food situation would change.

Much of the matériel to build trenches and gun emplacements, such as gabions and fascines, had to be made locally. On 18 December, a General Order directed that 'the soldiers of the regiments of the 1st, 3d, 4th, and Light Divisions, and Brigadier General Pack's Brigade, may be employed in making fascines and gabions and piquets'.[2] Someone in the army HQ felt that this was too vague and the next day one officer and forty-three men from each regiment within the divisions would be assigned the task.[3]

How this order was received by the Light Division is unknown, however by the end of the year it had 152 soldiers on command. Yet from the number of soldiers provided by each battalion the division let its subordinate commanders decide how they would support it. The 1st Battalion 52nd Foot responded enthusiastically, while other battalions did not.

---

1. *Redcoats of Wellington's Light Division: Unpublished & Rare Memoirs of the 52nd (Oxfordshire) Regiment of Foot*, p.157.
2. General Orders, dated 18 December 1811.
3. Jones, John, *Journal of the Sieges Carried on by the Army Under the Duke of Wellington Between the Years 1811 & 1814*, Vol. 1, p.91.

Table 2.1: Organisation 1 January 1812

Unit	Personnel	Rank	Location
Division HQ	Maj Gen Robert Craufurd	Commander	
	LT Charles Wood 52nd Foot	ADC	Fuenteguinaldo
	LT James Shaw 43rd Foot	ADC	
	LT John Bell 52nd Foot	DAQG	
	Maj Charles Rowan 52nd Foot	AAG	
	Charles Purcell	ACG	
	Wentworth Parker	CH	
1st Brigade	LTC Andrew Barnard	Acting Commander	Fuenteguinaldo
	Cpt Charles Beckwith 95th Rifles	Brigade Maj	
1st Bn 43rd Foot	LTC Charles McLeod	Commander	Fuenteguinaldo
RW 1st Bn 95th Rifles	Bvt Maj Alexander Cameron	Commander	Pastores & La Encina
Company 2nd Bn 95th Rifles	Cpt Samuel Mitchell	Commander	Pastores & La Encina
Company 2nd Bn 95th Rifles	Cpt John Hart	Commander	Pastores & La Encina
3rd Bn 95th Rifles	Cpt William Percival	Commander	Pastores & La Encina
3rd Caç Bn	LTC George Elder	Commander	Fuenteguinaldo
2nd Brigade	Maj Gen John Ormsby Vandeleur	Commander	Martiago
	LT Harry Smith 95th Rifles	Brigade Maj	
	LT William Armstrong 19th Light Dragoons	ADC	
1st Bn 52nd Foot	Maj Edward Gibbs	Commander	Martiago
2nd Bn 52nd Foot	LTC John Colborne	Commander	Agallas
LW 1st Bn 95th Rifles	Maj Peter O'Hare	Commander	La Atalaya
1st Caç Bn	Maj John Algeo	Commander	Robledillo de Gata

Table 2.2: Number of Other Ranks on Command 24 December 1811

Battalion	Number on Command
1st Bn 43rd Foot	35
1st Bn 52nd Foot	44
2nd Bn 52nd Foot	10
1st Bn 95th Rifles	11
1st Caç	36
3rd Caç	16

To encourage the soldiers to volunteer, they would be paid for each item that was made. The officer was paid 4s per day.[4] This was quite a bonus for a lieutenant who only made 6s 6d per day. For a soldier, who earned a shilling a day, being on this work party likely earned him 2s or 3s per day.

Table 2.3: Price Paid for Each Item Made[5]

Item	In Portuguese Money	In British Pounds
Large gabions 5ft 6in high by 4ft 8in diameter	15 Vintins	5.25 Pence
Small gabions 3ft in height by 2ft 3in diameter	4 Vintins	1.5 Pence
Large fascines 6ft by 1ft	2 Vintins	0.75 Pence
Tracing fascines 4ft long by 6in	1 Vintin	0.375 Pence
Sleepers for platforms, 15ft long, 6in by 4in squares	8 Vintins	3 Pence
Splinter-proof timbers 12–14ft long	8 Vintins	3 Pence

The order of the day did not initially specify how many of each were to be made, but before long the total number needed was sent out.

Table 2.4: Amount of Engineer Material Needed[6]

Item	Amount Needed
Large gabions 5ft 6in high by 4ft 8in diameter	30
Small gabions 3ft in height by 2ft 3in diameter	2,000
Large fascines 6ft by 1ft	2,500
Tracing fascines 4ft long by 6in	1,800
Fascine Pickets 3 and 4ft in length	7,000
Sleepers for platforms, 15ft long, 6in by 4in squares	200
Splinter-proof timbers 12–14ft long	400

4. *Redcoats of Wellington's Light Division: Unpublished & Rare Memoirs of the 52nd (Oxfordshire) Regiment of Foot*, p.155.
5. Jones, John, *Journal of the Sieges Carried on by the Army under the Duke of Wellington between the Years 1811 & 1814*, Vol. 1, p.90.
6. Ibid.

Instructions were also sent out for how to make the different items. The gabions, initially were made of green materials and those that were,

> 3 feet in height by 2 feet 3 inches in diameter; those of oak weighed 90 lbs., and those of willow 80 lbs. The former were found perfectly unmanageable; even at 2 feet, those of oak averaged 85lb, and those of willow 70 lbs., and were found still too heavy...fascines were made 6 feet, 9 feet, and 18 feet in length by 1 foot in diameter. The former averaged 50 lbs. weight and were found most useful under a heavy fire. The latter, being made of green boughs and twigs, were much too heavy.[7]

Although this seems like easy money for the troops, what had to be factored in the equation was the availability of material to make the items. All were made from wood, which was not readily available. The division had been billeted in the area for five months and easily accessible wood had long been collected to feed the innumerable fires that the men used to cook their food and to stay warm. The work details had to travel many kilometres to find the wood to make the items needed for the siege.

These work details had little impact on the soldiers who were not part of them. Despite knowing that orders to commence the siege would arrive soon, the soldiers and officers continued their daily routine of life in winter quarters. Some rifle officers, including Captain Jonathan Leach, celebrated the new year making

> an excursion, on the 3d of January, to Robadillia, a large village in one of the deepest and most secluded valleys of the Sierra de Gata, where a Spanish family resided with whom we had become acquainted on the other side of the mountains in the previous autumn. We sent on two servants with mules, on which we carried a change of clothes, tea, sugar, cigars, meat, &c. &c.; for, be it known, that in Spain, if you wish to fare moderately well whilst travelling, nothing of this kind should be left to chance.
>
> The snow was so deep on the mountains, that we passed them with infinite difficulty; and, but for the honour of the thing, might as well have left our guns behind us, as the only living animal we saw was a wild boar, going at the rate of thirty miles an hour, many gun-shots distant.
>
> The old don, his wife and daughters, received us kindly, and procured billets for us in the village. They beat up for volunteers, and having collected the village belles, and a fiddler or two, we danced with great glee; after which, we gave the fair ones a supper at our billets. This was followed by duets, trios, catches, and glees, and melodies of all sorts and kinds, both

7. Ibid, Vol. 3, pp.194–195.

> Spanish, Irish, Scotch, and English. Some young padres, with the crowns of their heads shaved, were amongst the party invited to accompany the ladies to our fête; and these lads were evidently much annoyed at the preference which the signoras evinced towards the heretical Englishmen; nor did they attempt to disguise their feelings. I am free to confess that I never had a great predilection for any of that idle, vagabond class; and in this I was by no means singular, for I found my comrades quite ready to join in any frolic or fun which might be proposed as just a punishment for their uncourteous conduct.
>
> When the amusements of the evening were over, and we had escorted our partners to their homes, we still found some of those clericos hanging about the street with lanterns in their hands. We suddenly opened a heavy fire of snow-balls on them, of the hardest and most terrific kind, which smashed their lanterns to atoms, and battered them from head to foot, to a degree beyond a joke. We heard their curses and execrations on Englishmen and heretics gradually die away as they ran from us and hid themselves in their respective habitations.
>
> Thus ended our frolic in Robadillia, which was soon followed by matters of a far different nature. Intelligence reached us that the Light Division was instantly to invest and lay siege to Ciudad Rodrigo, and that it was moving to El Bodon, Pastores, and other villages nearer that fortress. Having said farewell to our friends in Robadillia (not including the padres), we passed the whole day in floundering across the snowy mountains, and joined our battalion late at night at El Bodon.[8]

Late in the evening, on 3 January, orders were received by the division to move the next day to new billets in anticipation of supporting the siege. The orders could not have come at a worse time weatherwise. Winter had set in hard the previous month and although there was not much snow, the temperatures fell below freezing at night and rising only a little above freezing during the day. On the morning of 4 January, the weather worsened. The 1st Brigade marched out at 10:00 a.m. and spent the next three and half hours marching 16km in one of 'the most dreadful mornings possible. Hale [Hail] & rain with a violent gale from the northward' before reaching their new billets in La Encina.[9] Lieutenant John Cooke, 43rd Foot wrote afterwards that

> During this march a tremendous storm of sleet and snow took place; the snow froze and adhered to the horses hoofs, forming balls which

8. Leach, Jonathan, *Rough Sketches of the Life of an Old Soldier*, pp.242--244.
9. Duffy, John, *Journals of Majors John Duffy and John Maxwell Tylden of the 43rd Foot,* p.141, and Oglander, Henry, *The Journals of Captain Henry Oglander of the 43rd & 47th Foot*, p.113.

> raised them several inches from the ground. Fortunately, the march was short, as fatigue-parties of soldiers were obliged to return to prop up the weak and staggering baggage-animals, that had suffered previously from bad provender.[10]

The 2nd Brigade was not much better off. It moved 20km from its quarters in the vicinity of Martiago to El Bodón, which it had to share 'with Captain Ross Troop R.H.A., General Craufurd and his Staff, and the commissariat much crowded in this very dirty town.'[11]

After changing its billets, the Light Division continued to wait for orders to move towards Ciudad Rodrigo. The army's HQ had developed a plan so that a division would work on the siege lines for twenty-four hours and then be relieved the next day at noon by another division. The relieving force would replace the division currently on duty one battalion at a time so that the enemy would not take the opportunity to attack the besiegers during the confusion of the changeover. After being relieved, the soldiers would return to their quarters and have the next three days off. While on duty one brigade would work on the trenches and the other would provide a covering party to protect them from any sallies from the city by the defenders. There was space and equipment for only 1,000 troops to work on the trench works at a time. The brigade charged with building the trenches would have half its troops work for six hours and then be relieved by the other half of the brigade. While not working on the siege lines, the troops waiting for their shift to start would rest behind the siege lines, protected from the defenders' fire by the hill. Plans were made to have fires to keep the off-duty soldiers warm. Like many well-intentioned plans, this one made assumptions that could not be carried out since there was a lack of firewood in the area.

The other brigade would serve as the covering force. Its light troops would screen the workers and when possible, shoot at the defenders on the wall. One battalion would be kept at the ready to respond to any excursion by the defenders. The other battalions would be off duty. The units in the covering force would rotate the duty every several hours. At the end of twelve hours, the two brigades would switch duties, with the covering force working on the siege works and the brigade that worked on the trenches first becoming the covering force.

After a few days' delay, orders were finally given to start the siege works. The Light Division was the first to be tasked.

---

10. Cooke, John, *A True Soldier Gentleman: The Memoirs of Lt. John Cooke 1791–1813*, pp.100–101.
11. Ewart, John, *Peninsular War Diary of Captain John Frederick Ewart, 52nd Light Infantry, 1811–1812*, pp.53–54.

Table 2.5: Work Schedule For the Building of the Siege Works

Date	Unit
8 January	Light Division
9 January	1st Division
10 January	4th Division
11 January	3rd Division
12 January	Light Division
13 January	1st Division
14 January	4th Division
15 January	3rd Division
16 January	Light Division
17 January	1st Division

The division was ordered to be at the Great Teson, a large hill north of Ciudad Rodrigo, by noon on 8 January. This was easier said than done. It was billeted in an area about 20km south of the city and on the opposite side of the Águeda River. It would have to start marching before dawn, which was about 7:30 a.m. It would ford the river in the vicinity of La Caridad Monastery, which was about 5km south of the city, and then march about 10km through the countryside to the east and then north of the siege lines, staying out of cannonball range of the city. For the troops of the 1st Brigade, it would be about a 25–30km march while for the 2nd Brigade would be 30–35km march.

Table 2.6: Location of the Light Division Cantonments During the Siege of Ciudad Rodrigo

Unit	Location	Distance to Ford at La Caridad (km)
Division HQ	El Bodón	18
1st Brigade	La Encina	14
43rd Foot	La Encina	14
RW 1st Bn 95th (4 Companies)	Pastores	11
2nd Bn 95th (2 Companies)	Pastores	11
3rd Bn 95th (5 Companies)	La Encina	14
3rd Caç	Pastores	11
2nd Brigade	El Bodón	18
1st Bn 52nd Foot	El Bodón	18
2nd Bn 52nd Foot	El Bodón	18
LW 1st Bn 95th (4 Companies)	La Encina	14
1st Caç	El Bodón	18
Pack's Portuguese Brigade	Sanjuanejo	1

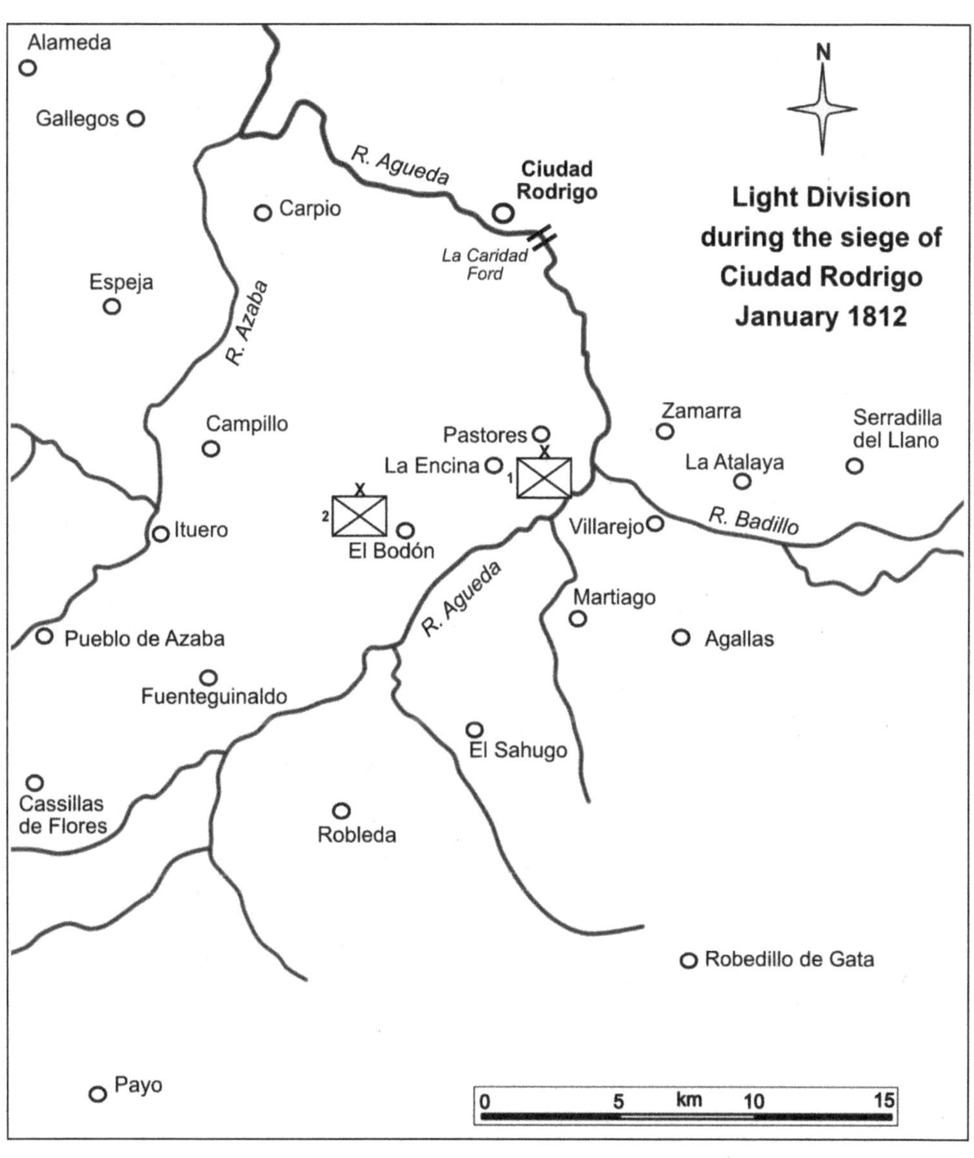
Light Division
during the siege of
Ciudad Rodrigo
January 1812
N
Alameda
Gallegos
R. Agueda
Ciudad
Rodrigo
Carpio
La Caridad
Ford
Espeja
R. Azaba
Campillo
Pastores
La Encina
1
2
Zamarra
Serradilla
del Llano
La Atalaya
Ituero
El Bodón
Villarejo
R. Badillo
Martiago
R. Agueda
Pueblo de Azaba
Agallas
Fuenteguinaldo
El Sahugo
Cassillas
de Flores
Robleda
Robedillo de Gata
Payo
0
5
km
10
15

The march itself should not have been that difficult. There was no need for the men to carry their full kit, since they would return to their billets the next day. They would only bring their weapons, rations, and their greatcoats and blankets. Everything else would be left in their cantonment area. The problem was crossing the Águeda River. There was no bridge close to them and they would have to ford it. The nearest ford was about waist deep and the water was just above freezing. The temperature generally dropped below freezing at night and the river often had ice in it. Rifleman Edward Costello wrote,

> Pieces of ice that were constantly carried down this rapid stream bruised our men so much, that, to obviate it the cavalry at length were ordered to form four deep across the ford, under the lee of whom we crossed comparatively unharmed, although by the time we reached our quarters, our clothes were frozen into a mass of ice.[12]

In an effort to keep their shoes and trousers dry, the men were ordered to remove them prior to fording the river and cross it 'sans culotte'.[13] Despite doing so, their uniforms got wet and there was no opportunity of drying them. Lieutenant John Dobbs, 1st Battalion 52nd Foot, said nights were particularly hard.

> In crossing the Aguada to take our tour of duty in the siege of Ciudad Rodrigo, we had to ford it, the water being up to our hips; and as there was a heavy hoar-frost during the whole period of the siege, and we lay on the bare ground for six hours during the night, with only a single blanket to cover us, we were sufficiently cooled; our blankets after the night were stiff enough to stand upright…[14]

Lieutenant Henry Oglander of the 43rd Foot wrote in his diary that

> we marched across country & consequently only crossed roads or accidentally & for a short distance only, followed their direction. The country in front of Rodrigo is nearly flat, excepting when broken by ravines & is everywhere open & fit for the action of cavalry, as far as the lines of hills which bounded this plain.[15]

Upon arriving shortly before noon at the Great Teson, 'several French officers made their appearance, and politely took off their hats and spoke to us.

12. Costello, Edward, *Adventures of a Soldier*, p.142.
13. Cooke, John, *A True Soldier Gentleman: The Memoirs of Lt. John Cooke 1791–1813*, p.101.
14. Dobbs, John, *Recollections of an Old 52nd Man*, pp.20–21.
15. Oglander, Henry, *The Journals of Captain Henry Oglander of the 43rd & 47th Foot*, p.115.

They of course were very anxious to know what all this meant.'[16] They would find out very soon, for the division's orders were changed within the hour. Instead of starting the siege works, the division was ordered to the Renaud Redoubt, which was about 500m to the southeast of the Great Teson.

The redoubt was almost square in shape with its walls facing almost north, south, east and west. The eastern wall was about 200m from the San Francisco Convent, while the southern wall was about 500m from the walls of the city. The northern wall faced uphill. While standing on the top of the Great Teson, due to the drop of the slope, it was not possible to see the southern wall. The north, east and west walls were protected by a 3m high parapet that had a strong wooden palisade on the lower half and dirt on the top half. In front of these walls was a 3m deep ditch that was about 4m wide. The ditch had deep water in towards the downhill side. The rear of the redoubt was protected by a low wall with a gate in it. The rear wall was also protected by wooden stakes placed into the wall at an angle.[17]

This redoubt had to be destroyed before digging could begin. Major George Napier, 2nd Battalion 52nd Foot, immediately volunteered to command the assault force, 'but Lord Wellington said whoever was the first field officer for duty should command, and as Lieutenant Colonel Colborne was the first, he got it.'[18] General Craufurd ordered each of the British battalions to provide two companies, commanded by the battalion's senior captains, for the assault. These orders were mostly complied with, but some units did not send both of their senior captains. The 43rd Foot's two senior captains were part of the assault, while the 52nd Foot's companies were commanded by three of the four senior captains in the two battalions. The 1st Battalion 95th Rifles, only provided its senior company commander. The 3rd Battalion 95th Rifles only provided one company. The two companies of the 2nd Battalion 95th Rifles were not tasked to provide a company, nor were the 1st and the 3rd Caçadores. Lieutenant Colonel George Elder, the commander of the 3rd Caçadores, asked General Craufurd to be allowed to supply some volunteers to the assault party. Craufurd agreed but limited it to one officer and twelve men. Elder ignored this and provided one officer and fourteen men. Craufurd wrote to Wellington after the assault 'I am confident that the 1st caçadores would have manifested the same spirit, but they were still detached on the Salamanca road at the time that the detachment was formed for the attack.'[19]

16. Simmons, George, *A British Rifleman: Journals and Correspondence During the Peninsular War and the Campaign of Wellington*, p.218.
17. Burgoyne, John, *Life and Correspondence of Field Marshal Sir John Burgoyne*, Vol. 1, p.155.
18. Napier, George, *At War With Wellington: The Peninsular War Letters of William, George and Charles Napier*, p.112.
19. *W.D.*, Vol. 5, p.463.

Table 2.7: The Light Division Assault Force on the Renaud Redoubt 8 January 1812

Personnel	**Unit/Position**
LTC John Colborne, 2nd Bn 52nd Foot	Commander
Maj Edward Gibbs, 1st Bn 52nd Foot	Second in command
Cpt John Duffy's Company	43rd Foot
Cpt James Fergusson's Company	43rd Foot
Cpt William Mein's Company	1st Bn 52nd Foot
Cpt Joseph Dobbs' Company	1st Bn 52nd Foot
Cpt William Jones' Company[20]	2nd Bn 52nd Foot
Cpt Augustus Merry's Company	2nd Bn 52nd Foot
Cpt Jeremiah Crampton's Company	1st Bn 95th Rifles
1LT Thomas M'Namara's Company	1st Bn 95th Rifles
Cpt James Travers' Company	3rd Bn 95th Rifles
LT Francisco (José) de Madureira Lobo's Detachment[21]	3rd Caç
2Cpt Edmund Mulcaster	Royal Engineers
1LT Alexander Thomson	Royal Engineers

After reviewing the troops, Colborne realised that the numbers were short. He turned to the brigade major, Lieutenant Harry Smith, to inquire why. Smith had thought the troop requirement was for 4 companies, instead of 400 men. When asked by Colborne, Smith replied 'I am sorry if I am mistaken' to which Colborne said 'Oh, never mind; run and bring another Company.'[22] Smith returned with First Lieutenant M'Namara's company, from the Left Wing of the 1st Battalion 95th Rifles.

Colborne's plan was to have the three rifle companies and Captain Merry's company of the 2nd Battalion 52nd Foot, to precede the assault force and line the glacis of the redoubt. Once there they were not to fire until the defenders fired first. Then they were to keep the defenders under a heavy fire to prevent them from firing on the assaulters. Captain Duffy's company of the 43rd Foot and Captain William Mein's company of the 1st Battalion 52nd Foot would form the assault force. Lieutenant Thomson was in charge of the men carrying the ladders. Captain Jones' company, 2nd Battalion 52nd Foot, was responsible for carrying the ladders and fascines. Lieutenant Thomson, Royal Engineers, would accompany Jones' company to show them where to place the ladders and fascines. The ladders had been constructed earlier that day from 'rafters

20. Jones was assigned to the 1st Battalion, but due to the lack of experienced company commanders in the 2nd Battalion he was placed in the 2nd Battalion at the time.
21. AHM 1-14-256-04 MS-54.
22. Smith, Harry, *The Autobiography of Sir Harry Smith*, p.55.

of an old house'[23] and were quite heavy. The reserve would consist of Captain Fergusson's company of the 43rd Foot and Captain Dobbs' company of the 1st Battalion 52nd Foot. Lieutenant Lobo's detachment of the 3rd Caçadores was likely assigned to the ladder carrying party.

The plan was to attack after dark. Sunset was at 5:00 p.m., but it would still be light until 6:30 p.m. There was a new moon, and it would not rise until 1:30 a.m. the next morning, so there would be very little illumination that night. The troops began forming about 7:00 p.m. on the reverse slope of the Great Teson and Lieutenant Colonel Colborne reviewed the plan with all his commanders. Captain Mulcaster, the senior Royal Engineer, suggested that the ladders were too heavy and cumbersome and they should wait until lighter ladders could be brought forward. Colborne said that they could not afford to wait, and the attack would be made with the heavy ladders.[24] At dusk an officer and two sergeants were sent forward to stand on the brow of the hill and be in a position so that they face the salient angle of the redoubt with the steeple of the city's cathedral behind it.[25] This would give the approaching troops the direction of the attack. At 8:00 p.m. the troops formed up and the covering companies moved over the hill to the slopes in front of the redoubt.[26]

Lieutenant George Barlow was in Jones' company, and immediately behind the covering screen. He wrote to his uncle after the fight that the covering party

> advanced in the best order & silence, cut off the enemy's advanced videttes and prevented any alarm. They were however discovered by the sentry on the parapet at the distance of about fifty yards, after receiving one volley from their guns and musketry...kept up so hot a fire that the French could not venture to show their heads above the parapet or retard them.[27]

In the dark the troops carrying the ladders and fascines became disordered and did not know where to place them. Barlow was sent by his company commander to find Lieutenant Colonel Colborne and learn where he wanted the ladders and fascines. In the confusion of the fight Barlow never found him and joined the assault instead.[28]

---

23. Freer, William, *With the 43rd in the Peninsula: The Letters of William Freer, Edward Freer and Daniel Gardner of the 43rd Foot (1808–15)*, p.96.
24. Colborne, John, 'Letter Describing Attack on the Upper Teson Redoubt, 1812', *Redcoats of Wellington's Light Division: Unpublished & Rare Memoirs of the 52nd (Oxfordshire) Regiment of Foot*, p.34.
25. Ibid.
26. Dawson, Henry, *Redcoats of Wellington's Light Division: Unpublished & Rare Memoirs of the 52nd (Oxfordshire) Regiment of Foot*, p.141.
27. Barlow, George Ulrich, *A Light Infantryman With Wellington: The Letters of Captain George Ulrich Barlow, 52nd and 69th Foot, 1808–1815*, p.105.
28. Ibid.

Captain Duffy, whose company was the lead company in the assault wrote in his diary that,

> we had formed at in the following order. 4 sections of Rifles and light infantry battalion to line the glacis & keep up a constant fire at the embrasures, a party of men with 15 ladders and about 30 fascines, then came the storming party under my own command consisting of 50 men of my own company, followed by the 50 men of the 52nd Regiment under Captain Mein…& we approached the battery as silently as possible and got pretty near before the enemy were aware of our intentions. The flanking parties immediately opened upon the enemy's guns which only fired one round. The other parties rushed on, we at the same time followed but found on arriving at the ditch that not a ladder was placed, the men entrusted with them having thrown them down some yards previous to their gaining the ditch. We had therefore to return for them. One was placed to the left of the palisade which answered as a bridge to clear the top. We then jumped down about 9 feet, got two ladders and in a few moments ascended the sides of the battery with a cheer. The enemy ran into one corner of the battery and to a guard house deep down in the fort where some firing took place, however in two minutes the fort was taken. During this time, we were in the ditch the French threw some shells over the ramparts which burst amongst our men & wounded several.[29]

Lieutenant Colonel Colborne also left an account of the fighting, although not written until 1859.

> The party with the ladders soon arrived and placed them in the ditch against the palisades, so that they were ready when Captain Mein of the 52nd, came up with the escalading companies. They got into the ditch by descending on the ladders and then placing them against its fraises.[30] The only fire from which the assailants suffered was from shells and grenades thrown over from the rampart. During these proceedings [Lieutenant John] Gurwood of the [2nd Battalion] 52nd, came from the gorge and mentioned that a company could get in by the gorge with ladders, I desired him to take any he could find. Thompson [Thomson] of the engineers had no opportunity of being of use, the whole arrangements were executed by the exertions of the captains of companies and the order preserved by them. We entered the redoubt by the ladders safely, no resistance or opposition was made. The company at the gorge had forced open the gate, or it had been opened by some of the defenders endeavouring to escape. Captain

29. Duffy, John, *Journals of Majors John Duffy and John Maxwell Tylden of the 43rd Foot*, pp.141–142.
30. Sharpened stakes protruding from the ramparts.

> Mein, I believe, was wounded from a shot from one of our own companies as he was mounting on the rampart.[31]

Major Gibbs went with Lieutenant Gurwood and a mixed force. Which units were with them is unknown. It was probably a mix of soldiers from both the two reserve companies and Lieutenant Lobo's Portuguese. Upon arriving at the gate, they were able to enter the redoubt. Colborne claimed that it was left open by the defenders trying to avoid capture by fleeing to the city. Lieutenant Barlow wrote in a letter home that the gate was blown open by a French grenade.[32] This is supported by a journal of the siege kept by the French engineer and found after Ciudad Rodrigo fell, that a 'sergeant of artillery, who, seeing no more hope, threw a lighted shell among the English soldiers, and, followed by a few comrades, made his way through the opening made in the English ranks to avoid the shell.'[33] Once the British and Portuguese were in the redoubt, the French garrison surrendered. The assault and capture of the redoubt took less than ten minutes. Upon its surrender, the British soldiers started cheering loud enough that the rest of the division, which had been observing the assault, knew the fort had been taken. Sources disagree about what this cheer consisted of. George Napier claims that '"England and St. George" was heard shouted loud and strong, and re-echoed by the division.'[34] However, Captain John Ewart, 1st Battalion 52nd Foot, wrote in his diary that it was three huzzas.[35]

Corporal Thomas Garretty was in Captain Fergusson's company of the 43rd Foot and was part of the reserve. He claims the reserve company was brought under fire and then entered the redoubt to secure prisoners.

> After the redoubt had been taken, I was employed with several others in escorting the prisoners to a place of safety. The garrison, it seems, had no expectation of this unceremonious visit; and when we entered the place I observed several packs of cards, with which the men had been amusing themselves. On returning, I unexpectedly came in contact with a French soldier, who by some means or other had escaped notice. I called out instantly,

31. Colborne, John, 'Letter Describing Attack on the Upper Teson Redoubt, 1812', *Redcoats of Wellington's Light Division: Unpublished & Rare Memoirs of the 52nd (Oxfordshire) Regiment of Foot*, p.34.
32. *W.D.*, Vol. 5, p.463, and Barlow, George Ulrich, *A Light Infantryman With Wellington: The Letters of Captain George Ulrich Barlow, 52nd and 69th Foot, 1808–1815*, p.105.
33. Burgoyne, John, *Life and Correspondence of Field Marshal Sir John Burgoyne*, Vol. 1, p.156.
34. Napier, George, *At War With Wellington: The Peninsular War Letters of William, George and Charles Napier*, p.112.
35. Ewart, John, *Peninsular War Diary of Captain John Frederick Ewart, 52nd Light Infantry, 1811–1812*, p.55.

> desiring him to surrender, which he did; but while in the act of conducting him to the others, a British Serjeant, who deserves to be named, but on whom compassionate silence shall be shown, stopped the prisoner for the sake of plunder. Enraged at this unjust and discreditable interference, I placed my gun on the ground, determined to knock down the interloper, and secure my captive. A scuffle accordingly ensued; when, in an instant, we found to our dismay, that further contention was needless. The Frenchman observing our quarrel, instantly took to his heels, and being exceedingly alert, was out of sight before I could fire at him.[36]

Once the redoubt was secured, Colborne moved his force down the Great Teson until it reached a small stream. There they stayed to provide a screen for the rest of the division who began to dig trenches. The screen stayed in the forward position until about 1:30 a.m. when the moon began to rise.

Lieutenant Colonel Colborne wrote in his after-action report that two officers and forty-seven rank and file were captured.[37] One howitzer and a 6- and an 8-pounder cannon were also taken. The Light Division's casualties, were light. Captain William Mein and Lieutenant John Woodgate, both in the 1st Battalion 52nd Foot, and Second Lieutenant Rutherford Hawksley, 3rd Battalion 95th Rifles, were seriously wounded. Mein was shot in the thigh. Woodgate was also wounded in the thigh but by a grenade. Hawksley died of his wounds on 11 January. Six British soldiers were killed and another seventeen wounded. Lobo's Portuguese detachment took heavy casualties, with four corporals and privates killed, and six corporals and privates wounded, out of fifteen who fought.[38]

Table 2.8: Light Division Casualties at the Assault on the Renaud Redoubt 8 January 1812

Unit	Officers		Sergeants		Other Ranks	
	KIA	WIA	KIA	WIA	KIA	WIA
43rd Foot	-	-	1	-	-	5
52nd Foot	-	2	-	-	5	5
95th Rifles[39]	-	1	-	-	1	7
3rd Caç	-	-	-	-	4	6
Total	-	3	1	-	10	23

36. Garretty, Thomas, *Memoirs of a Sergeant Late in the Forty-Third Light Infantry Regiment*, pp.146–147.
37. Colborne, John, 'Letter Describing Attack on the Upper Teson Redoubt, 1812', *Redcoats of Wellington's Light Division: Unpublished & Rare Memoirs of the 52nd (Oxfordshire) Regiment of Foot*, p.35.
38. AHM 1-14-256-04 MS-54.
39. Caldwell, George, and Cooper, Robert, *Rifle Green in the Peninsula*, Vol. 3, p.29.

In the Trenches 9 January–16 January

As soon as word was received that the redoubt had fallen, orders were given to begin digging the trenches. The engineers had laid out where they wanted them dug, but it was not easy. Besides being pitch dark and below freezing temperatures, the biggest problem was that the dirt on the Great Teson was 'very stony, and during open weather in winter, water rises at the depth of six inches below the surface.'[40] When the French realised that the trench work had begun, they opened fire with every gun that could bear. Rifleman Costello described what it was like to dig the ditches.

> Now was the time to cure a skulker, or teach a man to work for his 'life'. There we were, in twos, each provided with a pick-axe and shovel; now digging with a vengeance into the frozen mould [*sic*], and then watching the glances of the shot; and again sticking to work like devils, or perhaps pitching ourselves on our bellies to avoid their being 'purged' with grape and cannister.[41]

By daylight the trenches were deep enough to provide some protection, but the French artillery fire was heavier and more accurate.[42]

The division was relieved by the 1st Division beginning at about 11:00 a.m. and they marched more than 30km back to their cantonments. They had to ford the river once again and arrived back at their billets soaking wet. While passing the town, they were brought under fire and the horse General Craufurd was riding was killed.[43] The division was back on trench duty on 12 January. They began marching at 6:00 a.m. and upon arriving at the trenches found that two eleven-gun batteries were being constructed near the redoubt.[44] The 1st Brigade had the first duty in the trenches but were relieved at 5:00 p.m. by the 2nd Brigade.[45]

> We were employed all day in completing some batteries, and at night in laying the platforms for the battering artillery. The garrison kept up, as usual, an eternal fire of shot, shells, and grape, by which we lost many men.

40. Jones, John, *Journal of the Sieges Carried on by the Army Under the Duke of Wellington Between the Years 1811 & 1814*, Vol. 1, p.97.
41. Costello, Edward, *Adventures of a Soldier*, p.141.
42. Leach, Jonathan, *Rough Sketches of the Life of an Old Soldier*, p.246.
43. Ewart, John, *Peninsular War Diary of Captain John Frederick Ewart, 52nd Light Infantry, 1811–1812*, p.56.
44. Duffy, John, *Journals of Majors John Duffy and John Maxwell Tylden of the 43rd Foot*, p.142.
45. Ewart, John, *Peninsular War Diary of Captain John Frederick Ewart, 52nd Light Infantry, 1811–1812*, p.56.

> Some companies of our regiment were sent out of the trenches, after it was dark, to get as near the town as possible, and to fire at the artillery-men through the embrasures. If this operation was a disagreeable one to the enemy, it was far from a delectable one for us they threw fire-balls among us, which were composed of such combustible matter, that they could not easily be extinguished, and made every thing near them as visible as at broad day.[46]

On 15 January, the firing from the British guns had caused a breach to open in the walls. The troops knew that soon they would be called on to assault the city, unless it surrendered first. The division was once again in the trenches on 16 January. Lieutenant Oglander recorded in his diary that,

> Throughout the whole of this day a very thick fog prevailed, to such a degree indeed, that not only our batteries did not fire, but even the enemy's fired (excepting shells) but very seldom. The 1st Brigade furnished the working parties &c till sunset, when it was relieved by the 2nd, continued in the trenches till one the next morning. About sunset a flag of truce was sent to the governor carried by Colonel Macleod, to summon him to surrender, which he refused to do, in the common place times used on those occasions.[47]

The French shelling was quite intense once the fog lifted. Lieutenant George Simmons, 95th Rifles, wrote in his diary the next day that,

> I had charge of a party to carry earth in gabions, and plant them upon the advanced saps in places where the ground was an entire rock and could not be penetrated. The enemy fired grape, and consequently numbers fell to rise no more from the effects of it. I ran the gauntlet here several times, and brought gabions of earth, always leaving some of my poor fellows behind, when I returned for more, and glad enough I was when the Engineer said 'We have now sufficient.'[48]

Simmons was happy to record in his diary that he 'returned to quarters in a whole skin.'[49]

Lieutenant Cooke of the 43rd Foot also wrote about the shelling and the soldiers' humour dealing with the dangers of it,

---

46. Leach, Jonathan, *Rough Sketches of the Life of an Old Soldier*, p.247.
47. Oglander, Henry, *The Journals of Captain Henry Oglander of the 43rd & 47th Foot*, p.117.
48. Simmons, George, *A British Rifleman: Journals and Correspondence During the Peninsular War and the Campaign of Wellington*, pp.219–220.
49. Ibid, p.220.

> a furious fire of shot and shell opened on us, while digging a parallel close to the captured fort; the earth being thrown up on the town side. The land is arable, and bestrewn with loose stones, which were flying on all sides from the impulse given by the cannon balls, and the bursting of shells, which were exploding on every side, killing and maiming many soldiers.
>
> During the siege, the enemy threw a vast quantity of shells. One night two mortars kept up an incessant discharge; and the soldiers called out 'Here comes a shell from *big Tom*; and here comes another from *little Tom*.' All the cannon shot that flew over our trenches lodged on a hill one mile north of the town, at the base of which was a *spring*, where I saw a soldier killed while stooping down to fill his canteen with water. This hill, owing to its being so ploughed up with balls, was familiarly named by the soldiers *plumb-pudding hill*.[50]

The next day was a

> Very fine day. At one in the morning the 2nd Brigade was relieved by the 1st, which continued to work till it was replaced by the 2nd at daybreak. At ten the 1st Division arrived & we were gradually relieved, each regiment marching home independently. During yesterday & last night the trenches were rapidly advanced & completed; the sap was carried to within about 150 yards of the glacis, where a new battery was commenced & it was supposed to be completed tonight. The fire of our batteries began at daybreak & continued throughout the day with little interruption.[51]

Most of the accounts were of digging the trenches and only a few wrote about the covering party. Lieutenant John Kincaid, 95th Rifles, was in the party on 12 January at

> eight in the evening, when I was ordered to take thirty men with shovels to dig holes for ourselves, as near as possible to the walls, for the delectable amusement of firing at the embrazures [*sic*] for the remainder of the night. The enemy threw frequent fire-balls among us, to see where we were; but, as we always lay snug until their blaze was extinguished, they were not much the wiser, except by finding, from having some one pop off from their guns every instant, that they had got some neighbours whom they would have been glad to get rid of.[52]

---

50. Cooke, John, *True Soldier Gentleman: The Memoirs of Lt. John Cooke 1791-1813*, pp.101–102.
51. Oglander, Henry, *The Journals of Captain Henry Oglander of the 43rd & 47th Foot*, p.117.
52. Kincaid, John, *Adventures in the Rifle Brigade in the Peninsula, France, and the Netherlands from 1809–1815*, p.103.

One night Second Lieutenant John Fitzmaurice of the 1st Battalion 95th Rifles was part of the covering party and wrote that he and his friend played a joke on their company commander. They

> were engaged in picking off French gunners, being themselves exposed to a smart shell fire form the town. As soon as the flash of a gun was seen it was the duty of the commanding officer to give the order 'on our bellies men'; then after seeing the order duly obeyed to lay himself down in leisurely fashion. But the commanding officer on this occasion, was in the opinion of the subalterns, going through the manoeuvre in what they considered a 'dirty hurry', so having seen him throw himself down too hastily they armed themselves with clods and as soon as the worthy man was down, let him have a couple pretty smartly on his back. When all danger had passed up jumped the officer, 'Boys what an escape I have had; two bits of shell struck me and I am not killed!' They congratulated him on his good fortune and renewed the fun three or four times during the night, taking of course good care that none of the privates should see what they were up to.[53]

On the night of 16 January, troops were sent forward to shoot at the defenders. A 'covering party of 200 men under Major [George] Napier 52nd, who was slightly wounded and a good many men were killed and wounded during this night.'[54] Lieutenant Kincaid was also in the covering party that night.

> I was sent to take command of the highland company, which we had at that time in the regiment, and which was with the left wing, under Colonel Cameron. I found them on piquet, between the right of the trenches and the river, half of them posted at a mud-cottage, and the other half in a ruined convent, close under the walls. It was a very tolerable post when at it; but it is no joke travelling by daylight up to within a stone's throw of a wall, on which there is a parcel of fellows who have no other amusement but to fire at every body they see. We could not show our noses at any point without being fired at; but, as we were merely posted there to protect the right flank of the trenches from any sortie, we did not fire at them, and kept as quiet as could be, considering the deadly blast that was blowing around us. There are few situations in life where something cannot be learnt, and I, myself, stand indebted to my twenty-four hours' residence there, for a more correct knowledge of martial sounds than in the study of my whole life time besides. They must be an unmusical pair of ears that cannot inform the wearer

53. Fitzmaurice, John, *A Biographical Sketch of Major General John Fitzmaurice*, p.28.
54. Ewart, John, *Peninsular War Diary of Captain John Frederick Ewart, 52nd Light Infantry, 1811–1812*, p.57.

> whither a cannon or a musket played last, but the various notes, emanating from their respective mouths, admit of nice distinctions. My party was too small, and too well sheltered to repay the enemy for the expense of shells and round shot; but the quantity of grape and musketry aimed at our particular heads, made a good concert of first and second whistles, while the more sonorous voice of the round shot, travelling to our friends on the left, acted as a thorough bass; and there was not a shell, that passed over us to the trenches, that did not send back a fragment among us as soon as it burst, as if to gratify a curiosity that I was far from expressing. We went into the cottage soon after dark, to partake of something that had been prepared for dinner; and, when in the middle of it, a round shot passed through both walls, immediately over our heads, and garnished the soup with a greater quantity of our parent earth than was quite palatable. We were relieved, as usual, by the first division, at ten next morning; and, to avoid as much as possible the destructive fire from the walls, they sent forward only three or four men at a time, and we sent ours away in the same proportions.[55]

The last day the division was in the trenches was on 17 January. The Left Wing of the 1st Battalion 95th Rifles decided to take a short cut back to their cantonments. Instead of taking the long way around the city, they decided to cross the Águeda River on the east side of the city. They found 'that by crossing the river where we then were, and running the gauntlet for a mile, exposed to the fire of two pieces of artillery, that we should be saved the distance of two or three miles in returning to our quarters.'[56] Upon returning to their billets, the division received an order to be ready to return to the trenches the next day. However, this order was rescinded the following day and they were told to march on 19 January to 'the Convent of La Caridad and halt there until further orders.'[57]

Despite the horrendous weather and having to ford an icy river twice in thirty hours, and then work in wet clothes, the men appeared to be unaffected by the ordeal. Captain Ewart of the 1st Battalion 52nd Foot noted in his diary on 17 January that 'Most of the division were again thirty hours out and all the men suffered from having to ford the Agueda, taking off their shoes and stockings; the sick list, however, is wonderfully small, 1st 52nd not 30.'[58]

---

55. Kincaid, John, *Adventures in the Rifle Brigade in the Peninsula, France, and the Netherlands from 1809–1815*, pp.104-106.
56. Ibid, p.106.
57. Gairdner, James, *The American Sharpe: The Adventures of an American Officer of the 95th Rifles in the Peninsula & Waterloo Campaigns*, p.18.
58. Ewart, John, *Peninsular War Diary of Captain John Frederick Ewart, 52nd Light Infantry, 1811–1812*, p.57.

Despite spending many hours searching for the division's casualties from 8–18 January, we only found one set. Most of the battalions just included them in the monthly returns, so it was impossible to separate them. The one exception was the 3rd Caçadores.

Table 2.9: The 3rd Caçadores Casualties 8 January–18 January 1812

Date	Officers		Sergeants		Corporals and Privates	
	KIA	WIA	KIA	WIA	KIA	WIA
8 January[59]	-	-	-	-	4	6
12 January[60]	-	-	-	-	1	5
17 January[61]	-	-	-	-	-	2
Total	-	-	-	-	5	13

59. AHM 1-14-256-04 MS-54.
60. AHM 1-14-256-04 MS-52.
61. AHM 1-14-256-04 MS-53.

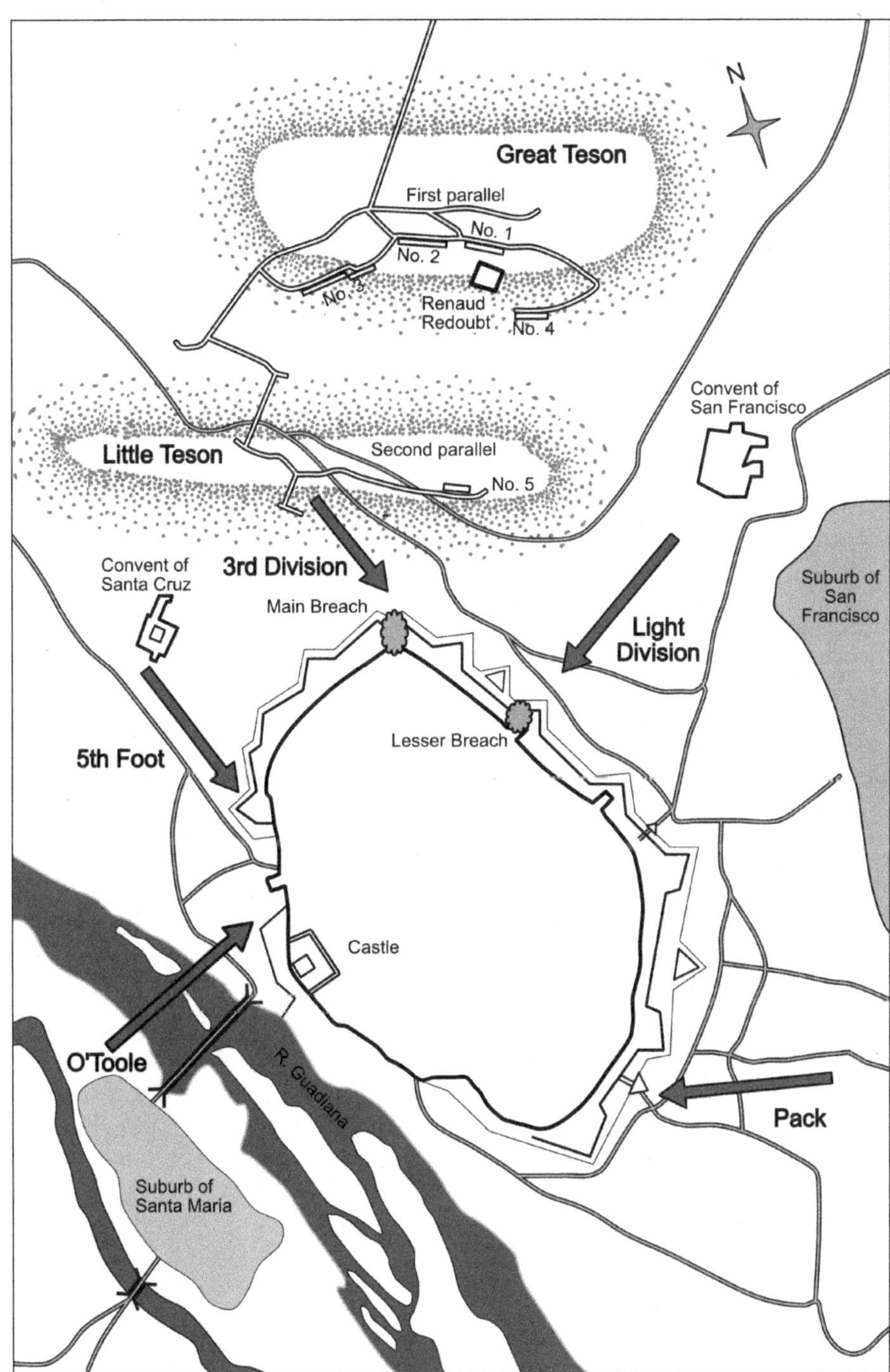

Assault on Ciudad Rodrigo 19 January 1812

Chapter 3

The Assault on Ciudad Rodrigo

> Nothing however could resist the impetuosity of the assailants who rushed over every obstacle, scaling two walls & passing as many ditches. The enemy as soon as they came in contact were driven into the Grand Square of the town at the point of the bayonet.
>
> Lieutenant George Barlow,
> 1st Battalion 52nd Foot[1]

The division received orders in the evening of 18 January to march to La Caridad Monastery the next day. It was on the road about 6:00 a.m. when the sky began to get light.[2] By noon the division had crossed the Águeda River and soon reached the monastery. Not having received further orders, the men built large fires to cook their rations and to dry their clothes.[3] The 1st and 3rd Caçadores did not march with the British troops, having been told to 'to await further orders in their respective quarters'.[4] General Craufurd became impatient at the lack of orders and told his aide-de-camp, Lieutenant James Shaw, to ride to the siege lines and find out what Wellington wanted them to do. Shaw

> found Lord Wellington's Staff near to the Convent of San Francisco and asked for His Lordship whom they pointed out, sitting near the convent and at some distance and alone, but they said I could not speak to him, as he was writing the orders for the assault. But this I had nothing to do with and went immediately up to him and informed him of the orders which I had received from General Craufurd. He stopped writing, listened attentively to what I said, gave the most clear and distinct orders as to the division and then returned [to] writing.[5]

1. Barlow, George Ulrich, *A Light Infantryman With Wellington: The Letters of Captain George Ulrich Barlow, 52nd and 69th Foot, 1808–1815*, p.57.
2. Nautical twilight was at 5:56 a.m.
3. Duffy, John, *Journals of Majors John Duffy and John Maxwell Tylden of the 43rd Foot*, p.143; Ewart, John, *Peninsular War Diary of Captain John Frederick Ewart, 52nd Light Infantry, 1811–1812*, p.58, and Oglander, Henry, *The Journals of Captain Henry Oglander of the 43rd & 47th Foot*, p.117.
4. Oglander, Henry, *The Journals of Captain Henry Oglander of the 43rd & 47th Foot*, p.117.
5. Shaw, James, *Riflemen of Wellington's Light Division in the Peninsular War 1808–14*, p.171.

Shaw returned to Craufurd at about 3:00 p.m. and the division marched to Ciudad Rodrigo. As they neared the city, they passed the encampment of the Guards Brigade of the 1st Division who came out to greet them and wish them success. In response, the band of the 43rd Foot began playing *The Downfall of Paris*.[6] The division moved behind the Great Teson and waited for their orders which finally arrived.

> The attack upon Ciudad Rodrigo must be made this evening at seven o'clock.
>
> The ditch must likewise be entered by a column on the left of the great breach, consisting of three companies of the 95th regiment, which are to issue from the right of the convent of St. Francisco. This column will be provided with three ladders, 12 feet long, with which they are to descend into the ditch, at a point which will be pointed out to them by Lieutenant [Peter] Wright [Royal Engineers]: on descending into the ditch, they are to turn to their right, and to proceed towards the main breach; they are to have 10 axes, to enable them to cut down the obstacles which may have been erected to impede the communication along the ditch, on the left of the breach.
>
> Major General Vandeleur's brigade, will issue out from the left of the convent of St. Francisco, and are to attack the breach to the left of the main breach; this column must have 12 ladders, each 12 feet long, with which they are to descend into the ditch, at a point which will be shown them by Captain [Charles] Ellicombe [Royal Engineers]: on arriving in the ditch, they are to turn to their left, to storm the breach in the fausse-braie, on their left, of the small ravelin, and thence to the breach in the tower of the body of the place; as soon as this body will have reached the top of the breach, in the fausse-braie wall, a detachment of five companies are to be sent to the right, to cover the attack of Major General M'Kinnon's brigade, by the principal breach, and as soon as they have reached the top of the tower, they are to turn to their right, and communicate with the rampart of the main breach; as soon as this communication can be established endeavour should be made to open the gate of Salamanca.
>
> Colonel Barnard's brigade will be formed behind the convent of St. Francisco, ready to support Major General Vandeleur's brigade; all these columns will have detached parties especially appointed to keep up a fire on the defences during the above.
>
> The men with ladders, and axes, and bags, must not have their arms; those who are to storm, must not fire.
>
> The different regiments and brigades to receive ladders are to send parties to the engineers' depôt to receive them, three men for each ladder.[7]

6. Cooke, John, *A True Soldier Gentleman: The Memoirs of Lt. John Cooke 1791–1813*, p.102.
7. Jones, John, *Journal of the Sieges Carried on by the Army Under the Duke of Wellington Between the Years 1811 & 1814*, Vol. 1, pp.139–41. The complete order can be found in Appendix 4.

There were two breaches in the wall. The main breach was to be attacked by the 3rd Division. About 200m to its left was the Lesser Breach, which the Light Division was to assault. According to Lieutenant Henry Oglander, 43rd Foot, 'the largest, which was sufficiently wide for ten men to advance abreast; was opposite to our trenches; the smaller, by which a front of six might mount, was opposite to the convent of San Francisco.'[8]

A few days prior to the assault, Major George Napier, 2nd Battalion 52nd Foot, petitioned Craufurd to allow him to command the storming party in the assault. Craufurd agreed. Lieutenant Harry Smith, the 2nd Brigade's brigade major, hearing that Lieutenant John Gurwood, 52nd Foot, had been given command of the forlorn hope, also went to Craufurd and volunteered to command the forlorn hope instead. Smith knew that if he survived the assault as its commander, he would be promoted to captain. Craufurd refused his request and said 'Why, you cannot go; you, a Major of Brigade, a senior Lieutenant, you are sure to get a Company. No, I must give it to a younger officer.'[9]

It was not until 19 January, when Lieutenant Shaw returned to the division waiting at La Caridad with orders for the assault that night, was Napier informed that he and Gurwood were chosen.[10] Once they were at the Great Teson, Craufurd ordered Napier

> to get one hundred volunteers from each British regiment in the division, with proportionate officers and non-commissioned officers, to form them up in front of the division, and take the command of them in order to lead the assault. I went to three regiments – viz., the 43rd, 52nd, and Rifle Corps, and said, 'Soldiers, I have the honour to be appointed to the command of the storming party which is to lead the Light Division to the assault of the small breach. I want one hundred volunteers from each regiment; those who will go with me come forward.' Instantly there rushed out nearly half the division, and we were obliged to take them at chance. I then formed them in companies of one hundred men each, Captain [James] Fergusson commanding the 43rd, Captain [William] Jones the 52nd...Captain [Samuel] Mitchel [2nd Battalion 95th Rifles] commanded the Rifles. These were preceded by what is called the *forlorn hope,* consisting of twenty-five men, two sergeants, and one subaltern, a lieutenant, because if he survives he gets a company. The officer who commanded in this instance was a great friend of mine, a very excellent gallant officer, Lieutenant [John] Gurwood, of the 52nd. As soon as all was formed, we marched at the head of the division in high spirits, and determined that nothing should stop

8. Oglander, Henry, *The Journals of Captain Henry Oglander of the 43rd & 47th Foot*, p.117.
9. Smith, Harry, *The Autobiography of Sir Harry Smith*, pp.56–57.
10. *W.D.*, Vol. 8, p.552.

> us from carrying the breach. I felt that I was on the point of fulfilling my old motto, 'Death or glory.' I knew if I failed it must be my own fault, as I had at my back three hundred British bayonets, wielded by as able hands and stout 'hearts of oak' as ever faced the enemy! that I had only to lead, to give the word, and all would be carried by British steel, let the opposition be ever so great. If I fell, I should fall as I wished; if I lived, most probably promotion, certainly glory, the soldier's greatest prize, would be my reward; and, above all, I knew I should receive the approbation of the commander of the army.[11]

Napier then 'gave orders that when the breach was carried, the 43rd party was to clear the ramparts to the right towards the great breach and the 52nd party to the left.'[12]

The mystery of why the 1st and 3rd Caçadores were not in the first movement orders was finally solved. They were 'to carry bags filled with long dry grass, in order, by throwing them into the ditch, to prevent any accident' when the troops jumped from the fausse-braie into the ditch below the walls.[13]

By 6:30 p.m. the division was formed up behind the convent of San Francisco.[14] There they were met by 'Lord Wellington, General Graham, with Marshal Beresford, and nearly all the general officers of the army.'[15]

Craufurd modified the orders that he received from Wellington. Instead of sending three companies from the 1st Battalion 95th Rifles, who were to move to the Main Breach once they were in the ditch, he ordered the four companies of the Right Wing of the 1st Battalion 95th Rifles to line the glacis and provide cover for the assaulting columns. Once the assault by the two columns reached the top of the glacis, they were to enter the ditch and move to the right. Furthermore, instead of assaulting with the 2nd Brigade in front and the 1st Brigade in reserve, he ordered both brigades to attack with the 1st Brigade on the right and the 2nd Brigade on the left.

Lieutenant Shaw, Craufurd's aide-de-camp, left a detailed description on how the division was formed for the assault. It

11. Napier, George, *At War With Wellington: The Peninsular War Letters of William, George and Charles Napier*, p.114.
12. Fergusson, James, *Men of Wellington's Light Division: Unpublished Memoirs of the 43rd (Monmouthshire) Regiment in the Peninsular War*, p.76.
13. Napier, George, *At War With Wellington: The Peninsular War Letters of William, George and Charles Napier*, p.115.
14. Cooke, John, *A True Soldier Gentleman: The Memoirs of Lt. John Cooke 1791–1813*, p.102.
15. Ewart, John, *Peninsular War Diary of Captain John Frederick Ewart, 52nd Light Infantry, 1811–1812*, pp.58–59.

> advanced to the assault in the following order three [*sic*] companies of the Rifles moved to the right to enter the ditch between the greater & lesser breaches. And the main column consisting of the 43rd and 52nd Regiments [and] part of the Rifles, marched directly for the lesser breach, preceded by a forlorn hope under Lieutenant Gurwood and 800 [*sic*] men as a storming party under Major Napier.
>
> The 43rd and 52nd Regiments were formed in columns of sections and were abreast of each other; the 43rd formed the right-hand column of sections, the 52nd the left-hand column of sections.
>
> The 43rd column of sections was formed right in front, the 52nd left in front. The 43rd was ordered on entering the breach to proceed in its column of sections along the rampart, towards the Main Breach, the 52nd in the opposite direction towards the Salamanca gate. Thus the 43rd, when it wheeled to the left & the 52nd to the right when on the rampart would form a line facing the town. The leading sections of the 43rd and 52nd it will be observed were abreast of each other, they were led respectively by Lieutenant Colonel Macleod & Lieutenant Colonel Colborne the commanders of those regiments, who in their advance followed up closely the storming party.[16]

The forlorn hope consisted of twenty-five men commanded by Lieutenant John Gurwood of the 2nd Battalion 52nd Foot. Assisting him, was Lieutenant Lawrence Steele, the most junior lieutenant in the 43rd Foot.[17] The storming party was supposed to consist of 3 officers and 100 men from each regiment. The 43rd Foot provided: Captain James Fergusson, and Lieutenants John Bramwell and John O'Connell.[18] There were at least five officers from the 52nd Foot: Captain William Jones (2nd Battalion), Lieutenants George Young (1st Battalion), Douglas Hamilton (2nd Battalion) and John Knox (2nd Battalion), and Ensign John Royle (1st Battalion).[19] The 95th Rifles provide two officers from the 1st Battalion: First Lieutenants William Johnston and John Kincaid; and one from the 2nd Battalion: Captain Samuel Mitchell.[20] Captain Rice Jones of the Royal Engineers would guide them to the breach.[21]

16. Shaw, James, *Riflemen of Wellington's Light Division in the Peninsular War* 1808–14, pp.171–172.
17. Fergusson, James, *Men of Wellington's Light Division: Unpublished Memoirs of the 43rd (Monmouthshire) Regiment in the Peninsular War*, p.76.
18. Ibid, p.75.
19. Booth, Charles, *Redcoats of Wellington's Light Division: Unpublished & Rare Memoirs of the 52nd (Oxfordshire) Regiment of Foot*, p.114.
20. Kincaid, John, *Adventures in the Rifle Brigade in the Peninsula, France, and the Netherlands from 1809–1815*, p.108.
21. Jones, Rice, *An Engineer Officer Under Wellington in the Peninsula*, p.124.

Eight sergeants and corporals from the two companies of the 2nd Battalion 95th Rifles volunteered for the forlorn hope and the storming party: Sergeants Joseph Bowley, Patrick Comarford, George Ecke, John Spencer, and Richard Tute; and Corporals Luke Derby, David Larkin, and John Nesbitt. Corporal Robert Fairfoot of the 1st Battalion 95th Rifles was also with them. Spencer, Tute, Derby, and Nesbitt were from Captain John Hart's company, while Bowley, Comarford, Ecke, and Larkin were assigned to Captain Samuel Mitchell's company.[22]

Preceding the whole formation were the four companies of the Right Wing of the 1st Battalion 95th Rifles commanded by Brevet Major Alexander Cameron. Initially, these riflemen would form a covering party for the assault columns. Their mission was 'to line the crest of the glacis, and fire upon the ramparts. Some companies of Portuguese, which were supposed to be unarmed, carrying bags filled with hay and straw, for throwing into the ditch, to facilitate the passage of the storming party.'[23] Napier states the 3rd Caçadores had the mission of carrying the bags.[24] Once the bags of grass were thrown into the ditch, those four companies, which included Captain Uniacke's company, was to move through the ditch to the right to link up with the 3rd Division at the Main Breach.

It appears that during the rush to get ready for assault, no unit was assigned the mission of carrying the 12-ft ladders. When Lieutenant Smith, the 2nd Brigade's brigade major, realised this prior to the assault, he went to the Left Wing of the 1st Battalion 95th Rifles and came to a fire near where Lieutenant George Simmons was, and said,

> One of you must come and take charge of some ladders if required, at the impulse of the moment I took with me the men required, and followed him to the Engineers' camp, where the ladders were handed to me. I marched with them to General Craufurd, who was with the advance. He attacked me in a most ungracious manner.
>
> 'Why did you bring these short ladders?'
>
> 'Because I was ordered by the Engineer to do so, General.'
>
> 'Go back, sir, and get others; I am astonished at such stupidity.'
>
> Of course I went back, but was sadly crestfallen. This is what I deserved for over-zeal. A Portuguese captain and his company were waiting for something to do, so I said, 'Here, my brave fellows, take these ladders,' and

22. Cope, William, *The History of the Rifle Brigade (The Prince Consort's Own) Formerly the 95th* p.97, WO 12/9523, WO 12/9583.
23. Kincaid, John, *Adventures in the Rifle Brigade in the Peninsula, France, and the Netherlands from 1809–1815*, p.109.
24. Napier, George, *At War With Wellington: The Peninsular War Letters of William, George and Charles Napier*, p.114.

> handed them over with every necessary instruction for the good of the service. I then instantly returned to the company I belonged to, which was posted at the head of the column ready to proceed.[25]

General Craufurd marched on the left of the division.

The division's two brigades were formed in separate columns that were close together. Each column had a three-man front,[26] with the senior captain's company at its head. The 1st Brigade's column was on the right. The 43rd Foot was in the lead, with Captain John Duffy's company in front. The 2nd Brigade's column was led by Major General Vandeleur. Joining him was Lieutenant Colonel Colborne, the commander of the 2nd Battalion 52nd Foot, and Captain Joseph Dobbs, the senior captain in the 1st Battalion 52nd Foot. With this small party was Lieutenant Harry Smith, the brigade major, and Lieutenant William Armstrong, Vandeleur's aide-de-camp. In the 1st Battalion 52nd Foot, Captain Dobbs' company was at the head of the column, followed by Captain Robert Campbell and his company. The other eight companies were formed behind them in order of their commander's seniority[27] although Captain John Ewart, who was fifth in seniority, claims his company was fourth.[28] Following them was the 2nd Battalion 52nd Foot, with Captain Augustus Merry and his company leading the battalion.

It is likely that the men from the caçadore battalions who were not assigned to carry the bags of grass and hay brought up the rear of the two columns.

The Walls

The northern walls of the city, the side that faced the Great Teson, were protected by a ravelin – a triangular fortification that was designed to split the attacking force and allow the defenders to fire on the flanks of the approaching assault columns. The sloping ground leading to the ravelin was called the glacis. Between the glacis and the ravelin was a 3m (10ft) deep ditch that was 6m (20ft) wide. The apex of the ravelin pointed to the glacis, while its base faced the walls of the fausse-braie. The wall on the side of the ditch that was between the glacis and the ravelin was called the counterscarp and was about 3m (10ft)

25. Simmons, George, *A British Rifleman: Journals and Correspondence During the Peninsular War and the Campaign of Wellington*, pp.220–221.
26. Duffy, John, *Journals of Majors John Duffy and John Maxwell Tylden of the 43rd Foot*, p.144, and Ewart, John, *Peninsular War Diary of Captain John Frederick Ewart, 52nd Light Infantry, 1811–1812*, p.59.
27. Dobbs, John, *Recollections of an Old 52nd Man*, p.33.
28. Ewart, John, 'Letter Describing the Storming of Ciudad Rodrigo', *Redcoats of Wellington's Light Division: Unpublished & Rare Memoirs of the 52nd (Oxfordshire) Regiment of Foot*, p.94.

high. The ditch on either side of the ravelin's apex led to the ditch before the fausse-braie. This ditch had puddles of water in it, but none were deep enough to be an obstacle to infantry. The fausse-braie was about 6m (20ft) high and was designed to protect the wall of the city from artillery fire. Between the wall and the fausse-braie was an 8m-wide ditch that was dry. The wall of the city was about 10m (32ft) high, of which only the lower 6m were protected by the fausse-braie.

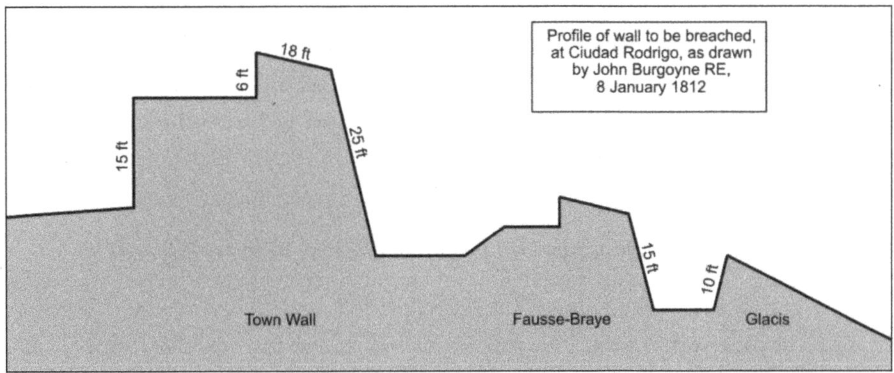

Note: This original sketch does not show the ravelin where the Light Division attacked.

The Defenders

General of brigade Jean Barrié, the commander of the garrison, had about 2,000 men to defend the city, including a battalion each from the 34th Léger and 113th Line Regiments, two companies of artillery, and fifteen engineers and sappers. According to a document found in the quarters of Captain Jean-Pierre Cathala,[29] the garrison's chief engineer, the plan called for a company of voltigeurs to defend the Lesser Breach. Exits from the ramparts near the breach were to be blocked with carriages and wood. The reserves were to remain 'within reach of the breaches, or were distributed around the perimeter of the place to repel attempts at escalation. The governor positioned himself between the two breaches with his staff and around sixty men forming his reserve.'[30] Before the siege began, numerous guns had been placed on the walls around the city. Most of the guns that could fire on the breaches had been put out of action by 19 January.

29. Belmas, J., *Journaux des sièges dans la péninsule de 1807 à 1814*, Vol. 4, p.283.
30. Jones, John, *Journal of the Sieges Carried on by the Army Under the Duke of Wellington Between the Years 1811 & 1814*, Vol. 1, p.126.

The Breaches

The Allies began their bombardment at 4:00 p.m. on 14 January. Their goal was to knock a hole in the wall of the city, that the troops could use to enter the city. The wall was to some extent protected by the fausse-braie which was supposed to absorb the cannonballs that were shot at the wall. However, it was several metres shorter than the wall and there was a danger that the balls would miss the fausse-braie and hit the wall. The Main Breach was near the corner of the wall close to the cathedral. A smaller breach, also called the Lesser Breach, was blown in the wall about 200m to the left of the Main Breach. Although the division's mission was to assault the Lesser Breach, there were two breaches that had to be crossed to get into the city: one in the fausse-braie and the wall.

Description of the Breaches the Light Division Was to Assault

The artillery had knocked about 3m (10ft) off the top of the city's wall, leaving 7m (22ft) of the wall intact. The gap in the wall at the top was about 6m (19ft) wide. The rubble caused by the artillery continuous pounding of the wall had fallen into the ditch below it, creating a ramp 8m (26ft) long that was stopped by the back wall of the fausse-braie. This ramp had a slope between 40° and 50°. The fausse-braie had been reduced to about 3m (10ft) in height with a breach about 6m wide at the top. Its ramp had a slope between 30° and 40°. The defenders placed the barrel to a 6-pounder cannon at the top of the breach. The barrel was 180cm (71in) long and blocked much of the opening to the ramparts.

The ramps leading to the top of the breaches were made of dirt, stones blocks, rocks, concrete, and broken cannonballs. It was very unstable and the footing was treacherous. Climbing on it would cause mini avalanches hitting the climbers below. Scrambling up a 45° slope would be very difficult with two hands, but the soldier would be carrying his musket or rifle with its bayonet fixed in one hand, so he would only have the use of one hand to pull himself up. If he slipped there was a real danger of being impaled on the bayonets of those behind him or bowling over the soldiers on the slope below. These were just the dangers from the slope. There was a good chance that he would also have to face grapeshot from artillery, musket fire and grenades from the defenders, as well rocks being dropped on him from above.

At the Main Breach, the defenders created a retrenchment by fortifying the houses to be able to fire on the top of the breach and lining the space at the bottom of the ramparts with caltrops and other sharp objects to prevent the assaulters from jumping off the back of the 5m high ramparts. At the Lesser

Breach there were no retrenchments to prevent the attacker from entering the city other than blocking the stairs leading down to the city from the ramparts.

The Assault

Shortly before the assault was to begin, Wellington sent for Lieutenant Colonel Colborne and Major Napier. Wellington wanted to ensure that Napier knew exactly where the breach was

> and pointing out, as well as the light would permit, the spot where the foot of the breach was, he said to me, 'Now do you understand the way you are to lead, so as to arrive at the breach without noise or confusion?' I answered, and we then went back to the regiment; and just before I moved on, some staff officer present said, 'Why, your men are not loaded; why do you not make them load?' I replied, 'Because if we do not do the business with the bayonet, without firing, we shall not be able to do it at all, so I shall not load.' I heard Lord Wellington, who was close by, say, 'Let him alone; let him go his own way.'[31]

The division stood in the cold behind the convent of San Francisco waiting until 7:00 p.m. when the assault would kick off. For some, their minds turned to thoughts of what awaited them. Rifleman Edward Costello volunteered to be in the storming party and

> with three others I had, as I then considered, the good fortune to be chosen from our company. This was an occasion, as may be believed, momentous and interesting enough in the life of a soldier, and so we seemed to consider it. We shook hands with a feeling of friendly sincerity, while we speculated as to the chances of outliving the assault, and, if truth must be told, the chances of plunder in the town. We were at this time in the trenches in front of the city, from whence proceeded a very smart fire of shot and shell, probably to give us an idea of the warm reception we might expect on our visit at night.[32]

Twenty-year-old Second Lieutenant John Fitzmaurice, 1st Battalion 95th, took time before the assault to step out of the trenches with his company commander, Captain John Uniacke, to look at the walls of the city. Uniacke turned to him and said,

---

31. Napier, George, *At War With Wellington: The Peninsular War Letters of William, George and Charles Napier*, pp.114–115.
32. Costello, Edward, *Adventures of a Soldier*, pp.143–144.

> 'Look there Fitz, what would our mothers say' (they were both widows' sons) 'if they saw what was preparing for us?'
>
> 'Far better they should not,' replied his friend;
>
> 'but what an extravagant fellow you are to have put on that beautiful new pelisse for such a night as this.'
>
> Fitzmaurice laughed and responded with 'I shall be all the better worth taking.'[33]

Craufurd took time to address the forlorn hope and the storming party. 'Soldiers! the eyes of your country are upon you. Be steady, be cool, be firm in the assault. The town must be yours this night. Once masters of the wall, let your first duty be to clear the ramparts, and in doing this keep together.'[34]

The Assault of the Forlorn Hope and the Storming Party

Despite the assault being well planned by Wellington, there was no indication that the subordinate units were briefed on what to expect. Nor were units tasked to carry ladders, and there were some questions about who was supposed to be carrying the sacks of hay and grass. Furthermore, it does not appear that the officers and men knew that there were two breaches they would have to scale nor that the ravelin could be by-passed by moving through the ditch to the left of the right. Three Royal Engineer officers were assigned to the division for the assault. Captain Rice Jones was to go with the storming party, Captain Charles Ellicombe with the main column, and Lieutenant Peter Wright was with the five companies of the 95th Rifles in the covering party. Their mission was to guide the division to the breaches.[35] Despite having these guides, once the assault began, confusion reigned everywhere.

The covering party and the Portuguese from the 3rd Caçadores carrying the sacks of grass and hay moved out, followed by the forlorn hope and the storming party. Several accounts claim that the caçadores never arrived with the sacks to break their fall. Major Napier, the commander of the storming party believed that Lieutenant Colonel George Elder, the 3rd Caçadores commander, never received the order to do so.[36] Corporal Thomas Garretty, 43rd Foot, who was in the storming party, said the men with him were too impatient to wait for the troops carrying the sacks, and jumped into the ditch before they arrived.[37]

33. Fitzmaurice, John, *A Biographical Sketch of Major General John Fitzmaurice*, p.27.
34. Ibid, p.144.
35. Jones, Rice, *An Engineer Officer Under Wellington in the Peninsula*, p.124.
36. Napier, George, *At War With Wellington: The Peninsular War Letters of William, George and Charles Napier*, p.114.
37. Garretty, Thomas, *Memoirs of a Sergeant Late in the Forty-Third Light Infantry Regiment*, p.148.

Rifleman Costello wrote later that the Portuguese stopped advancing across the glacis when they began taking casualties from the defenders.[38]

The forlorn hope, which had the mission of drawing the initial fire of the defenders, got lost after descending into the ditch between the glacis and the ravelin. They thought they had reached the fausse-braie and were using the ladders to climb to the top of the ravelin. Once there they crossed the ravelin they found that the storming party had beat them to the undefended breach in the fausse-braie. By the time it reached the breach in the main wall, the storming party was already climbing the rubble of the Lesser Breach.[39] Lieutenant Gurwood started climbing but 'was knocked down by a hand grenade to the bottom of the breach, he mounted again & received a slight wound in the head which stunned him for some minutes & had a second roll [down the breach], a third time he succeeded in getting [a] footing on the breach.'[40]

The storming party, with Captain James Fergusson and his 100 men was in the front and the first to reach the breach in the wall. Fergusson wrote,

> we advanced rapidly across the glacis & descended into the ditch near the ravelin under a heavy fire. We found the forlorn hope placing ladders against the face of the work and to which spot our party turned when the engineer officer called out 'You are wrong this is the way to the breach in the fausse braie which leads to the breach you are to attack'[41]

Rifle Lieutenant Kincaid confirmed the confusion among the storming party as they tried to find their way in the dark.

> We had some difficulty at first in finding the breach, as we had entered the ditch opposite to a ravelin, which we mistook for a bastion. I tried first one side of it and then the other, and seeing one corner of it a good deal battered, with a ladder placed against it, I concluded that it must be the breach, and calling to the soldiers near me, to follow. I mounted with the most ferocious intent, carrying a sword in one hand and a pistol in the other; but, when I got up, I found nobody to fight with, except two of our own men, who were already laid dead across the top of the ladder. I saw, in a moment, that I had got into the wrong box, and

38. Costello, Edward, *Adventures of a Soldier*, p.148.
39. Fergusson, James, *Men of Wellington's Light Division: Unpublished Memoirs of the 43rd (Monmouthshire) Regiment in the Peninsular War*, pp.75–76.
40. Dawson, Henry, *Redcoats of Wellington's Light Division: Unpublished & Rare Memoirs of the 52nd (Oxfordshire) Regiment of Foot*, p.147.
41. Fergusson, James, *Men of Wellington's Light Division: Unpublished Memoirs of the 43rd (Monmouthshire) Regiment in the Peninsular War*, p.76.

was about to descend again, when I heard a shout from the opposite side, that the breach was there; and, moving in that direction, I dropped myself from the ravelin, and landed in the ditch, opposite to the foot of the breach, where I found the head of the storming party just beginning to fight their way into it.[42]

The storming party went through the ditch on either side of the ravelin, where they reached the ditch in front of the fausse-braie. Fergusson called on his

men to come on, we ascended the breach in the fausse braie and soon reached the breach in the body of the place without the use of ladders. We remained for a few moments on the breach until we had collected about twenty or thirty officers & men when we cheered & rushed in carrying the breach. A gun stretched across the entrance, near which some of the enemy were bayonetted and among the number some deserters from the Light Division in arms defending it against their countrymen. A soldier of the name of Jonathan [Israel] Wild 43rd Regiment was the first man that mounted the breach in the fausse braie, but no individual could claim being the first that entered the breach in the body of the place. It was a simultaneous rush of from twenty to thirty of us, some men of the 3rd Battalion Rifles among the number who had been ordered to line the crest of the glacis.[43]

Corporal Garretty, 43rd Foot, was in the storming party.

It was now our turn. [We] had three hundred yards to clear; but, impatient of delay, we did not wait for the hay-bags, but swiftly ran to the crest of the glacis, jumped down the scarp, a depth of eleven feet, and rushed up the faussebraye, under a smashing discharge of grape and musketry. The bottom of the ditch was dark and intricate, and the forlorn hope took too much to their left; but the storming party went straight to the breach, which was so contracted, that a gun placed lengthwise across the top nearly blocked up the opening. Here the forlorn hope rejoined the stormers; but when two thirds of the ascent were gained, the leading men, crushed together by the narrowness of the place, staggered under the weight of the enemy's fire.[44]

It was at this point Napier was wounded and the momentum of the attack stalled. He wrote later that,

---

42. Kincaid, John, *Adventures in the Rifle Brigade in the Peninsula, France, and the Netherlands from 1809–1815*, pp.110–111.
43. Fergusson, James, *Men of Wellington's Light Division: Unpublished Memoirs of the 43rd (Monmouthshire) Regiment in the Peninsular War*, p.76.
44. Garretty, Thomas, *Memoirs of a Sergeant Late in the Forty-Third Light Infantry Regiment*, pp.148–149.

> When about two-thirds up, I received a grape shot which smashed my elbow and great part of my [right] arm; and on falling, the men, who thought I was killed, checked for a few moments, and forgetting they were not loaded commenced snapping their muskets. I immediately called out 'Recollect you are not loaded; push on with the bayonet.' Upon this the whole gave a loud 'hurrah,' and driving all before them, carried the breach, and wheeling as I had given orders to the right and left soon drove off the enemy.[45]

Climbing up the breach was dangerous and not just from being shot, stabbed by a sword or bayonet, or pummeled with stones. Captain Rice Jones, the Royal Engineer who was acting as the guide for the storming party, was among the first to try and climb the breach. He slipped and fell head first down the beach, before he got halfway up it. He got up and tried a second time and made it to the top. He 'escaped this rough treatment with a slight scratch of a bayonet on my thigh, and a contusion on my breast.'[46] Gurwood, who commanded the forlorn hope, was wounded twice while climbing the breach. The first by a grenade that sent him flying down to the bottom of the breach. He got on his feet and climbed the breach a second time, was hit in the head and rolled down the breach again. There he laid stunned for a few minutes and by time he climbed to the top of the breach a third time, the breach was in British hands.[47]

The Wounding of General Craufurd

As the troops moved forward Craufurd and Lieutenant Shaw, his aide-de-camp, wrote they kept

> to the left of the column, proceeded directly to the crest of the glacis, about sixty yards to the left of where the column entered the ditch and from that spot, at the highest pitch of his voice, continued giving instructions to the column. This brought upon him an intense fire of musketry from the opposite parapets of the fausse braie and rampart and at a very short distance, for the ditch of the fausse braie was very narrow and even the main ditch was very narrow and the place had no covered way. He was thus exposed to a double fire of infantry at a very short distance, the superior slope of the parapet of the fausse braie being in the same line as the slope of the glacis, he could not remain many minutes where he was without being hit,

45. Napier, George, *At War With Wellington: the Peninsular War Letters of William, George and Charles Napier*, p.115.
46. Jones, Rice, *An Engineer Officer Under Wellington in the Peninsula*, p.124.
47. Dawson, Henry, *Redcoats of Wellington's Light Division: Unpublished & Rare Memoirs of the 52nd (Oxfordshire) Regiment of Foot*, p.141.

accordingly he was struck by a musket ball, which passed through his arm, broke through the ribs, passed through part of the lungs and lodged in or at the spine; and he not only fell, but the shock was so great that on falling he rolled over down the glacis. There was not a soul with him but myself, there was no one even near us. I immediately took hold of him and half dragged and half carried him to where there was an inequality of ground in which he was out of the direct fire from the place.[48]

The Assault of the Columns

Captain Duffy and his company of 43rd soldiers led the right column and upon reaching the top of the glacis ran into the rifles in the covering party. He wrote in his diary that,

> The attack at the great breach began too soon, as it was intended that our division was to have commenced it. The enemy opened a heavy fire of grape & musquetry which swept the glacis as we past. Owing to some mistake, a stop took place at the counterscarp of some companies of Rifles not extending as directed and General Craufurd called out for the 43rd to disengage to the right & lead, in which was complied with by myself & part of the company. The rest by mistake kept in the column & I believe the cassadores [caçadores] with the bags of hay impeded their progress. We were therefore obliged to sound the bugle to advance & then rush on. We descended the counterscarp about 9 feet then ascended the fausse-braye [*sic*] and down to the ditch. The breach was perfectly practical but we ascended with but little opposition about 40 feet.

Lieutenant John Cooke, also of the 43rd Foot, was in the right column. He

> heard the town-clock strike seven, and at the same time saw a match lighted in one of the embrasures – (very awful!) at that moment the 'forlorn hope,' headed by Lieut. Gurwood, of the 52d, and the storming party (composed of three hundred soldiers, with a proportion of officers) moved on, carrying a number of bags, filled with dried grass, to lessen the depth of the fausse braie and the ditch. In a few minutes they were on the brink of the ditch, and the fire of the town opened briskly on them. There was a sort of check, but no longer than might be expected, as they had to scramble in and out of the fausse braie, and then to jump into the dry ditch; but having gone too far to the left, the advance got on the wrong side of the tower, which was not breached, and the soldiers, for a few seconds, were knocking with

48. Shaw, James, *Riflemen of Wellington's Light Division in the Peninsular War 1808–14*, p.172.

> the butt-ends of their fire locks against the wall, crying out 'Where's the breach?' for although the enemy were firing rapidly from the top of the wall, still the troops, on first descending to the bottom of the ditch, were in total darkness. This state of suspense lasted, however, a very short time, for two soldiers, stumbling on the loose rubbish, called out 'Here's the breach,' and Lieut. Gurwood led up it; but the French swore they should not enter, and fought most desperately on the crest of the breach, throwing down large stones and missiles, and keeping up a most deadly fire.[49]

At the top of the breach was a 6-pounder cannon that had swept the fausse-braie. Bugler William Green, 95th Rifles, was part of the covering force but raced forward with the columns to reach the breach. Additionally, there was a second 6-pounder artillery piece covering both the fausse-braie and the breach.

> Some of us got up to the gun, it was loaded again, and the French gunner was in the act of applying the match, when one of our men knocked him down with the butt of his rifle. If we had been one moment later many of us would have been sent into eternity, as we were close up to the muzzle.[50]

Clearing the Ramparts

By the time the division reached the top of the breach it had lost any resemblance of two columns and was more a mob than a formation. The 1st Brigade was supposed to move to the right to support the 3rd Division's attack on the Main Breach by clearing the ramparts between the Lesser and Main Breach. Captain John Uniacke, 1st Battalion 95th Rifles, had orders to establish communications with the 3rd Division, which was attacking the Main Breach, once he reached the glacis of the fortifications. He chose to liberally interpret his orders by moving with the storming party in the assault on the Lesser Breach and once reaching the top of the breach he took his company down the ramparts to the right to clear any French who was resisting the assault. Things were chaotic on the walls. Lieutenant Harry Smith saw Uniacke disappear along the walls to the right. Despite being the brigade major of the 2nd Brigade and having no authority over any of the 1st Brigade's units, Smith grabbed a

> company of the 43rd and rushed on the flank, and opened a fire which destroyed every man behind the works. My conduct caused great annoyance

49. Cooke, John, *A True Soldier Gentleman: The Memoirs of Lt. John Cooke 1791–1813*, pp.103–104.
50. Green, William, *Where Duty Calls Me: The Experiences of William Green of Lutterworth in the Napoleonic Wars*, p.33.

> to the Captain, Duffy [the company commander whose company was the lead company in the right column], with whom I had some very high words; but the Company obeyed me, and then ran on with poor Uniacke's Company to meet the 3rd Division, or rather clear the ramparts to aid them.[51]

Mixed in with them were soldiers from the 52nd Foot.

They were not far from the Main Breach when the expense magazine (a place that temporarily stored gunpowder used to by the artillerymen on the wall) blew up and caused massive casualties among the attackers both in the Light and the 3rd Divisions. Among the casualties was Major General Henry Mackinnon, a brigade commander in the 3rd Division, who was killed

> on the spot and many soldiers, awfully scorching others. I [Harry Smith] and Uniacke were much scorched, but some splinters of an ammunition chest lacerated him and caused his death three days after the storm. Tom, my brother, was not hurt. I shall never forget the concussion when it struck me, throwing me back many feet into a lot of charged fuses of shells, which in the confusion I took for shells. But a gallant fellow, a Sergeant MacCurrie [Hugh McCurry], [1st Battalion] 52nd Regiment, soon put me right, and prevented me leaping into the ditch. My cocked hat was blown away, my clothes all singed; however the sergeant, a noble fellow, lent me a catskin forage-cap, and on we rushed to meet the 3rd Division, which we soon did. It was headed by a great, big thundering Grenadier of the 88th [Foot], a Lieutenant [James] Stewart, and one of his men seized me by the throat as if I were a kitten, crying out, 'You French' – Luckily, he left me room in the windpipe to d [damn] his eyes, or the bayonet would have been through me in a moment.[52]

After reaching the top of the breach, Major General Vandeleur and Lieutenant Colonel Colborne directed men from the two battalions of the 52nd Foot to clear the ramparts to the left. As they led the men to the left, the French defenders fired a volley into the densely packed troops causing heavy casualties, including Vandeleur and Colborne. After firing the volley, the French soldiers broke and fled into the city.

Rifleman Costello and some riflemen joined the 52nd and charged along the rampart to the left. It nearly cost him his life.

> The French as they retired kept up an occasional fire along the ramparts; while running forward I came against a howitzer, and with such force

51. Smith, Harry, *The Autobiography of Sir Harry Smith*, p.57.
52. Ibid, pp.57–58.

> that it actually tumbled me over, and I found myself prostrate across the body of a wounded French officer; beside him was a cannoneer of his own in the act of assisting him. The latter instantly seized me, and a fearful struggle ensued, till bent almost double by the height, and heavy person of the Frenchman I began to think that after all my escapes my game was over; at this crisis a few of our men came rushing up, one of which was my old 'chum' Wilkie. The cannoneer in his turn was fastened on, and tripped instantaneously by the side of his master. But poor Wilkie the next minute, himself staggered against the howitzer mortally wounded! I flew to his support. But seizing me hastily by the hand, and giving it a deadly squeeze, 'Ned,' he articulated, 'it's all up with me' and relaxing his grasp, he fell back and expired. The officer perceiving my agitation, and fearful of my retaliating on him, handed me over his gold watch.[53]

Taking the City

Once the ramparts were taken the French soldiers lost their will to fight. They abandoned the walls and fled to any place they thought would provide them with some cover. Chief of Battalion Pierre Fourtines, commander of the 34th Léger troops, rallied some of his troops in the main square of the city, but they were either killed or captured. Fourtines was severely wounded and would die on 19 February. Friendly fire between the Light and the 3rd Divisions occurred in the approaches to the square but it quickly died out.[54]

Lieutenant Gurwood, after climbing the breach a third time proceeded down from the ramparts to the city below. He grabbed two soldiers from the 52nd Foot and went to the castle that overlooked the main gate to the city. Inside the courtyard of the castle was the commander of the forlorn hope that assaulted the Main Breach, Lieutenant William Mackie of the 88th Foot, who was accepting the surrender of the city from two French staff officers. Gurwood ignored him and went inside the main room of the castle and accepted the surrender of General Barrié, who handed him his sword. Gurwood escorted Barrié to the Main Breach and presented him to Wellington, who let Gurwood keep the sword. By taking Barrié to Wellington, Gurwood received all the credit for accepting the surrender, while Mackie received none.

After the city surrendered the victorious troops spent the next twelve hours sacking the city.

---

53. Costello, Edward, *Adventures of a Soldier*, pp.146–147.
54. Ewart, John, *Peninsular War Diary of Captain John Frederick Ewart, 52nd Light Infantry, 1811–1812*, p.59, and Martinien, Aristide, *Tableaux par Corps et par Batailles des Officiers Tués et Blessés pendant les Guerres de l'Empire (1805–1815)*, p.463.

Chapter 4

The Sack of Ciudad Rodrigo

> To describe the scene which took place afterwards, is more than I am equal to. Firing into windows, bursting open doors, setting fire to houses, in fact sacking the town, stripping the inhabitants of their gold chains, earrings, trinkets & valuables of every kind, getting drunk and doing everything that soldiers are capable of after having carried a town by storm.
>
> Lieutenant Henry Dawson, 1st Battalion 52nd Foot[1]

Climbing the breach was slow, hard work. Between the darkness and the confusion about where to go once the men were in the ditches, the leaders lost control of their formations. By the time the first men of the Light Division had reached the top of the Lesser Breach the division had become a mob. Major Napier laid wounded about two-thirds of the way up the breach wrote later about the chaos:

> During all this time the troops of the Light Division kept pouring into the place through the breach, and I kept cheering them on as well as I could, but I got terribly bruised and trampled upon in the confusion and darkness. However, very soon 'Victory! England for ever!' was shouted by thousands, and then I knew all was right, and I waited patiently in the breach till all had passed.[2]

Even after the fighting had stopped, men still climbed the breach to get into the city. The officers and NCOs did their best to direct their men where to go once they reached the top of the breach, and even though chaos reigned the leaders had some success. The mob became three distinct groups that had a mixture of men from different regiments, usually from the same brigade, but not always. The regimental officers had loose control over them and got them moving in the right direction. Lieutenant Colonel Charles McLeod, the commander of the 43rd Foot, 'with the assistance of some other officers, managed to collect on

1. Dawson, Henry, *Redcoats of Wellington's Light Division: Unpublished & Rare Memoirs of the 52nd (Oxfordshire) Regiment of Foot*, pp.141–142.
2. Napier, George, *At War With Wellington: The Peninsular War Letters of William, George and Charles Napier*, p.116.

the rampart about 200 soldiers of our regiment and was exhorting them to keep together.'[3] The right column, consisting of the 43rd Foot and a few companies of the 95th Rifles, was initially checked by the explosion that decimated its lead troops, but the men poured off the ramparts and chased the fleeing French towards the Town Plaza. The left column, after losing its brigade commander, and one of its two battalion commanders turned to the left and after clearing the ramparts of the defenders, descended into the town and stopped at the Town Plaza. The surviving riflemen of the storming party moved to the left, stayed on the ramparts and circled around until it reached the Main Breach, when it finally descended into the town, and began rounding up prisoners.[4]

Once the French had surrendered in the Town Plaza, what little control the officers had ended and the soldiers went on a rampage of destruction. Their first goal was to find alcohol. To prevent this, Lieutenant Colonel McLeod 'detached officers with guards, to take possession of all the stores they could find, and to preserve order. These parties ultimately dissolved themselves. If they had not done so, they would have been engaged in the streets with our own troops.'[5] Lieutenant George Barlow, 2nd Battalion 52nd Foot, confirmed that they placed a guard 'over the spirit magazine in time to prevent its seizure. Fifty pipes of good cognac were there found, with a quantity of other commissariat articles.'[6]

Word quickly spread about the alcohol and soon it was every man for himself. Rifleman Costello was among the first to find the store.

> The first place I found myself drawn to by some comrades, was a large white house that had been used as a commissary's store by the French: here a crowd had assembled to break it open, when they were warned off by a sentinel, a German, who was posted to guard the premises. Not heeding his threat, the throng rushed at the door. The poor sentry, true to his trust, attempted to oppose their entrance, and the following minute was run through the body by a bayonet. The house contained several puncheons of spirits, which the men present immediately tapped, by striking in the heads. All now soon became madly drunk; and several wretches, especially, those mounting the steps that had been placed against the butts, to enable them to obtain the rum, fell into the liquor head-foremost and perished, unnoticed by the crowd. Several fights took place, in which the drunkenness

3. Cooke, John, *A True Soldier Gentleman: The Memoirs of Lt. John Cooke 1791–1813*, p.106.
4. Kincaid, John, *Adventures in the Rifle Brigade in the Peninsula, France, and the Netherlands from 1809–1815*, p.113.
5. Cooke, John, *A True Soldier Gentleman: The Memoirs of Lt. John Cooke 1791–1813*, p.106.
6. Barlow, George Ulrich, *A Light Infantryman with Wellington: The Letters of Captain George Ulrich Barlow, 52nd and 69th Foot, 1808–1815*, p.107. A pipe measured 550 litres. This store held 27,500 litres or 6,049 gallons of brandy.

> of the parties alone prevented mischief; and to crown the whole, a light falling into one of the barrels of spirit, the place was set on fire, and many poor wretches, who from the quantity of liquor they had swallowed, were incapable of moving, were consumed in the flames.[7]

Captain Ewart, 1st Battalion 52nd Foot, wrote in his diary about the debauchery of the troops and the inability of the officers to get them under control. 'During the whole night the soldiers committed many excesses, setting fire to some houses, plundering many, particularly after finding some large stores of very good French brandy, bread, pork &c, and it was impossible to get them into any order for a long time.'[8]

Corporal Garretty, 43rd Foot, later recalled that once the men left the ramparts

> after which, throwing off the restraints of discipline, frightful excesses were committed. The town was fired in three or four places; the soldiers menaced their officers, and shot each other; many were killed in the market-place; intoxication soon increased the disorder; and at last, the fury rising to an absolute madness, a fire was wilfully [*sic*] lighted in the middle of the great magazine, when the town, and all in it, would have been blown to atoms, but for the energetic courage of some officers and a few soldiers, who still preserved their senses.[9]

These soldiers were led by Captain William Jones, the senior surviving officer in the 2nd Battalion 52nd Foot. According to a tale that was passed down through the regiment over the years that Jones, also known as 'Jack Jones,' took the surrender of a French officer and used him to find

> quarters for his men, – and having placed some of them in a large store, the French officer led the way into the church, in front of which Lord Wellington and some of the staff were collected. Some fire had been lighted already (supposed by Portuguese soldiers) on the pavement, and the Frenchman entering, and seeing the fire, instantly started back, exclaiming, '*Sacré bleu*!' and ran out with looks of the utmost horror. Jones, not understanding French, did not catch the idea. '*Sacré bleu*' puzzled him, until, going further in, he saw powder about the floor and powder-barrels near the fire. '*Sacré bleu*' became at once identified with powder, and he immediately got the help

---

7. Costello, Edward, *Adventures of a Soldier*, p.148.
8. Ewart, John, *Peninsular War Diary of Captain John Frederick Ewart, 52nd Light Infantry, 1811–1812*, p.60.
9. Garretty, Thomas, *Memoirs of a Sergeant Late in the Forty-Third Light Infantry Regiment*, pp.149–150.

> of two or three of his men (whose names are not known), and carried with his own hands the powder-barrels out of the way of immediate danger.[10]

Lieutenant George Barlow, 2nd Battalion 52nd Foot, gave a slightly different perspective on the cause of the fires.

> Very little booty was however to be gained, inasmuch as the whole town had been deserted by everyone previous to its first occupation by the French, who had pulled down the houses for firewood and our shot has demolished the whole of those nearest the ramparts. The night was moreover miserably cold & our troops crowded into the ruined houses to make fires. These rotten edifices soon caught the flames and the conflagration became dreadful.[11]

The threat of fire was not only the danger in town. Many of the drunk soldiers still retained their weapons and had no inhibition about shooting them. At one point 'many commenced firing, without any ostensible cause; some fired in at the doors and windows, some at the roofs of houses, and others at the clouds; and, at last, some heads began to be blown from their shoulders in the general hurricane.'[12]

Some soldiers, after witnessing the horrors where the alcohol was stored, went wandering, looking for food and a place to sleep. Costello

> went with a comrade, to look for a house where we might obtain refreshment and take up our quarters for the night. This, after some search, we found in the domicile of a doctor, whom we took from under a bed clasped in the arms of a very pretty girl whom he called his niece, like himself, [who was] almost 'Distill'd to jelly with th' effect of fear!' This, however, we soon dispelled, and were rewarded for our pains with a good supper crowned by a bowl of excellent punch that at the time, in own minds, compensated for all the sufferings we had endured in the trenches during the siege.[13]

Restoring Order

Lieutenant Colonel McLeod eventually gave up trying to bring his soldiers from the 43rd Foot under control, finally ordering Captain Duffy to stay at the Lesser Breach to keep any soldiers from going into the town to join the

---

10. Moorsom, William, *Historical Record of the Fifty-Second Regiment*, pp.161–162.
11. Barlow, George Ulrich, *A Light Infantryman With Wellington: The Letters of Captain George Ulrich Barlow, 52nd and 69th Foot, 1808—1815*, p.107.
12. Kincaid, John, *Adventures in the Rifle Brigade in the Peninsula, France, and the Netherlands from 1809–1815*, p.119.
13. Costello, Edward, *Adventures of a Soldier*, p.149.

looters.[14] Lieutenant Wyndham Madden joined him and was told to climb back down the Lesser Breach

> with twenty-five men, ordering him to continue at the foot of it during the night, and to prevent soldiers leaving the town with plunder. At eleven o'clock I went to see him; he had no sinecure, and had very judiciously made a large fire, which, of course, showed the delinquents to perfection, who were attempting to quit the town with plunder, in the garb of friars, nuns, or enveloped in silk counterpanes, or loaded with silver forks, spoons, and church plate, all of which was of course taken from them, and was piled up, to hand over to the proper authorities on the following day. He told me that no masquerade could, in point of costume and grotesque figures, rival the characters he stripped that night.[15]

Madden wrote to his mother two days later that,

> indeed, the whole was a scene of horror and plunder and I never wish to see it repeated, although I am not sorry to have been present at such a service. As soon as the place was in our power, I was placed on guard at the breach where I remained until relieved late yesterday. Many of our officers have got horses and mules, William[16] has got two beautiful animals. He has promised to give me one of them.[17]

Lieutenant Cooke also tried to bring his men under control, but soon gave up.

> When the troops had sipped the wine and the Cogniac [*sic*] brandy in the stores, the extreme disorders commenced. To restore order was impossible; a whole division could not have done it. Three or four large houses were on fire, two of them were in the market-place, and the town was illuminated by the flames. The soldiers were drunk, and many of them for amusement were firing from the windows into the streets. I was talking to the regimental barber, private Evans, in the square, when a ball passed through his head. This was at one o'clock in the morning. He fell at my feet dead, and his brains lay on the pavement. I then sought

---

14. Duffy, John, *Journals of Majors John Duffy and John Maxwell Tylden of the 43rd Foot*, p.144.
15. Cooke, John., *A True Soldier Gentleman: The Memoirs of Lt. John Cooke 1791–1813*, pp.107–108.
16. His brother William Madden was a captain in the 1st Battalion 52nd Foot.
17. Madden, Wyndham, *Men of Wellington's Light Division: Unpublished Memoirs of the 43rd (Monmouthshire) Regiment in the Peninsular War*, pp.179–180. This bragging about his brother getting horses is a bit ironic considering Madden spent the night forcing plundering soldiers to drop their loot before they could leave the city.

> shelter, and found Colonel M'Leod with a few officers in a large house, where we remained until daylight.[18]

Lieutenant Colonel Barnard, the senior Light Division officer in the town, joined with Lieutenant General Thomas Picton, the commander of the 3rd Division, to bring order out of the chaos. They were concerned that the drunken soldiers shooting their guns and setting fires to sit around while consuming their liquor would accidently kill civilians and burn down the town.

> Sir Thomas Picton, with the power of twenty trumpets, began to proclaim damnation to every body, while Colonel Barnard, Colonel Cameron, and some other active officers, were carrying it into effect with a strong hand; for, seizing the broken barrels of muskets, which were lying about in great abundance, they belaboured every fellow, most unmercifully, about the head who attempted either to load or fire, and finally succeeded in reducing them to order. In the midst of the scuffle, however, three of the houses in the square were set on fire; and the confusion was such that nothing could be done to save them; but, by the extraordinary exertions of Colonel Barnard, during the whole of the night, the flames were prevented from communicating to the adjoining buildings.[19]

Around midnight the soldiers ran out of steam and many were too exhausted to continue their partying. The officers and NCOs began to gather their troops. The men of the1st Battalion 95th Rifles, according to Lieutenant George Simmons, were sent to the ramparts where they 'made fires, as the night was a clear and frosty one. Some men brought me wine, ham, and eggs. I soon made a hearty meal, and washed it down with some good French Burgundy, putting my feet to the fire, and enjoyed as calm a sleep as I ever did in my life before, for three or four hours.'[20]

Lieutenant Kincaid sat on the ramparts and reflected on surviving the assault and the state of his uniform.

> There is nothing in this life half so enviable as the feelings of a soldier after a victory. Previous to a battle, there is a certain sort of something that pervades the mind which is not easily defined; it is neither akin to joy or fear, and, probably, anxiety may be nearer to it than any other word in the dictionary:

18. Cooke, John, *A True Soldier Gentleman: The Memoirs of Lt. John Cooke 1791–1813*, p.108.
19. Kincaid, John, *Adventures in the Rifle Brigade in the Peninsula, France, and the Netherlands from 1809–1815*, pp.115–116.
20. Simmons, George, *A British Rifleman: Journals and Correspondence During the Peninsular War and the Campaign of Wellington*, p.222.

> but, when the battle is over, and crowned with victory, he finds himself elevated for a while into the regions of absolute bliss! It had ever been the summit of my ambition to attain a post at the head of a storming party – my wish had now been accomplished, and gloriously ended; and I do think that, after all was over, and our men laid asleep on the ramparts, that I strutted about as important a personage, in my own opinion, as ever trod the face of the earth; and, had the ghost of the renowned Jack-the-giant-killer itself passed that way at the time, I'll venture to say, that I would have given it a kick in the breech without the smallest ceremony. But, as the sun began to rise, I began to fall from the heroics; and, when he showed his face, I took a look at my own, and found that I was too unclean a spirit to worship, for I was covered with mud and dirt, with the greater part of my dress torn to rags.[21]

French Prisoners

Prisoners were a major problem. Over 1,500 French soldiers were still alive when the city fell. They were scattered throughout the city and were reluctant to place themselves in the hands of the drunken men. Around 10:00 p.m. Captain Ewart was ordered by Lieutenant Colonel Barnard, the senior surviving officer in the division, to take 2 companies to a large barracks and guard 700 prisoners that had been collected there. Ewart was able to round up some of his soldiers to do so, but fell far short of two companies' worth of men.[22]

Lieutenant Kincaid also began to collect prisoners. At the first street he came to after he descended from the ramparts,

> a French officer came out of a door and claimed my protection, giving me his sword. He told me that there was another officer in the same house who was afraid to venture out, and entreated that I would go in for him. I, accordingly, followed him up to the landing-place of a dark stair, and, while he was calling to his friend, by name, to come down, 'as there was an English officer present who would protect him,' a violent screaming broke through a door at my elbow. I pushed it open, and found the landlady struggling with an English soldier, whom I immediately transferred to the bottom of the stair head foremost. The French officer had followed me in at the door, and was so astonished at all he saw, that he held up his hands, turned up the whites of his eyes, and resolved himself into a state of the most eloquent silence. When he did recover the use of his tongue, it was

21. Kincaid, John, *Adventures in the Rifle Brigade in the Peninsula, France, and the Netherlands from 1809–1815*, pp.116–117.
22. Ewart, John, *Peninsular War Diary of Captain John Frederick Ewart, 52nd Light Infantry, 1811–1812*, p.60.

> to recommend his landlady to my notice, as the most amiable woman in existence. She, on her part, professed the most unbounded gratitude, and entreated that I would make her house my home for ever; but, when I called upon her, a few days after, she denied having ever seen me before, and stuck to it most religiously. As the other officer could not be found, I descended into the street again with my prisoner.[23]

Kincaid continued towards the Town Plaza and left the officer with the other prisoners there.

Captain Ewart remained on guard throughout the night

> Making good fires and having got a good cloak from my servant, without which I should have been very cold (as we all stormed in scarlet of course) and this morning the total of the prisoners collected at this place besides many others, amounted to 980, some of whom were wounded, but it was impossible to get them dressed. At noon I was ordered to deliver them over to the 3rd Cacadores [*sic*], as well as 64 officers who had been collected at the governor's house and I set off after the regiment with my guard for El Bodon.[24]

In the morning the prisoners were lined up and began to march out of the town. As they passed near the Lesser Breach

> a great explosion took place a few yards to the right of the *small breach*, blowing up the *terre-plein* of the rampart, four yards in breadth and ten in length. This fatal explosion (which was accidental, owing to some sparks of fire igniting some barrels of gunpowder in a casement,) happened while the French garrison were marching out of the city by the *small breach*, which had become so hard, owing to such numbers of soldiers walking up and down it, as to make the ascent nearly impracticable. The French, as well as the British soldiers, were carried up into the air, or jammed amongst the rubbish, some with heads, arms, or legs sticking out of the earth. I saw one of the unfortunate soldiers in a blanket, with his *face*, *head*, and *body*, as black as a coal, and cased in a black substance like a shell; his features were no longer distinguishable, and all the hair was singed from off his head, but still the unfortunate man was alive. How long he lived in this horrible situation I cannot say.[25]

---

23. Kincaid, John, *Adventures in the Rifle Brigade in the Peninsula, France, and the Netherlands from 1809–1815*, p.114.
24. Ewart, John, *Peninsular War Diary of Captain John Frederick Ewart, 52nd Light Infantry, 1811–1812*, p.60.
25. Cooke, John, *A True Soldier Gentleman: The Memoirs of Lt. John Cooke 1791–1813*, p.110.

Corporal Garretty had just left the town via the breach when the explosion occurred.

> Unhappily, the slaughter did not end with the battle; for the next day, as the prisoners and their escort were marching out by the breach, an accidental explosion took place, and numbers of both were blown into the air. The personal sufferings of the soldiers were severe, as the service had been unusually dangerous. While in the front ditch near the glacis, a live shell exploded within a few paces of the spot on which I stood: we threw ourselves flat on the ground, but, though nearly suffocated by the dust it threw around, no material injury was inflicted either on myself or comrades.[26]

The Departure of the Light Division

About 9:00 a.m. on the day after the assault, the Light Division left Ciudad Rodrigo and returned to its billets. The hungover soldiers presented quite a spectacle as they marched out the gate towards the bridge. They were 'dressed in all the varieties imaginable, some with jackboots on, others with frock-coats, epaulettes, &c., and some with even monkies [*sic*] on their shoulders'.[27] As they approached the bridge over the Águeda River, they met the lead elements of the 5th Division that was coming to repair the breaches in the walls. Much to the delight of the soldiers, the 5th Division 'immediately formed upon the left of the road, presented arms, and cheered us as we went along.'[28] Among those who watched them depart was Wellington and his staff. Upon seeing them Wellington had the

> curiosity to ask the officer of the leading company, what regiment it was, for there was scarcely a vestige of uniform among the men, some of whom were dressed in Frenchmen's coats, some in white breeches, and huge jack-boots, some with cocked hats and queues; most of their swords were fixed on the rifles, and stuck full of hams, tongues, and loaves of bread, and not a few were carrying bird-cages! There never was a better masked corps![29]

Unfortunately, there is no record of what Wellington thought of their dress.

The division marched back to their billets near El Bodón where the inhabitants turned out to greet them with vivas. Some of the troops continued to drink

26. Garretty, Thomas, *Memoirs of a Sergeant Late in the Forty-Third Light Infantry Regiment*, p.150.
27. Costello, Edward, *Adventures of a Soldier*, p.151.
28. Ibid.
29. Kincaid, John, *Adventures in the Rifle Brigade in the Peninsula, France, and the Netherlands from 1809–1815*, pp.117–118.

on the march. One soldier was so drunk that he fell out of the formation and set 'himself down to sleep in the wood that separates the road from Gallegos. Poor fellow, it was his last sleep, for on the roll being called, a party was sent in search of him, and discovered his body under a tree, torn to pieces by the wolves, which greatly infested that part of Spain.'[30] Another soldier died after returning to his quarters through his own stupidity. He had

> the misfortune to carry his death in his hands, under the mistaken shape of amusement. He thought that it was a cannon-ball, and took it for the purpose of playing at the game of nine-holes,[31] but it happened to be a live [howitzer] shell. In rolling it along it went over a bed of burning ashes, and ignited without his observing it. Just as he had got it between his legs, and was in the act of discharging it a second time, it exploded, and nearly blew him to pieces.[32]

Captain Jonathan Leach's Conclusion About the Sack of Ciudad Rodrigo

Leach, a company commander in the 1st Battalion 95th Rifles, wrote

> When a town is stormed, it is inevitable that excesses will be, as they ever have been, committed by the assailants, more particularly if it takes place at night. It affords a favourable opportunity for the loose and dissolute characters, which are to be found in all armies, to indulge in every diabolical propensity. That this was the case to a certain extent, on the night in question, no one will deny; but, at the same time, I feel convinced that no town taken by assault ever did or ever will suffer less than Rodrigo. It is true that soldiers of all regiments got drunk, plundered, and made great noise and confusion in the streets and houses, in spite of every exertion on the part of the officers to prevent it; but bad and revolting as such scenes are, I never heard that either the French garrison, when it had once surrendered, nor any of the inhabitants, suffered personal indignities or cruelty from the troops.[33]

Leach's attitude may reflect that some of the officers and NCOs took part in the looting or directly benefited from. For example a prized family heirloom of Lieutenant John Fitzmaurice, 95th Rifles, was a silver snuff box taken 'from

30. Costello, Edward, *Adventures of a Soldier*, pp.152 and 157.
31. A children's game similar to tic-tac-toe.
32. Kincaid, John, *Adventures in the Rifle Brigade in the Peninsula, France, and the Netherlands from 1809–1815*, p.119.
33. Leach, Jonathan, *Rough Sketches of the Life of an Old Soldier*, p.250.

the table of General Barrié, the French Governour.'[34] An anonymous sergeant in the 43rd Foot wrote in his memoirs thirty-five years later that he went into a French storehouse and 'got my haversack full of silver plate, which the French had plundered from the churches.'[35] Then there are Lieutenants Simmons and Madden, the first dining on food given to him by his soldiers that was looted from the town, while the second expected to share of his brother's taking of two horses.

34. Fitzmaurice, John, *A Biographical Sketch of Major General John Fitzmaurice*, p.27.
35. Hamilton, Anthony, *Hamilton's Campaign With Moore and Wellington During the Peninsular War*, p.115. This source is credited to Sergeant Anthony Hamilton. However, according to the regimental quarterly payrolls for 1812, there was no Anthony Hamilton. The memoirs are filled with too many plausible anecdotes to be a work of fiction. The author was probably writing under a pseudonym.

Chapter 5

Light Division Casualties During the Siege of Ciudad Rodrigo

> The greater portion of the light division lay at the foot of the *small breach* in the ditch; hence it was that they fought on the slope, and rolled down in succession as they were killed.
>
> Lieutenant John Cooke, 43rd Foot[1]

Within hours of Ciudad Rodrigo surrendering, members of the Light Division returned to the Lesser Breach to look for missing comrades and relatives. Rifleman Costello had sobered up when he went looking for his friend 'Wilkie', whom he had found in the Lesser Breach. He used some of the loot he took the night before to bribe some drunken soldiers to assist him in burying his friend.

> I found him, at length, cold and stiff, the bullet having entered his breast close under the left shoulder. He was stripped! But I easily distinguished him by the likeness he bore to his sister; old times then burst vividly o'er my recollection, and as I stood over his prostrate remains, a few moments brought to mind all the scenes in which he had been so active a coadjutor, my quondam [former] recruit, bed-fellow, press-man, and pot companion, lay stretched before me clotted and besmeared with his blood, a single drop of which, at one time, was even more valued by me than the whole of my own more lucky current. The remembrance of his sister, much as my profession had tended to wipe her off my mind, now resumed its almost pristine freshness; my eyes dimmed for a second, and perchance one solitary proof of my weakness might have left its scalding course behind it, but I felt only as a soldier. I held my own life as it were in my hand, ready to part with it, at even a moment's notice, and I presumed as much of all belonging to me.
>
> The proceeds of the storming 'business' had enabled me to gain over a few half drunken soldiers, who had been staggering near me stupidly staring at my anxiety. We buried poor Wilkie in the glacis, near the breach, the whole wreck around us displaying the veriest [*sic*] monument ever reared to the memory of a soldier![2]

1. Cooke, John, *A True Soldier Gentleman: The Memoirs of Lt. John Cooke 1791–1813*, p.126.
2. Costello, Edward, *Adventures of a Soldier*, pp.149–150.

After burying his friend Wilkie, Costello soon heard that Captain Uniacke had been killed and that,

> his remains lay on the suburbs, in a house next to that where those of our brave old General were stretched out. Several of the men of his company crowded about his person, hoping for he was still living, and sensible; that he yet might return amongst us. But his arm had been torn from the socket, and he died some few days afterwards. Here let me pay a brief, though sincere tribute to his memory; though young in years [he was 22 years old] – he was gallant, daring, and just to all whom he commanded. During the Peninsular war our men had divided the officers into two classes; the 'come on,' and the 'go on;' for as Tom Plunkett in action once observed to an officer, 'The words go on don't befit a leader, Sir.' To the honour of the service, the latter, with us Rifles, were exceedingly few in numbers. But amongst the former, none were seen so often in the van as Uniacke; his affability and personal courage had rendered him the idol of the men of his company.[3]

Lieutenant Cooke found

> Captain [Joseph] Dobbs, of the 52d, on his back, at the foot of the breach, and stripped of his uniform. An officer at first thought he was a Frenchman, who had tumbled headlong during the strife from the top of the breach; but, while he was holding a piece of lighted wood, to contemplate, with admiration, his extremely placid and handsome countenance, even in death, a captain of the 52d knew it to be the body of poor Dobbs. On lifting him up, the blood flowed copiously from his back, a musket ball having entered at the breast, and passed through his body.[4]

Cooke also came across the body of

> a tall athletic soldier of the 52d lay amongst the dead at the foot of the breach, on his back; his arms and legs being at their full extent. The top of his head, from the forehead to the back part of his skull, was split in twain, and the cavity of the head entirely emptied of the brains, as if a hand-grenade had exploded within, and expanded the skull, till it had forced it into a separation with the parts ragged like a saw, leaving a gaping aperture nine inches in length, and four in breadth. For a considerable time I looked on this horrible fracture, to define, if possible, by what missile or instrument so wonderful a wound could have been inflicted; but without being able to come to any conclusion as to the probable cause.[5]

3. Costello, Edward, *Adventures of a Soldier*, p.150–151.
4. Cooke, John, *A True Soldier Gentleman: The Memoirs of Lt. John Cooke 1791–1813*, p.122.
5. Ibid, p.129.

Corporal Garretty found a wife searching for her husband.

> It was in the ditch, among the unburied dead. Nothing struck me more forcibly than the conduct of a soldier's widow. Suspecting that her husband had fallen, she traversed this vale of death to seek him. Never shall I forget the anguish of her soul when she discovered the much loved remains. The brave man had fallen covered with wounds. His countenance was sadly disfigured, and suffused with blood. She fell upon his face and kissed his faded lips. She then gazed at the lifeless form, repeated her embraces, and then gave way to the wild and ungovernable grief which struggled for expression.[6]

For Captain Leach, daybreak

> presented a horrid sight, and unfit to be contemplated in cold blood. Many objects, of both parties, lying near the spot where the magazine had exploded, were frightful to a degree. Bodies without limbs, and limbs without bodies, were scorched and scattered about in different directions; and the houses near the breaches were filled with such of the wounded as were able to crawl away from the ramparts, with a view to find shelter from the severe frost, which numbed their wounds.[7]

The Casualties

Unfortunately, it appears that only the 3rd Caçadores submitted casualty reports for the days they occurred. The other units waited until Ciudad Rodrigo was taken and then submitted a report for all casualties from 8–20 January. Except for officers, it is very difficult to determine whether the casualty occurred during the siege or the assault. The 3rd Caçadores casualties show that they did take part in the assault.

Table 5.1: The 3rd Caçadores Casualties During the Assault on Ciudad Rodrigo 19 January–20 January 1812[8]

Killed or Died of Wounds			Wounded			Total
Officers	Sergeants	Men	Officers	Sergeants	Men	
-	-	6	1	1	18	26

6. Garretty, Thomas, *Memoirs of a Sergeant Late in the Forty-Third Light Infantry Regiment*, pp.149–150.
7. Leach, Jonathan, *Rough Sketches of the Life of an Old Soldier*, pp.250–251.
8. AHM 1-14-256-04 MS-50.

Table 5.2: Light Division Casualties From 8 January–19 January 1812

Division	Battalion	Killed or Died of Wounds			Wounded			Total
		Officers	Sgts	Men	Officers	Sgts	Men	
	Staff	1	-	-	-	-	-	**1**
1st Brigade	43rd Foot[9]	1	1	13	2	2	35	**54**
	1st Bn 95th Rifles[10]	-	-	1	3	-	16	**20**
	2nd Bn 95th Rifles[11]	-	-	-	2	-	4	**6**
	3rd Caç[12]	-	-	6	1	1	18	**26**
2nd Brigade	Staff	-	-	-	1	-	-	**1**
	1st Bn 52nd Foot[13]	1	-	8	4	1	33	**47**
	2nd Bn 52nd Foot[14]	-	1	3	1	-	5	**10**
	3rd Bn 95th Rifles[15]	-	-	-	2	-	4	**6**
	1st Caç[16]	-	-	2	-	-	24	**26**
	Total	3	2	33	16	4	139	197

Light Division Officer Casualties

Major General Robert Craufurd was,

> struck by a musket ball, which passed through his arm, broke through the ribs, passed through part of the lungs and lodged in or at the spine…after lying for a few minutes in this situation, he said to me that he was mortally wounded and that he felt that he was just dying. I expressed my grief that he had such a feeling and a hope that he was mistaken, in answer to which he reiterated his opinion that he was just dying. I then asked him if I could do anything for him. To this he replied that I could not, as all his affairs were fully settled. I then asked him if he had anything to communicate to Lord Wellington. After considering a little he said that he did not recollect anything that he had to communicate to Lord Wellington and that there was only one thing I could do for him, which was to 'say to Mrs Craufurd that he was quite sure that they would meet in heaven'. After this he lay for

9. Levinge, Richard, *Historical Records of the Forty-Third Regiment Monmouthshire Light Infantry 1739 to 1867*, p.160.
10. Verner, Willoughby, *History & Campaigns of the Rifle Brigade: 1800–1813*, Vol. 2, pp.348–349.
11. Ibid.
12. AHM 1-14-256-04 MS-49 to AHM 1-14-256-04 MS-54.
13. Moorsom, William, *Historical Record of the Fifty-Second Regiment*, pp.158–159.
14. Ibid.
15. Verner, Willoughby, *History & Campaigns of the Rifle Brigade: 1800–1813*, Vol. 2, pp.348–349.
16. AHM 1-14-256-04 MS-55.

> some time quiet and without speaking, recovering himself in some measure from this quiet, he said that he felt a little better. I then proposed to attempt to raise him and that if possible he should proceed to the suburb. To this he agreed and leaning heavily upon me he succeeded in getting to the convent of San Francisco, on our approach to which we met a medical officer of the Rifles who made enquiry as to the wound and thought that the arm alone was injured and he pointed out the place in the San Francisco where General Craufurd should be taken for examination. There he was taken and examined by some medical officers. During that examination, I had gone to look for a house to which he might be taken and on my return, met one of the surgeons who had examined the wounds; he said that the wounds were so serious as to leave no hope of the general's life being preserved. From the San Francisco he was removed to a house very near it.[17]

Craufurd was under the care of Assistant Surgeon Thomas Walker of the 52nd Regiment.[18] Due to the severity of his wounds Staff Surgeon George Guthrie was brought in within an hour to examine him. He found that

> from the general anxiety manifested, I was satisfied with the severity of the injury. The symptoms were not at first urgent [often the case with severely injured people]; but their continuance and augmentation, in spite of the most rigorous antiphlogistic treatment [i.e. anti-inflammatory management, bleeding vigorously, a cathartic, emetic, a low diet and also opiates], led, in a few days, to his death.[19]

Craufurd died at 10:00 a.m. on 24 January.[20] Surgeon Guthrie performed an autopsy on him and he found that,

> on examination of the body, the ball was found lying in the diaphragm [*sic*]; the cavity of the chest contained a very large quantity of turbid scrum; false membranes had formed on the lung [layers of deposited infected serum and thickened, inflamed lining of the lung, the pleura], which was compressed towards the spine, and at the upper part retained the mark of an injury as from a ball which had not force enough to penetrate and lodge.[21]

Craufurd was buried the next day in the Lesser Breach. A description of his funeral can be found in Appendix III: Major General Craufurd's Funeral.

---

17. Shaw, James, *Riflemen of Wellington's Light Division in the Peninsular War 1808–14*, pp.172–173.
18. Ibid, p.173.
19. Crumplin, Michael, *Guthrie's War: A Surgeon of the Peninsula & Waterloo*, p.72.
20. Shaw, James, *Riflemen of Wellington's Light Division in the Peninsular War 1808–14*, p.173.
21. Crumplin, Michael, *Guthrie's War: A Surgeon of the Peninsula & Waterloo*, p.72.

Major General John Vandeleur was shot in the shoulder and the musket ball was lodged under his collarbone. He was brought to the forward aid station at the San Francisco Convent and sat on a stone waiting his turn to be treated.[22] His wound was very serious and he eventually went to Portalegre to recover. He would have rheumatism in his shoulder for the rest of his life.[23]

The 43rd Foot

Lieutenant John Bramwell was wounded by a ball that nicked his femoral artery. There was some hope that he might survive but he died of his wounds on 27 January 1812.[24]

Captain James Fergusson was severely wounded by a musket ball close to the spine and slightly in the foot. The surgeons decided to not remove the ball since it was not causing problems.[25]

Lieutenant Cook Tylden Pattenson

> made a terrible figure of by the explosion of some gunpowder...[that] scorched his face and one hand very badly and he had scarcely recovered his astonishment at this summersault over the wall, when he received a pretty deep graze from the splinter of a shell or a ball in his counterpart [buttocks], but he is likely to recover completely and be as beautiful as ever.[26]

Despite the severity of his wounds, he was carried as present for duty in the monthly returns.

The 52nd Foot

Lieutenant Colonel John Colborne (2nd Battalion 52nd Foot) was shot in the right arm, just under the epaulette. The bullet broke

> the head of the bone right off in the socket. To this the attention of the surgeons was of course directed. Some months after Colborne complained of a pain four inches below where the ball entered, and suppuration took place,

22. Napier, George, *At War With Wellington: The Peninsular War Letters of William, George and Charles Napier*, p.116.
23. McGuigan, Ron and Burham, Robert, *Wellington's Brigade Commanders*, p.286.
24. Macleod, Charles, *Men of Wellington's Light Division: Unpublished Memoirs of the 43rd (Monmouthshire) Regiment in the Peninsular War*, p.17.
25. Ibid, p.18. and Hall, John, *Biographical Dictionary of British Officers Killed and Wounded, 1808–1814*, p.202.
26. Macleod, Charles, *Men of Wellington's Light Division: Unpublished Memoirs of the 43rd (Monmouthshire) Regiment in the Peninsular War*, p.18.

> and by surgical treatment the bone was gradually exposed. The ball, after breaking the arm above, had descended and broken the arm four inches below, and was firmly embedded in the bone. The pain he suffered in the extraction of the ball was more even than his iron heart could bear. He used to lay his watch on the table and allow the surgeons five minutes' exertions at a time, and they were three or four days before they wrenched the ball from its ossified bed.[27]

Colborne lost much of his range of movement in his shoulder joint but eventually was able to move his lower arm and hand.[28] He was evacuated to Gallegos and then to Coimbra. He travelled to Lisbon with George Napier but was too ill to travel further. He was eventually evacuated to England arriving there on 4 June.

Later in his life, Colborne described his wounding to his daughters.

> The worst wound I ever had I received at Ciudad Rodrigo. A bullet from the walls hit my right shoulder and passed some way down my arm. This was about 20 minutes, I suppose, after the attack had begun. I was knocked down by the wound at the moment, but I was able to go into the town. I had another wound in my leg at the same time, but the first was so bad that I did not think of that. I was taken the next day to a convent, and three weeks after I was carried on 20 men's shoulders to Coimbra, in Portugal. That journey in the open air was perhaps a good thing for me, though it took a week and gave me a great deal of pain at the time. I always had an appetite and could eat. The surgeon said, 'I think you must do well, you always have such an appetite.' A part of the gold wire of my epaulette was carried into the wound, and for long after, whenever I moved, this wire gave me the greatest torture. I could not lie on my side on the left shoulder, as it hurt the other to be raised, and it was dreadful pain to lie on my back, the bones in my back being quite sore. They were obliged to raise my bed off the ground on one side to give me ease. The day after the wound a surgeon came and cut the wound across and across, probing for the ball. When the ball was taken out, 15 months after, it did not hurt me so much. I was so accustomed to be probed in every direction, it did not seem much. In spite of the probing they could not find the ball, and then inflammation came on and the arm swelled, and they could do nothing...I stayed several months in Coimbra, and by the end of that time all the bits of wire were taken out.[29]

Captain Joseph Dobbs (1st Battalion 52nd Foot) was buried in the Lesser Breach, close to Craufurd.[30] Major George Napier eulogised Dobbs in his memoirs.

---

27. Smith, Harry, *The Autobiography of Sir Harry Smith*, p.59.
28. Ibid.
29. Moore Smith, George, *The Life of John Colborne*, pp.174–177.
30. Hall, John, *Biographical Dictionary of British Officers Killed and Wounded, 1808–1814*, p.168.

> Never fell a braver soldier in the flower of youth, beloved and regretted by all who knew him. He was open, generous, and warm-hearted, enthusiastic in his profession, and just sufficiently romantic to make him enter into any project with spirit and ardour. An Irishman, like them he was gay and cheerful, with a spirit of honour marked by the most scrupulous integrity. When his purse was full, it was open to all, and shared with his comrades; when empty, he only regretted it because he was thus deprived of the power of giving to all round him; but being empty, his high and independent spirit would make him submit to any personal deprivation rather than be under pecuniary obligations to any man. Such was my lamented friend Joe Dobbs. Arduous in his professional duties, honourable in his dealings with all men, generous, kind, and cheerful with his comrades, high spirited and daring, he met a soldier's glorious death while in the act of cheering his men to victory.[31]

Lieutenant John Gurwood (2nd Battalion 52nd Foot) was slightly wounded in the head while climbing the Lesser Breach but was carried as present for duty in the monthly returns.

Captain William Mein (1st Battalion 52nd Foot) was severely wounded by a musket ball in the thigh during the assault on the Renaud Redoubt on 8 January. He was evacuated to a hospital in Gallegos and on 8 February sent to a hospital in Coimbra.

Major George Napier (2nd Battalion 52nd Foot) had his right elbow shattered by a musket ball.[32] As he waited patiently on the Lesser Breach for help, he heard his

> name called several times, and upon answering, the Prince of Orange, Lord March [Lieutenant Charles Lennox, Earl of March], and Lord Fitzroy Somerset came up to me, and the Prince taking off his sash…they tied up my arm, and with the help of a sergeant and some men I got down and proceeded to the old ruined convent, where I found numbers wounded and the surgeon very busy with his knife.[33]

Prior to the assault, Napier had a premonition that he would lose an arm and asked his friend, Assistant Surgeon Thomas Walker to perform the surgery. When it came time to amputate his right arm Napier

31. Napier, George, *At War With Wellington: The Peninsular War Letters of William, George and Charles Napier*, p.119.
32. Rowan, Charles, 'Letter Regarding Wounding of Major George Napier at Ciudad Rodrigo', *Redcoats of Wellington's Light Division: Unpublished & Rare Memoirs of the 52nd (Oxfordshire) Regiment of Foot*, p.91.
33. Ibid, p.116.

> reminded my friend Walker, who was there, of his promise to me a few hours before, and begged he would be so good as to perform the operation; but he told me he could not, as there was a staff surgeon present, whose rank being higher, it was necessary he should do it, so Staff Surgeon [George] Guthrie cut it off. However, for want of light, and from the number of amputations he had already performed, and other circumstances, his instruments were blunted, so it was a long time before the thing was finished, at least twenty minutes, and the pain was great. I then thanked him for his kindness, having sworn at him like a trooper while he was at it, to his great amusement.[34]

There was no room in the house where he had his arm removed, so Napier went

> wandering and stumbling about the suburbs for upwards of an hour, I saw a light in a house, and on entering I found it full of soldiers, and a good fire blazing in the kitchen. As I went towards the fire I saw a figure wrapped up in a cloak sitting in the corner of the chimney place apparently in great pain. Upon nearer inspection I found this was my friend John Colborne, who had received a severe wound in the shoulder. As soon as I could get a bed I went into it, but sleep was impossible, for the pain increased, and the inflammation got so high that in a couple of hours I was quite delirious, and remained so for the next twenty-four hours, after which I fell asleep and began gradually to get better. In the room above me was General Craufurd, dying from a wound, the shot having passed through his arm, entered his chest, and lodged in his lungs. He suffered dreadfully, his moans were very distressing to me, and more particularly so in consequence of his daily, nay, I may almost say, hourly, sending down messages to me to know how I was, and to express his approval of my conduct, and his regret that he should never see me again.[35]

Napier was evacuated to Gallegos on 25 January, a distance of about 25km. While moving to the hospital there

> it was necessary, as I was the only officer still remaining there, that I should be carried in a blanket by eight or ten men as I was too ill to bear a cart. The troops being all drawn up to receive the body of General Craufurd I had to pass through them, and as I went through my own regiment I was greeted by many a kind look and exclamation of approbation and pity from the men who had so gallantly supported me in the assault…The day was intensely hot…and by the time I arrived at my journey's end my poor

34. Napier, George, *At War With Wellington: The Peninsular War Letters of William, George and Charles Napier*, pp.114 and 116.
35. Ibid, pp.116–119.

> bearers and myself were completely knocked up. I was so ill and delirious that night that the surgeons thought I should have died. A few days restored my strength, but what most contributed to my recovery was a visit from Lord Wellington, who brought me the English newspapers; told me my battalion (the 2nd of the 52nd) was ordered home and that I should go also and…recommended me for the medal which would be struck upon the occasion, and also for the rank of lieutenant colonel…About three weeks after the loss of my arm I commenced my journey towards Lisbon. The first day I left my room I mounted my horse and rode sixteen miles in a hot sun, and in a few days arrived at Coimbra, where I found my friend Colonel Colborne in bed suffering dreadful pain from his wound, while, comparatively, I was not suffering anything. Here we stayed some time, till Colborne was able to travel by easy journeys to Lisbon. When we arrived there he was so ill and weak that it was impossible he could undergo the fatigue of the voyage, so I embarked in the *Agincourt*…and after being sick and miserable for upwards of six weeks, I landed at Plymouth.[36]

Lieutenant John Woodgate (1st Battalion 52nd Foot) was severely wounded by a grenade in the thigh during the assault on the Renaud Redoubt on 8 January. He was evacuated to a hospital in Gallegos and on 15 February sent to a hospital in Lisbon.

The 95th Rifles

Lieutenant John Cox (1st Battalion 95th Rifles) was severely wounded by musket ball which 'parted the bone of the upper arm.'[37] He was initially kept in the division hospital, but by March was evacuated to a hospital in Abrantes. By May he was sent to England to recover.

Second Lieutenant William Hamilton (1st Battalion 95th Rifles) was severely wounded in the pelvis. He wrote to his father on 12 March that he was 'nearly recovered from the wound I received at Ciudad Rodrigo, the ball entered into the hench bone [pelvis] and came out inside my thigh, I am still lame but as the officers of this division are all mounted, I am able to do my duty I think and that is enough for me.'[38]

Lieutenant Walter Bedell (2nd Battalion 95th Rifles) was wounded, but the extent of his wound is unknown. He was sent to England on 11 April to recover.

---

36. Ibid, pp.120–121.
37. Cox, John, *Riflemen of Wellington's Light Division in the Peninsular War 1808–14*, p.111, and Cope, William, *The History of the Rifle Brigade (The Prince Consort's Own) Formerly the 95th*, p.97.
38. Hamilton, William, *Riflemen of Wellington's Light Division in the Peninsular War 1808–14*, p.125.

Captain Samuel Mitchell (2nd Battalion 95th Rifles). According to some sources he was severely wounded in the leg.[39] The severity or extent of his wound is unknown. However, the monthly theatre returns list him present for duty until March when he was seconded to the Portuguese Army.

Captain John Uniacke (1st Battalion 95th Rifles) was seriously wounded by the explosion on the ramparts near the Main Breach. Lieutenant Simmons wrote in his diary that 'Poor Uniacke got round the corner just in time enough to get scorched from head to foot in a fright [*sic*] manner and died a few hours after in great agony.'[40]

Uniacke was well loved by his troops and they wanted him to have a decent burial. They were determined that he be buried in consecrated ground. This was a problem since the only consecrated ground in the area was in a churchyard and the Spanish priests objected, calling him a heretic. Sergeant Fairfoot told the priests that Uniacke was Irish, and they assumed he was Catholic, and he was buried under 'the finest tree in the churchyard of Galleagos [*sic*].'[41]

> [His] company received orders to pay the last tribute to our Captain Uniacke. We marched under the command of the lieutenant, and arrived at Gallegos about twelve o'clock. The men having plenty of money, which they had obtained at Rodrigo, got drinking, and actually while conveying the body to the grave, stumbled under the weight of the coffin, and the lid not having been nailed down, out rolled the mangled remains of our brave captain, to the consternation of a number of French officers, en parole (prisoners from Rodrigo). One more careless than the rest viewed the occurrence with a kind of malicious sneer, which so enraged our men, that one of them taking the little tawny-looking Italian by the nape of the neck, kicked his hind-quarters soundly for it.[42]

Some sources state that Lieutenant Alexander McGregor, 2nd Battalion 95th Rifles, was severely wounded during the storming of Ciudad Rodrigo. This is correct, but he was seconded to the 4th Caçadores on 8 January and was serving with them while wounded.

The 3rd Caçadores

Lieutenant António Correia Leitão was severely wounded during the assault on the town.[43]

---

39. Hall, John, *Biographical Dictionary of British Officers Killed and Wounded, 1808–1814*, p.412.
40. Simmons, George, *A British Rifleman: Journals and Correspondence During the Peninsular War and the Campaign of Wellington*, p.222.
41. Fitzmaurice, F.M., *Recollections of a Rifleman's Wife, at Home and Abroad*, pp.183–184.
42. Costello, Edward, *Adventures of a Soldier*, pp.156–157.
43. AHM 1-14-256-04 MS-50.

Chapter 6

Winter Quarters 21 January–25 February 1812

Once again, the Light Division's senior leadership was devastated by heavy casualties. The division's commander had been killed and was replaced by its senior brigade commander, Major General Vandeleur. However, Vandeleur had been seriously wounded and it was not known how long he would be able to stay in command. The 2nd Brigade had lost its only lieutenant colonel, and one of the four majors still assigned to the brigade had lost an arm and was headed home. In the event that the brigade had to go into the field, the brigade would be commanded by a major, and the two battalions of the 52nd Foot would be commanded by captains. Its caçadore battalion was still missing its commander and was commanded by a major.

Table 6.1: Organisation 21 January 1812

Division	Personnel	Position	Location
Division HQ	Maj Gen John Ormsby Vandeleur	Acting Commander	
	LT Charles Wood 52nd Foot	ADC	Fuenteguinaldo
	LT James Shaw 43rd Foot	ADC	
	LT John Bell 52nd Foot	DAQMG	
	LT William Armstrong 19th Light Dragoons	ADC	
	Maj Charles Rowan 52nd Foot	AAG	
	Charles Purcell	ACG	
	Wentworth Parker	Chaplain	
1st Brigade	LTC Andrew Barnard	Acting Commander	Fuenteguinaldo
	Cpt Charles Beckwith 95th Rifles	Brigade Major	

Division	Personnel	Position	Location
1st Bn 43rd Foot	LTC Charles McLeod	Commander	Fuenteguinaldo
RW 1st Bn 95th Rifles	Bvt Maj Alexander Cameron	Commander	Pastores & La Encina
Company 2nd Bn 95th Rifles	Cpt Samuel Mitchell	Commander	Pastores & La Encina
Company 2nd Bn 95th Rifles	Cpt John Hart	Commander	Pastores & La Encina
3rd Bn 95th Rifles	Cpt William Percival	Commander	Pastores & La Encina
3rd Caç Bn	LTC George Elder	Commander	Fuenteguinaldo
2nd Brigade	Maj Edward Gibbs	Acting Commander	El Bodón
	LT Harry Smith 95th Rifles	Brigade Major	El Bodón
1st Bn 52nd Foot	Cpt Robert Campbell	Commander	El Bodón
2nd Bn 52nd Foot	Cpt William Jones	Commander	El Bodón
LW 1st Bn 95th Rifles	Maj Peter O'Hare	Commander	La Encina
1st Caç Bn	Maj John Algeo	Acting Commander	El Bodón

The question for many of the officers was who would replace Craufurd? Rumors were going around the division that the adjutant general, Major General Charles Stewart, would be the next commander. Lieutenant George Barlow, 52nd Foot, wrote home that 'He was reckoned as good an officer of light troops as any in the British army, even during the lifetime of General Craufurd and under his command the division, will I am sure continue to maintain its such high character.'[1] Vandeleur also wanted the command and on 3 February he wrote to Wellington asking that he be appointed the commander, based on his service as a brigade commander in the division during the previous four months. Wellington had the adjutant general reply to him on 5 February with a sympathetic letter stating that he 'would be happy if he had it in his power to avail himself of your talents and experience in command of the Light division' but that there were too many others senior to him who also had as valid of a claim to the command.[2] There were nine major generals who commanded infantry brigades and six commanding cavalry brigades that were senior to Vandeleur. This was also a problem for Stewart, who was promoted to major

1. Barlow, George Ulrich, *A Light Infantryman With Wellington: The Letters of Captain George Ulrich Barlow, 52nd and 69th Foot, 1808–1815*, pp.127–128.
2. *W.D.*, (enlarged ed.), Vol. 5, p.504.

general only eighteen months before. Wellington was also considering Major Generals Henry Clinton and Charles Alten,[3] but they too were promoted to major general on the same day as Charles Stewart. Clinton was the highest on the promotion list followed by Stewart, then Alten.

Stand-To

News had reached the French in Salamanca that Ciudad Rodrigo had fallen and on 25 January Wellington was informed that a French force was on the move. French cavalry was reported in Tamames, about 40km from Ciudad Rodrigo. Wellington's units in the vicinity of Ciudad Rodrigo were placed on alert and given three days' rations of biscuits, which were withdrawn the next day. The division was kept on alert and even after the threat disappeared no orders were issued to stand down. However, on 29 January the division was ordered to send enough baggage animals to the depot in Celorico to bring back new camp equipment that would replace missing or worn-out items. The fact that their pack animals would be making a 200km round trip was a good indicator to the officers that they would not be moving for some time.[4]

Winter Quarters

Heavy rains, strong winds, and cold temperatures plagued the division for much of late January until 6 February when the rain finally stopped. However, the roads had been turned into bogs and the rivers were high, but still passable at fords.[5] The duty was very relaxed, and many officers took the time to explore the countryside in the vicinity of Ciudad Rodrigo and Almeida. The officers of the 2nd Brigade even had time to hold a ball on 6 February, although the scarcity of women may have put a damper on the festivities.[6]

Life was not as good for the soldiers as it was for the officers. Lieutenant Colonel McLeod, the commander of the 43rd Foot, wrote on 4 February to Brevet Major William Napier, who was in England recovering from a wound. 'We are in bad quarters, particularly for the men, who are obliged to go leagues to cut wood and bring it home on their shoulders in the worst weather.'[7] For

---

3. Ibid, p.487.
4. Oglander, Henry, *The Journals of Captain Henry Oglander of the 43rd & 47th Foot*, p.122.
5. Duffy, John, *Journals of Majors John Duffy and John Maxwell Tylden of the 43rd Foot*, pp.145–146, and Oglander, Henry, *The Journals of Captain Henry Oglander of the 43rd & 47*th *Foot*, p.124.
6. Ewart, John, *Peninsular War Diary of Captain John Frederick Ewart, 52nd Light Infantry, 1811–1812*, p.72.
7. Macleod, Charles, *Men of Wellington's Light Division: Unpublished Memoirs of the 43rd (Monmouthshire) Regiment in the Peninsular War*, p.19.

some soldiers, long overdue prize money for the 1807 Siege of Copenhagen was finally paid to them. Corporal Garretty, 43rd Foot, was one of the fortunate ones.

> I received, in conjunction with others, who were similarly entitled, my share of prize-money, on account of the property captured some years before at Copenhagen. Some arrears of pay were also supplied by the hands of Major [Joseph] Wells. A little good advice was kindly subjoined. We were exhorted to save our money, to avoid excesses, and spend with economy. But alas! how hardly shall they that are rich keep in the path of moderation and humility. The cash burnt in our pockets. The intimations so civilly given were altogether wasted, and might as well have been addressed to our knapsacks. No sooner did opportunity offer, than the wine-houses washed away, not only all our good advices, but the whole of our hard earned pittance so recently distributed. When a man is determined to indulge in liquor, he is almost sure to find some justification for it.[8]

Garretty's prize money was £3 13s 6d. His monthly pay was 15s after his 6d per day for rations was deducted. His prize money was the equivalent of almost five months of his monthly take home pay. After receiving both his prize money and pay, he had £4 8s 6d or about six months' pay to fund his drinking!

On 31 January, the division moved to new quarters.

Table 6.2: Location of the Light Division 31 January 1812[9]

Unit	Location
Division HQ	Fuenteguinaldo
1st Bn 43rd Foot	El Bodón
RW 1st Bn 95th Rifles	La Encina
Company 2nd Bn 95th Rifles	La Encina
Company 2nd Bn 95th Rifles	La Encina
3rd Bn 95th Rifles	La Encina
3rd Caç Battalion	Ituero de Azaba and Campillo de Azaba
2nd Brigade	Pueblo de Azaba
1st Bn 52nd Foot	Pueblo de Azaba
2nd Bn 52nd Foot	Pueblo de Azaba
LW 1st Bn 95th Rifles	Pueblo de Azaba
1st Caç Bn	Pueblo de Azaba

8. Garretty, Thomas, *Memoirs of a Sergeant Late in the Forty-Third Light Infantry Regiment*, p.152.
9. Ewart, John, *Peninsular War Diary of Captain John Frederick Ewart, 52nd Light Infantry, 1811–1812*, p.71.

Dealing With Deserters

At least eighteen British deserters were captured at the fall of Ciudad Rodrigo. Among them were nine men from the Light Division.

- 43rd Foot: Private Thomas Price.
- 52nd Foot: Corporal Robert Fuller, who was reported to have deserted between 25 October and 24 November 1811.
- 52nd Foot: Private James Cummings, who deserted on 6 December 1811.
- 52nd Foot: Private John Malone, who deserted on 9 December 1811.
- 52nd Foot: Private Patrick O'Neil, who deserted on 6 December 1811.
- 52nd Foot: Private William Robinson, who deserted on 24 November 1811. None of the 52nd men were in the same company.
- 95th Rifles: Rifleman Miles Hodgson deserted on 10 December 1811.
- 95th Riffles: Riflemen Malcolm McInnes and William Mills deserted sometime in 1811 and had been dropped from the payrolls.

In the General Orders of 8 February 1812, Major General James Kempt was appointed the president of a general court martial that would try them. Captain Stephen Goodman, 48th Foot, deputy judge advocate general, was also appointed. The court was formed with fourteen officers[10] from the 3rd Division.

The court martial was held at Nave de Haver on 12 and 13 February. The charges were 'desertion to the enemy, and being taken on the assault and capture of the garrison of Ciudad Rodrigo, on the evening of the 19th January, 1812.'[11] The prisoners pleaded not guilty. They gave as their defence that 'they had several months' pay due, which they saw no prospect of ever receiving'.[12] Not helping them were allegations that during 'attack of the breaches in assaulting the place, they were distinctly heard crying out to one another, "Now here comes the light division; let us give it them, the rascals," or something to that effect, and had, it is said, done more injury to the assailing party than twice their number of Frenchmen.'[13]

The court found all nine guilty and sentenced them to 'be shot to death, at such time and place as his Excellency the Commander of the Forces may be pleased to direct…The prisoners will be sent to their Regiments, and the Commander of the Forces will send orders respecting the execution of their sentences.'[14]

10. For a general court martial to give a sentence of death it had to be composed of thirteen officers. Normal practice was to have fourteen officers on it in case one of them fell sick.
11. General Orders, dated 17 February 1812.
12. Leach, Jonathan, *Rough Sketches of the Life of an Old Soldier*, p.253.
13. Surtees, William, *Twenty-Five Years in the Rifle Brigade*, p.134.
14. General Orders, dated 17 February 1812.

On 17 February, the division was formed into the sides of a square on a plain near Ituero de Azaba.

> The graves of the hapless beings occupying a part of the fourth face of the square. When all was ready, and a firing party from each regiment had been formed in the centre, the provost-marshal went to the guard-tent, where the prisoners were in waiting, to conduct them to the place of execution. They soon after appeared, poor wretches, moving towards the square, with faces pale and wan, and with all the dejection such a situation is calculated to produce. Their arms had been pinioned one by one as they came out from the guard-tent, and all being ready, the melancholy procession advanced towards the centre of the square. The proceedings of the court which tried them, together with the sentence, and the approval of the Commander of the Forces, was read by the Assistant Adjutant-general, in the hearing of the whole division; which concluded, the prisoners were marched round in front of every regiment, that all might see and avoid their unhappy fate. They were then moved towards their graves…the chaplain of the division had been with them in the guard-tent some little time previously to their leaving it, and when they quitted as above described, he followed them at a considerable distance, apparently ashamed of his peculiar calling, and the duty incumbent on him in such a conjuncture. They were led, as I said before, towards their graves; and when they reached the bank of earth in front of each, they were made to kneel down with their faces fronting the square, and then being one after another blindfolded, and left for a few moments to their own reflections or their prayers.[15]

The men who were to be executed included the nine deserters from the Light Division and Private George Cameron, Royal Horse Artillery. Private James Cummings, 52nd Foot, had been wounded while fighting alongside the French at Ciudad Rodrigo had to be carried to the field and placed on the ground.[16] At this point Wellington chose to pardon one man from each regiment: Privates Thomas Price and James Cummings, and Rifleman Miles Hodgson, who had been wounded at Bussaco in 1810. Rifleman Costello was glad that Hodgson had been pardoned but could not understand why Cummings had been. Costello believed that Cummings had 'been mainly instrumental…in getting the others to desert with him…He had been particularly noticed at Rodrigo in one of the breaches, most actively employed, opposing our entrance, and cheering on the besieged to resist us'.[17]

15. Surtees, William, *Twenty-Five Years in the Rifle Brigade*, pp.134–135.
16. Costello, Edward, *Adventures of a Soldier*, p.158.
17. Ibid.

After the three pardoned men were returned to their battalions,

> the provost-marshal proceeded to the firing party, who had been previously loaded, and directing the men of each regiment to fire at their own prisoner, he advanced them to within about ten or twelve paces of the wretched men, and giving the signals by motion for their making ready and firing, the whole fired at once, and plunged the unhappy criminals into eternity. There was, indeed, one melancholy exception to this. One of the prisoners belonged to the troop of horse artillery attached to the division, and it seems the provost, in giving his orders for the soldiers of each regiment to fire at their own man, had not recollected that the artillery had no men there to fire. He was thus left sitting on his knees, when the others had fallen all around him.[18] What his feelings must have been it is in vain to guess; but, poor fellow, he was not suffered long to remain in suspense, for a reserve party immediately approaching, they fired and stretched him also along with his companions in crime and misery; and in such of the others as they perceived life still remaining, they also immediately put an end to their sufferings, by placing their muskets close to their body, and firing into them. One poor man, when he received his death wound, sprung to a considerable height, and giving a loud shriek, he fell, and instantly expired.[19]

Lieutenant Harry Smith was the brigade major of the day and was responsible for overseeing the execution. He later wrote that the provost-marshal did not specify

> that a certain number of men should shoot one culprit, and so on, but at his signal the whole party fired a volley. Some prisoners were fortunate enough to be killed, others were only wounded, some untouched. I galloped up. An unfortunate Rifleman called to me by name – he was awfully wounded – 'Oh, Mr. Smith, put me out of my misery,' and I literally ordered the firing party, when reloaded, to run up and shoot the poor wretches. It was an awful scene.[20]

After the men were executed the division 'was formed into column, and marched round in front of the bodies, where each soldier might distinctly perceive the sad

18. Costello claims the man was from 'the 52nd, who, strange to say, remained standing and untouched. His countenance, that before had been deadly pale, now exhibited a bright flush. Perhaps he might have imagined himself pardoned; if so, however, he was doomed to be miserably deceived, as the following minute two men of the reserve came up and fired their pieces into his bosom, when giving a loud scream, that had a very horrible effect upon those near, he sprang forward into his grave', *Adventures of a Soldier*, pp.158–159.
19. Surtees, William, *Twenty-Five Years in the Rifle Brigade*, pp.135–136.
20. Smith, Harry, *The Autobiography of Sir Harry Smith*, pp.59–60.

and melancholy effects of such a fatal dereliction of duty. They were then, without more ado, thrown into their graves, which were filled up without delay, and the division separating, each regiment marched to its quarters.'[21]

Departure of the 2nd Battalion 52nd Foot

On 23 February, the 2nd Battalion 52nd Foot was ordered to return to England. Almost half of its other ranks were sick or hospitalised and it was missing over 50 per cent of its officers, including its battalion commander and two majors. Before the battalion departed, it transferred 10 sergeants, 7 buglers, and 482 other ranks to the 1st Battalion 52nd Foot. In exchange it received five sergeants, two buglers, and sixty-nine other ranks from the 1st Battalion that were no longer fit for duty.[22]

Eight officers were also transferred to the 1st Battalion: Captain Augustus Merry; Lieutenants George Barlow, Douglas Hamilton, and Charles Dawson; Ensigns William Moore, William Ogilvy, and Henry Wallis; and Acting Paymaster William Chalmers.[23]

Lieutenant Charles Wood, who had been Craufurd's aide-de-camp, was attached as a deputy assistant adjutant general to the adjutant general's department on 25 February.[24]

Sometime during the month Lieutenant Colonel Thomas Beckwith returned to the division and resumed command of the 1st Brigade.

Promotions

Several officers were promoted for their actions during the siege. These promotions were dated 6 February 1812. Lieutenant John Gurwood was promoted to captain in the Royal African Corps. Majors Edward Gibbs and George Napier, both of the 52nd Foot, were promoted to brevet lieutenant colonel. Captains John Duffy 43rd Foot and William Mein 52nd Foot were promoted to brevet major. Brevet rank, also known as army rank, was different to regimental rank. If the officer was serving on the staff outside of his regiment, he would have the pay and privileges of his brevet rank. An officer could continue to be promoted in brevet rank, without being promoted in regimental rank. By the end of the Peninsular War, there were officers who were regimental captains but had been promoted to brevet lieutenant colonel.

21. Surtees, William, *Twenty-Five Years in the Rifle Brigade*, p.136.
22. General Orders, dated 25 February 1812.
23. WO 17/2469.
24. General Orders, dated 25 February 1812.

Rumors of Moving South

By the middle of February rumors began to spread that the army would soon be marching south towards Badajoz. On 11 February, the 1st Division was the first to depart and was followed by the 3rd and 4th Divisions. In anticipation of receiving orders to move south, Major General Vandeleur ordered all the battalions to begin drilling three hours every day.[25] This caused some consternation among the officers about the shape of their baggage animals. The army had been in the same area for the past ten months and fodder for their horses was scarce. Should the division be the last to march, any available fodder along the route would have been consumed by the previous divisions. Captain Leach, 95th Rifles, wondered

> how we were to persuade our scarecrows of baggage-horses and mules to perform the journey in winter, when there was no green forage on the ground, nor any hay, straw, or corn to be procured in the line of country through which our route lay. I well remember purchasing, before we set out, a fanega of wheat (weighing about seventy pounds) for eleven Spanish dollars, and thought myself fortunate in being able to procure it at that price; so completely had every thing of the kind been consumed, or bought up by the commissariat for the staff, cavalry, and artillery. In addition to the wheat, we purchased for our quadrupeds, at an enormous price, small cakes of Indian corn-flour, which the Portuguese peasantry eat.[26]

On 24 February, orders were finally issued to the Light Division to march south towards Badajoz on 26 February.

---

25. Ewart, John, *Peninsular War Diary of Captain John Frederick Ewart, 52nd Light Infantry*, p.73.
26. Leach, Jonathan, *Rough Sketches of the Life of an Old Soldier*, p.253.

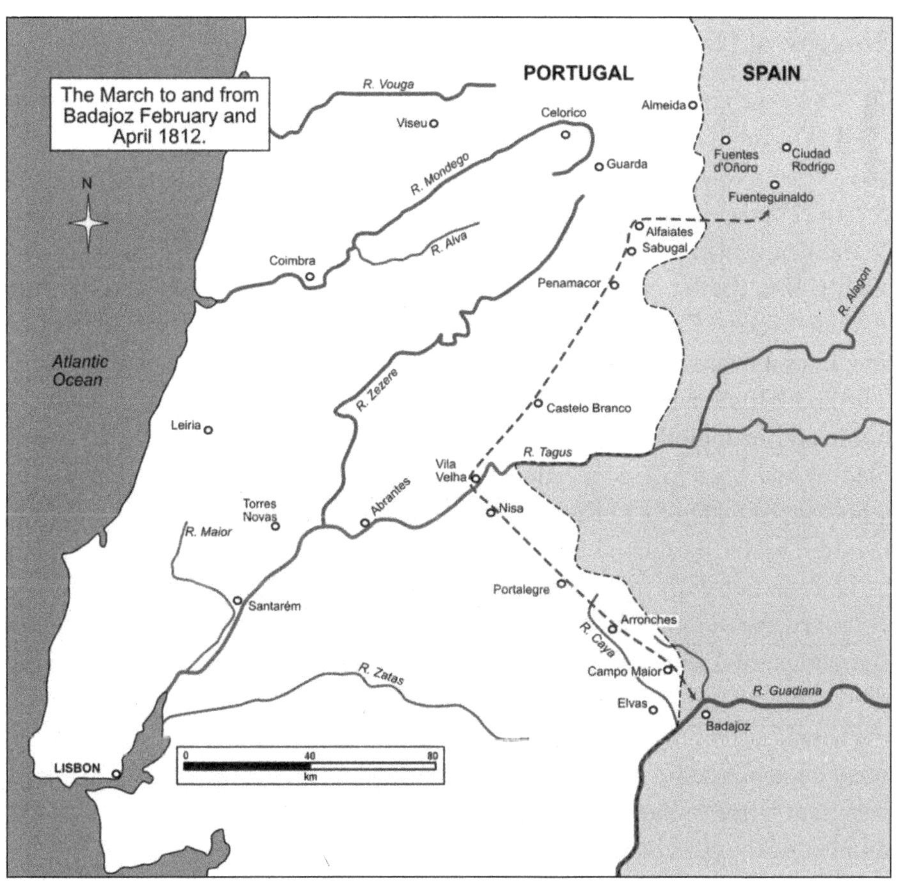
The March to and from Badajoz February and April 1812.
PORTUGAL
SPAIN
R. Vouga
Viseu
Celorico
Almeida
Guarda
Fuentes d'Oñoro
Ciudad Rodrigo
Fuenteguinaldo
R. Mondego
R. Alva
Coimbra
Alfaiates
Sabugal
Penamacor
R. Alagon
Atlantic Ocean
R. Zezere
Castelo Branco
Leiria
R. Tagus
Vila Velha
Abrantes
Nisa
Torres Novas
R. Maior
Portalegre
Santarém
Arronches
R. Caya
Campo Maior
R. Zatas
R. Guadiana
Elvas
Badajoz
LISBON
0
40
80
km
N

Chapter 7
The Road to Badajoz

Strength of Division

For much of February the Light Division rested and recovered its strength. During that time two events happened that affected the total number of troops available to march south to Badajoz. The first was the departure of the 2nd Battalion 52nd Foot. It was a sickly unit almost from the time it arrived in the Peninsula in March 1811. Upon its departure, its healthy soldiers were drafted into the 1st Battalion 52nd Foot, while the 1st Battalion sent its unfit soldiers back to England with the 2nd Battalion. This gave the 1st Battalion an additional 460 soldiers. Yet not all these soldiers were fit to go on campaign. The 2nd Battalion reported 275 sick in January. In February, it sent 153 soldiers home and had another 17 in the hospital too sick to move, plus 12 who had died or had been killed in action. That meant at least ninety-three of those who were transferred to the 1st Battalion had been hospitalised the month before. The 1st Battalion had 191 (23 per cent) of its other ranks listed as sick in January, but with the influx of over 480 troops from the 2nd Battalion in February, the number of sick rose to 333 other ranks or 26 per cent of the 1st Battalion's total strength. The second event was the arrival of replacements for the 1st Battalion 95th Rifles. These were the first soldiers to fill its ranks since the battalion arrived in the Peninsula thirty months before. The three sergeants, three buglers, and fifty-eight other ranks were offset by seven other ranks who were sent home broken in health. The arrival of these replacements caused the number of the battalion's sick to decrease by 3 per cent.

Sickness still haunted the division. At the beginning of the year, its sick rate was 20 per cent. By the end of February, it was still at 20 per cent, with 930 other ranks not fit for duty. If the 139 other ranks who were wounded during the Siege of Ciudad Rodrigo are subtracted from the total, that leaves 739 (16 per cent) or 1 man in 6 who was sick.

Then there were the officers. An examination of the monthly theatre returns for February shows 170 officers present with their battalions, who were not on the battalion staff.

Table 7.1: Number of Light Division Officers as Shown in the February 1812 Theatre Returns

Unit	LTC	Maj	Cpt	LT	Ens	Total
43rd Foot	1	2	8	24	3	**38**
1st Bn 52nd	-	1	9	17	11	**38**
1st Bn 95th	-	1	6	19	8	**34**
2nd Bn 95th (2 Companies)	-	-	2	3	1	**6**
3rd Bn 95th (5 Companies)	1	-	4	11	2	**18**
1st Caç	1	1	5	6	5	**18**
3rd Caç	1	1	5	6	5	**18**
Total	4	6	39	86	35	170

These numbers, however, are misleading. In the theatre returns, in addition to the number of officers in each British battalion, it lists the name of every officer assigned to the battalion and his status. Was he with the battalion? Hospitalised? On the staff or detached duty? The by-name list provides a different number, which is 13 per cent less than what the gross numbers show.

Table 7.2: Number of Officers That Are Named as With the Battalion in February 1812 Theatre Returns

	LTC	Maj	Cpt	LT	Ens	Total	Difference
43rd Foot	1	1	6	20	2	**30**	8 Less
1st Bn 52nd	1	1	7	13	8	**30**	8 Less
1st Bn 95th	-	1	6	17	8	**32**	2 Less
2nd Bn 95th (2 Companies)	-	-	2	2	1	**5**	1 Less
3rd Bn 95th (5 Companies)	1	-	4	10	2	**17**	1 Less
1st Caçadores	-	1	5	6	5	**17**	1 Less
3rd Caçadores	1	1	5	6	5	**18**	None
Total	4	5	35	74	31	149	21 Less

What is important about this is how few officers were with their battalion – only 75 per cent of its authorised officers would be marching with the colours. Particularly worrisome was the number of vacancies among the senior officers. The division was missing 50 per cent of its lieutenant colonels, 45 per cent of its majors, and 25 per cent of its company commanders. It did have almost 90 per cent of its lieutenants, but only 61 per cent of its ensigns and second lieutenants.

The division began the march to Badajoz with about 4,100 men when the battalion, brigade, and division staff officers are counted.

Table 7.3: Light Division Strength 1 March 1812

Unit	Officers Present					NCOs		Rank and File			
	LTC	Maj	Cpt	LT	Ens	Sgt	Buglers	With the Colours	Sick	On Command	Total
43rd Foot	1	1	6	20	2	66	23	863	222	45	**1,130**
1st Bn 52nd	1	1	7	13	8	69	26	905	333	42	**1,280**
1st Bn 95th	-	1	6	17	8	53	20	621	95	28	**744**
2nd Bn 95th (2 Companies)	_	_	2	2	1	10	2	149	25	_	**174**
3rd Bn 95th (5 Companies)	1	_	4	10	2	26	10	242	107	7	**356**
1st Caç		1	5	6	5	33	15	373	72	91	**536**
3rd Caç	1	1	5	6	5	34	12	444	76	14	**534**
Total	**4**	**5**	**35**	**74**	**31**	**291**	**108**	**3,597** [1]	**930** [2]	**227**[3]	**4,754**

The new organisation of the division was as per the following table.

Table 7.4: Organisation of the Light Division 1 March 1812

Unit	Personnel	Position
Division HQ	Maj Gen John Ormsby Vandeleur	Acting Commander
	LT James Shaw 43rd Foot	ADC
	LT William Armstrong 19th Light Dragoons	ADC
	LT John Bell 52nd Foot	DAQMG
	Maj Charles Rowan 52nd Foot	AAG
	Charles Purcell	ACG
	Wentworth Parker	CH
1st Brigade	LTC Thomas Beckwith	Commander
	Cpt Charles Beckwith 95th Rifles	Brigade Maj
1st Bn 43rd Foot	LTC Charles McLeod	Commander
RW 1st Bn 95th Rifles	Maj Peter O'Hare	Commander
2nd Bn 95th Rifles	Cpt Samuel Mitchell	Commander
2nd Bn 95th Rifles	Cpt John Hart	Commander
3rd Bn 95th Rifles	LTC Andrew Barnard	Commander
3rd Caç Bn	LTC George Elder	Commander

1. This is 75 per cent of the total rank and file of the division.
2. This is 20 per cent of the total rank and file of the division.
3. This is 5 per cent of the total rank and file of the division.

Unit	Personnel	Position
2nd Brigade	Bvt LTC Edward Gibbs	Acting Commander
	Cpt Harry Smith 95th Rifles	Brigade Maj
1st Bn 52nd Foot	Cpt Robert Campbell	Acting Commander
LW 1st Bn 95th Rifles	Bvt Maj Alexander Cameron	Commander
1st Caç Bn	Maj John Algeo	Acting Commander

The March South

It would take the division three weeks to march the 350km from its cantonments in the vicinity of Fuenteguinaldo to the outskirts of Badajoz. The route would take the soldiers through the Serra da Estrela, which has some the highest mountains in Portugal. Towards the end of the march, they would have to cross the Tagus River on the pontoon bridge at Vila Velha, which because of the steep approaches to and from it, could delay movement. Since it was still winter, the weather was cold, with the possibility of snow and rain. The impact of the weather would not just be on the roads, but also on where the soldiers could be billeted every night. Bivouacking in the open risked the soldiers becoming sick due to exposure, exhaustion, and not being able to dry their uniforms. To prevent this, arrangements had been made for the division to stop each night in villages and towns, whenever possible.

The roads wound through the mountains and in some places were good, but in others very bad. The rain and snow did not help their condition. Also affecting the roads was the amount of traffic that recently travelled over them. Three divisions had used them in the previous two weeks. Thousands of men moving along them would place much wear and tear on them, while the heavy baggage carts and the artillery train would cause considerable damage. The heavy rains had only made the road conditions worse.

Another factor that impacted the length of the daily march was the time of the year. Although it was late winter, the amount of daylight for marching was about twelve hours per day. Sunrise was around 6:00 a.m. and sunset was about 6:00 p.m. However, time had to be allowed for the troops to be assigned to their quarters, distribute rations, and most importantly, find firewood to cook their food, dry their clothes, and warm their billets. The same route had been used by the other divisions and the easy to obtain firewood and fodder had long since been taken. The troops would have to go some distance after the end of the day's march to find both. To alleviate this, the two brigades would initially take different roads.

The 1st Brigade's Route to Castelo Branco[4]

- 26 February: The brigade began its movement at about 6:30 a.m. and marched 43km through stormy weather. Its route took it via Quinta de Aguila to Nave de Haver and on to Vilar Maior where it stopped for the night.
- 27 February: The brigade was on the road at 6:30 a.m. and marched 30km through Bismula to Rendo. The weather was fine.
- 28 February: It rained the previous night, but the rain had stopped by the time the brigade began its march. Its route took them to Sabugal then to Santo Estêvão, and on to the Vale de Lobo where it bivouacked after a 32km march.
- 29 February: The weather was sunny. The 43rd Foot delayed its start until 7:30 a.m. due to having to investigate a complaint that one of its men was involved in a robbery. The brigade marched 25km to Meimoa and then to Pedrógão de São Pedro.
- 1 March: This was an easy day for the brigade. Its movement began at 8:00 a.m. and the march ended at Aldeia de Santa Margarida after only 7km. The likely reason for being so short was that there was a bottleneck at the crossing of the Tagus River by the divisions that had preceded them.
- 2 March: The brigade was on the road by 7:00 a.m. and made another easy march via São Miguel de Acha. It reached its destination, Lousã, by 11:00 a.m. after marching only 22km.
- 3 March: It should have been an easy 20km march to Castelo Branco via Escalos de Cima, but it was not. The brigade left Lousã at 6:30 a.m. The road was in poor condition and got worse the closer it got to Castelo Branco. There the brigade linked up with the 2nd Brigade.

The 2nd Brigade's March to Castelo Branco[5]

- 26 February: The brigade marched 40km from their billets in the vicinity of Pueblo de Azaba to Casillas de Flores to Forcalhos and then to Alfaiates where it spent the night. The weather was cold and rainy.
- 27 February: The weather was good; however, the roads were not. The brigade marched 20km via Souto, Torre, and stopped in Sabugal.
- 28 February: The weather continued to be good. The road from Sabugal was narrow and rocky till Sortelha, where the brigade HQ and the

4. Oglander, Henry, *The Journals of Captain Henry Oglander of the 43rd & 47th Foot*, pp.131–133.
5. Gairdner, James. *The American Sharpe: The Adventures of an American Officer of the 95th Rifles in the Peninsula & Waterloo Campaigns*, pp.20–21; Ewart, John, *Peninsular War Diary of Captain John Frederick Ewart, 52nd Light Infantry, 1811–1812*, pp.74–75, and Simmons, George, *A British Rifleman: Journals and Correspondence During the Peninsular War and the Campaign of Wellington*, p.224.

52nd Foot spent the night, after travelling 12km. The Left Wing of the 95th Foot and the 1st Caçadores continued another 9km to Casteleiro. Initially the terrain was gentle but soon it became 'exceedingly wild rocky and uncultivated.'[6]

- 29 February: The brigade left Sortelha at dawn and took a fair road 12km to Escarigo where the HQ, 52nd Foot, and 1st Caçadores spent the night. The 95th Rifles marched another 11km to Capinha.
- 1 March: The brigade marched 40km to Alpedrinha via Capinha. The 95th Rifles, which had spent the night in Capinha, only had to march 29km.
- 2 March: The brigade was on the road by 7:00 a.m. and marched 25km on a good road to Alcains via Lardoso. The weather continued to be very good. The houses were found to be 'tolerably good, but very dirty.'[7]
- 3 March: The 2nd Brigade was on the road at 8:00 a.m. and marched in good weather 14km on a good road to Castelo Branco. There they found the previous divisions to have left the quarters filthy.[8] They beat the 1st Brigade to the town and likely got the best quarters.[9]

The March to Castelo de Vide[10]

- 4 March: Castelo Branco was overcrowded, and the quarters were in poor condition. Many of the buildings housed the army's sick. It was supposed to be a rest day, however Lieutenant Colonel Beckwith was granted permission to continue marching his brigade south. It departed at 6:30 a.m. and marched 13km via Represa to Retaxo where it spent the night. The 2nd Brigade spent the night in Castelo Branco.
- 5 March: The 1st Brigade marched 40km to Nisa via the pontoon bridge across the Tagus River at Vila Velha. It left Retaxo at 5:30 a.m. and was at the bridge three hours later. Due to traffic, it halted for an hour before crossing and arrived at Nisa at 2:30 p.m. The 2nd Brigade marched 16km to Sarnadas de Ródão where its HQ and the 52nd Foot

6. Gairdner, James, *The American Sharpe: The Adventures of an American Officer of the 95th Rifles in the Peninsula & Waterloo Campaigns*, p.20.
7. Ewart, John, *Peninsular War Diary of Captain John Frederick Ewart, 52nd Light Infantry, 1811-1812*, p.75.
8. Ibid.
9. Ibid.
10. Oglander, Henry, *The Journals of Captain Henry Oglander of the 43rd & 47th Foot*, pp.134-137; Gairdner, James, *The American Sharpe: The Adventures of an American Officer of the 95th Rifles in the Peninsula & Waterloo Campaigns*, pp.21-22; Ewart, John, *Peninsular War Diary of Captain John Frederick Ewart, 52nd Light Infantry, 1811-1812*, pp.75-76 and Simmons, George, *A British Rifleman: Journals and Correspondence During the Peninsular War and the Campaign of Wellington*, p.224.

stopped for the day. The village was too small to hold all the troops, so the Left Wing of the 1st Battalion 95th Rifles stayed in Retaxo, while the 1st Caçadores went to Atalaia.

- 6 March: The weather was very warm and the 1st Brigade marched 23km to Castelo de Vide. The 2nd Brigade arrived at Nisa after marching 40km and crossing the Tagus River.
- 7 March: The 1st Brigade stayed in Castelo de Vide. The 2nd Brigade left Nisa about 6:00 a.m. and marched to Castelo de Vide. The quarters were tight and the Left Wing of the 1st Battalion 95th Rifles was placed in farmhouses outside the town, while the battalion HQ and the Right Wing were billeted in Escusa about 5km away.
- 8–13 March: The division spent the next seven days resting in Castelo de Vide. The 1st Battalion 95th particularly enjoyed their quarters. Lieutenant Gairdner described them as excellent and very comfortable.[11] Several officers took the time to explore the mountains near the town. By the end of the week, the weather turned cold and on 11 March, right after sunset, heavy snow fell for an hour.

The Court Martial of Rifleman Joseph Allman

In addition to the nine deserters found at the taking of Ciudad Rodrigo, another deserter from the Light Division was caught in January 1812. Rifleman Joseph Allman had deserted on 18 November 1811 and was in Ciudad Rodrigo when the siege began. Knowing that if the Allies took the town, he would be court martialed and likely executed, Allman fled from the city for Salamanca. He was caught by Spanish guerrillas and turned over to the British in late February. A general court martial was convened on 4 March with Major General Vandeleur as its president and Lieutenant Harry Smith as the deputy judge advocate. All of the court's fourteen members were drawn from the Light Division,[12] including Captain John Duffy, 43rd Foot.[13]

The trial was held in Castelo de Vide. Allman was found guilty and sentenced to death. The execution was carried out on 10 March. The division paraded near the town to witness the execution. Prior to being shot, Allman 'protested against their right to shoot him, until he first received the arrears of pay which was due at the time of his desertion.'[14]

11. Gairdner, James, *The American Sharpe: The Adventures of an American Officer of the 95th Rifles in the Peninsula & Waterloo Campaigns*, p.21.
12. General Orders, dated 7 March 1812.
13. Duffy, John, *Journals of Majors John Duffy and John Maxwell Tylden of the 43rd Foot*, p.147.
14. Kincaid, John, *Adventures in the Rifle Brigade in the Peninsula, France, and the Netherlands from 1809–1815*, p.122.

Rifleman Edward Costello and Allman were in the same company in the 1st Battalion 95th Rifles, and Costello was assigned to guard him.

> I knew him well: he was an exceedingly fine looking fellow, and up to the period of his unhappy departure from duty, noted for possessing the best qualities of a soldier. Some harshness on the part of an officer was the cause of [his] desertion; but from the circumstance of his previous good character, and the fact of his having been marched as a prisoner for many days together during our march from Rodrigo, it was commonly thought he would be pardoned. I happened to be on guard over him the night prior to his execution. The prisoner was playing at cards with some of the men in the evening, when the provost of the division entered the guard-room, and gave him the intelligence that he was doomed to suffer at ten o'clock the next morning. Sudden and utterly unexpected as the announcement was, [his] face was the only one that showed scarcely any emotion. 'Well,' he remarked to those around him, 'I am quite ready.' A short time afterwards he sent for the pay sergeant of the company he belonged to, from whom he received the arrears of pay that were due to him. This he spent on wine, which he distributed among the men of the guard. Noticing one man with very bad shoes, [he] observed his own were better, and taking them off he exchanged them for the bad pair, saying, 'They will last me as long as I shall require them.'
>
> The morning turned out showery, the division formed in three sides of a square, and the guard, headed by the band with [Allman] in front, slowly marched round; the muffled drum beat in dull time the Dead march, and the swell of its solemn harmony, though it filled the eyes of every man present, only seemed to strengthen the glance of the doomed. He led the van of his funeral procession, like one who was to live for ever his step was as firm and more correct than any, and I thought at the time, a finer soldier never stepped. Poor [Allman], I shall never forget when he halted at his own grave, the heavy rains had filled it half with water, which he noticed with a faint smile, and observed, 'Although a watery one, I shall sleep sound enough in it.' He then stood upright in a fine military position, while the Brigade Major read aloud the proceedings of the court-martial. The provost came to tie the handkerchief round his eyes, when he coolly remarked, 'There is no occasion – I shall not flinch.' Being told it was customary, he said, 'Very well, do your duty.' Before this last office was performed, he turned round, and calling most of the guard by name, bade them farewell. As I nodded to him in return, I fancied it was to a dead man, for in two minutes he was no more. The intrepid and cool manner in which he met his fate, drew forth a general feeling of admiration.[15]

15. Costello, Edward, *Adventures of a Soldier*, p.24–25.

The March Continues[16]

On 14 March, the division received orders to march immediately to Portalegre and then on to Elvas, which was 80km away. They were to be in Elvas in two days. The 2nd Brigade led the division and departed at noon and was followed by the 1st Brigade at 1:00 p.m. They arrived in Portalegre about 5:00 p.m. The march orders had taken the division by surprise and detachments had been sent out to collect firewood and forage prior to receiving the orders. Among those absent was Lieutenant Gairdner, who as the 1st Battalion 95th Rifles' orderly officer 'went out at 10 o'clock with the bat men for forage and on my return at about 2 o'clock I found that the regiment had marched to Portalegre. There were orders left for me to bring on the baggage to Portalegre, I got off at about 3 o'clock but did not get into Portalegre until after dark.'[17]

While at Portalegre, Major General Vandeleur went on sick leave to recover from his wounds. Lieutenant Colonel Beckwith took command of the division.

The following day the division was on the move at sunrise. The 1st Brigade stopped in Assumar after marching 23km, while the 2nd Brigade marched 25km to Arronches. On 16 March, the 1st Brigade departed at 5:30 a.m. and the 2nd Brigade left at 6:00 a.m. The 32km route took them through Santa Eulália. The road was good; however it rained for much of the march. The 1st Brigade arrived at Elvas about 2:00 p.m. and the 2nd Brigade arrived shortly after that.

---

16. Oglander, Henry, *The Journals of Captain Henry Oglander of the 43rd & 47th Foot*, pp.137–138; Gairdner, James, *The American Sharpe: The Adventures of an American Officer of the 95th Rifles in the Peninsula & Waterloo Campaigns*, pp.22-23; Ewart, John, *Peninsular War Diary of Captain John Frederick Ewart, 52nd Light Infantry, 1811–1812*, p.77, and Simmons, George, *A British Rifleman: Journals and Correspondence During the Peninsular War and the Campaign of Wellington*, pp 224–225.
17. Gairdner, James, *The American Sharpe: The Adventures of an American Officer of the 95th Rifles in the Peninsula & Waterloo Campaigns*, pp.22–23.

Chapter 8

The Siege of Badajoz 17 March–5 April 1812

Badajoz was going to be very difficult to take. Captain John T. Jones, the brigade major of the Royal Engineers at the siege, described Badajoz as being

> situated on the left bank of the Guadiana; which river is there from 300 to 500 yards broad, and washes one-fourth of the enceinte, rendering it nearly inattackable [*sic*]. The 1st defences along the river are confined to a simple and badly flanked rampart, with an exposed revetment, but on the other sides consist of eight spacious and well-built regular fronts, having a good counter-scarp, covered-way, and glacis, but the ravelins incomplete. The scarp of the bastions exceeds 30 feet in height, and that of the curtains varies from 23 to 26 feet. In advance of these fronts are two detached works: one, called the Pardaleras, at 200 yards distance, is a crown work; its escarps are low, its ditches narrow, and its rear badly closed: the other, called the Picurina, is a strong redoubt, 400 yards in advance of the town… On the northeast of the town, at the angle formed by the junction of the river Rivillas with the Guadiana, rises a hill to the height of more than 100 feet, the summit of which is crowned by an old castle; and its walls, naked, weak, and but partially flanked, here form part of the enceinte of the place.
>
> The space contained within the castle is considerable, and various projects have at different times been under consideration for occupying it with a citadel or some interior defensive post; but nothing had ever been carried into effect. Indeed the defences of the castle had been unaccountably neglected; two or three field-pieces only being mounted on its walls, and those without the shelter of proper parapets. Immediately opposite to the castle, on the right bank of the Guadiana, at the distance of 500 yards, are situated the heights of Christoval, rising to nearly the elevation of the castle; and as the terreplein or interior space of the castle is an inclined plane towards the Guadiana, every part of it is seen from the Christoval heights. To prevent a besieger readily availing himself of this advantage in any attack of the town, a fort has been constructed on them: its figure is nearly that of a square of 300 feet; the scarp, which is well built of stone, is 20 feet in height, and mostly well covered by a reveted counterscarp.

> The communication between the town and Fort Christoval is very open to interruption; being either by a bridge 600 yards in length, subject to be enfiladed or by boats for which there is no security.[1]

Wellington tried to take the city in 1811, so the French had a good idea of its weaknesses and took steps to strengthen it and repair the damage done then. According to Colonel Jean Lamare, the commander of the French engineers in the city, ravelins in front of the bastions had been repaired, and galleries were dug in counterscarps and in the terreplains of the bastions on the western approaches. These would be filled with gunpowder and blown up should the enemy move over them. In a masterful use of the terrain, two masonry dams were constructed to block the flow of the Rivillas stream and flood the approaches to the eastern walls. This would channel the attacker into better defended parts of the city. 'The castle, which had been attacked during the previous sieges, had been carefully closed. Magazines of provisions and ammunition were established in it, and our only powder magazine was there. The breach made by the English in the first siege had been completely repaired.'[2] The French wanted to rebuild palisades to protect the covered ways that were destroyed in 1811, but no source of wood was close enough to do so.[3]

To defend the city, the French had a garrison of about 5,000 troops.

Table 8.1: French Garrison of Badajoz 16 March 1812[4]

Command Staff		**Total**
General of Division Armand Philippon	Governor	1
LT Duhamel	ADC to Philippon	1
LT Demeuve	ADC to Philippon	1
General of Brigade Michel Veiland	Second in Command	1
Cpt Massot	ADC to Veiland	1
LT Saint-Vicent	ADC to Veiland	1
Chevalier Charpentier	Commandant	1
M. De Grasse	Staff Officer	1
LT Denisot	Town Adjutant	1
Colonel Gaspard Thierry		1
Colonel Pineau		1

1. Jones, John, *Journal of the Sieges Carried on by the Army Under the Duke of Wellington Between the Years 1811 & 1814*, Vol. 1, pp.11–12.
2. Lamare, Jean, *An Account of the Second Defense of the Fortress of Badajoz by the French in 1812*, pp.6–8.
3. Ibid. p.9.
4. Ibid. No page listed.

Command Staff		**Total**
Colonel Picoteau	Artillery Commander	1
Chief of Battalion l'Espganol	Second in Command	1
Cpt Guiraud	Artillery Officer	1
Cpt d'André-Saint-Victor	Artillery Officer	1
1 LTC and 3 Cpts	Spanish Artillery Officers	3
Colonel Jean Lamare	Commander of Engineers	1
Chief of Battalion Truilhier	Second in Command	1
Cpt Lefaivre	Engineer	1
Cpt Meynhart	Engineer	1
Sub-Inspector of Reviews Pazius		1
Commissary Vienné		1
Garde Magazine L. Coupin		1
Troops		
Artillery		233
	1st Company 2nd Regiment	
	1st Company 12th Regiment	
	Artificer Detachment	
Engineers		265
	2nd Company 2nd Bn of Miners	
	1st Company 2nd Bn of Sappers	
	Part of 5th Company 2nd Bn of Sappers	
Infantry		
	3rd Bn 9th Light Infantry	2,680
	3rd Bn 28th Light Infantry	
	1st Bn 58th Line Infantry	
	3rd Bn 88th Line Infantry	
	3rd Bn 103rd Line Infantry	
	2 Companies 64th Line Infantry	
	Hesse Darmstadt Crown Prince Infantry With Artillery Bsattery	900
	Spanish Infantry	50
Cavalry	Dragoons and Chasseurs	50
Artillery Drivers and Military Equipage		130
Total Combatants		4,333
Civil Officers, Sutlers, Sick and Servants		667
Total		5,000

The garrison had enough food to withstand a thirty to forty day siege, however the 'town's people were still worse supplied.'[5]

Badajoz had a prewar population of 16,000.[6] However, 'according to the local archives, the last census of the occupied population was made by the French on 17 March. This amounted to 300 families (about 1,200 / 1,500 people), most of whom apparently left the city between that date and 4 April, when the communications were definitely cut by the besiegers.'[7]

This exodus from the city was confirmed by the French engineer Colonel Lamare, however his numbers of the people who refused to evacuate are much higher.

> The former sieges had obliged many opulent families to quit the place, in order to avoid the danger and famine which threatened them; the fresh appearance of the English again, induced a great number of all classes to remove to a distance. Old men, women, and children were then to be seen loaded with their property, and flying on every road; they quitted their homes with tears, and often looked back with regret on their unhappy city, which they saw was about to be exposed a third time to all the calamities inseparable from war. There only remained about four or five thousand of the inhabitants, amongst whom were a number of indigent persons who, in spite of the sad prospect which the future presented to them, could not bring themselves to quit their abodes.[8]

Wellington's Plan to Take Badajoz

A reconnaissance by Royal Engineer officers had revealed that the counterguard[9] protecting the wall between Santa Maria Bastion 6 and La Trinidad Bastion 7 on the eastern side of the fortress had not been completed. It was protected by Fort Picurina, which was situated on the high ground about 500m on the other side of the Rivillas stream, which had been flooded by a dam. To be able to fire on the walls of Badajoz, Wellington would have to take Fort Picurina first. The plan was to dig trenches

> against the place in which enfilading batteries might be established to keep under the fire of all the faces and flanks bearing on the Picurina hill: also

5. Ibid, p.10.
6. Ibid, p.3.
7. Ortiz, Fernando, 'Civilian Casualties During the Sack of Badajoz 1812', *The Napoleon Series Online.*
8. Lamare, Jean, *An Account of the Second Defense of the Fortress of Badajoz by the French in 1812*, pp.11–12.
9. A position that is placed to protect a bastion or a wall from enemy artillery.

> to throw up batteries on the left of the parallel to injure the front defences of Fort Picurina, and to plunge into its interior with small charges, fired at high elevations, so as to break down the palisades along its gorge.[10]

Wellington's intention was to take Fort Picurina by assault on the first night. Once this was accomplished, his troops were

> to throw up breaching batteries in the most eligible situations on the Picurina hill, to breach the right face of the bastion Trinidad; and as the attack would not admit of the opposite flank of the bastion of Sta. Maria being silenced by enfilade fire, it was proposed to breach it also at the same time with the face. Further, as from the distance of the breaching batteries, several days would be required to render the breaches practicable, during which time the garrison might retrench them, it was proposed, as soon as the great breaches should become practicable, to turn the fire of all the breaching guns upon the curtain between them, and make a third breach in it, which would from its situation turn the defences of the other two. The obstacle of the inundation to be avoided by forming the columns for the assault behind the hills to the south and west of it. The covered-way and ditch to be entered as at Rodrigo.[11]

Each division was tasked to provide a certain number of men to dig the trenches and to form the covering party, which had the job of protecting the troops building the siege works by responding to any sorties by the garrison. The number of men required for the trench work varied by the day, but the covering party usually needed 2,000 men. The shifts usually ran from 6:00 a.m. to 6:00 p.m. and then 6:00 p.m. to 6:00 a.m. Fewer men were needed on the night shift. Unlike during the Siege of Ciudad Rodrigo, where a division had the duty every fourth day, at Badajoz a division was told the day before how many men it would have to provide the following day. The Light Division organised its men into six-hour shifts. The covering party was commanded by Major General James Kempt, a brigade commander in the 3rd Division. Beginning on 20 March, the troops for the covering party came from only one division.

Lieutenant Kincaid, 1st Battalion 95th Rifles, wrote that since

> we had a smaller force employed than at Rodrigo; and the scale of operations was so much greater, that it required every man to be actually in the trenches six hours every day, and the same length of time every night, which,

10. Jones, John, *Journal of the Sieges Carried on by the Army Under the Duke of Wellington Between the Years 1811 & 1814*, Vol. 1, p.153.
11. Ibid, pp.153–154.

> with the time required to march to and from them, through fields more than ankle deep in a stiff mud, left us never more than eight hours out of the twenty-four in camp, and we never were dry the whole time.[12]

Kincaid's description of the long hours and miserable conditions might be exaggerated, but probably not by much.

No copies of the work schedule from the quartermaster general are known to exist. However, some of the numerous diaries and letters written by Light Division officers and soldiers cover the days and times they were on duty. In addition to them, there were the monthly payrolls which listed when a soldier was killed or died from wounds. Unfortunately, if a soldier was wounded, the payrolls do not list a date he was wounded. They only list whether he was hospitalised on 24 March or 24 April. For the 1st and 3rd Caçadores, we used their daily casualty returns to determine the dates they were on duty. The following are the days and times that we know the Light Division either provided work or covering parties. There may have been more.

Table 8.2: Light Division Work Schedule During Siege of Badajoz 17 March–5 April 1812

Date	Day Shift 6:00 a.m. to 6:00 p.m.		Night Shift 6:00 p.m. to 6:00 a.m.	
	Work Party	Covering Party	Work Party	Covering Party
17 March			43rd Foot	
18 March	43rd Foot	52nd Foot		RW 1st Bn 95th Rifles
19 March	43rd Foot	52nd Foot		LW 1st Bn 95th Rifles
20 March	43rd Foot/52nd Foot			43rd Foot
21 March	RW 1st Bn 95th Rifles		43rd Foot	43rd Foot/52nd Foot
22 March		43rd Foot/52nd Foot	43rd Foot	
23 March			52nd Foot	
24 March				43rd Foot/52nd Foot
25 March		43rd Foot/52nd Foot	43rd Foot/52nd Foot RW 1st Bn 95th Rifles	
26 March	RW 1st Bn 95th Rifles			

12. Kincaid, John, *Adventures in the Rifle Brigade in the Peninsula, France, and the Netherlands from 1809–1815*, p.125.

Date	Day Shift 6:00 a.m. to 6:00 p.m.		Night Shift 6:00 p.m. to 6:00 a.m.	
	Work Party	Covering Party	Work Party	Covering Party
27 March		43rd Foot		43rd Foot
28 March		Light Division Has Duty		Light Division Has Duty
29 March				
30 March	52nd Foot RW 1st Bn 95th Rifles	3rd Caç	43rd Foot	3rd Caç
31 March	43rd Foot	3rd Caç		
1 April		3rd Caç	1st Caç	
2 April			1st Caç	52nd Foot
3 April		43rd Foot 1st and 3rd Caç		
4 April		RW 1st Bn 95th	43rd Foot	1st Caç
5 April		3rd Caç	1st Caç	

The Siege Begins

Captain John Jones, brigade major, Royal Engineers[13] stated, 'A few hours before we began the work, the weather which had so long been fine, broke, and there came on a deluge of rain, which has continued nearly ever since…Our trenches have all of them two and three feet of water in them, and there is no prospect of a change in the weather.'

The Light Division broke camp at Elvas and was on the march at daybreak.[14] Because it was 17 March, the bands played the jig 'Saint Patrick's Day' in the saint's honour. They crossed the Guadiana River on a pontoon bridge about 5km southwest of Badajoz.[15] The division marched east and bivouacked in an area about 4km south of the city, near the road to Torquemada,[16] in sight of Fort Pardaleras.[17] Their bivouacs were not good and had very few comforts, if any. These 16,000 men of the four Anglo-Portuguese divisions, plus hundreds of artillery men and engineers competed for the few supplies that could be found. Badajoz had been besieged three times in the past fourteen months and

13. Unpublished private letter from Jones to his brother, Captain George Jones, Royal Navy, dated 24 March 1812.
14. Sunrise was at 6:00 a.m.
15. Duffy, John, *Journals of Majors John Duffy and John Maxwell Tylden of the 43rd Foot*, p.148.
16. We have not been able to identify a town with this name near Badajoz. The road was likely modern-day N-432.
17. Cooke, John, *A True Soldier Gentleman: The Memoirs of Lt. John Cooke 1791–1813*, p.114.

everything was in short supply. The besieging armies had stripped the area of any trees and torn down most of the buildings outside the walls. Firewood was so scarce that the French garrison had to dig up the roots of the olive trees that had once grown near the city. The nearest forest of any size was 40km away.[18] Officers were used to supplementing their rations by purchasing food from the local people but that was no longer possible. Lieutenant Charles Booth, 52nd Foot, wrote to his uncle that the only food available was rations because the 'country is entirely eaten up by the army…Bread long since and even meat now has ceased to be supplied by the country people.'[19] Lieutenant Barlow, also from the 52nd Foot, wrote to his uncle about how miserable the living conditions were.

> The season at this time of the year is not very pleasant for those who live under canvas; a great deal of rain has lately fallen accompanied with high & tempestuous winds, Water must be fetched from a considerable distance & that not of the best; and which in summer must be particularly unwholesome, from being stagnant. It is a considerable distance to the Guadiana and the whole country around a sandy, barren flat, almost as naked as the palm of my hand and almost destitute of wood for fires & cooking.[20]

Digging the Trenches

The troops arrived at their bivouacs by mid-afternoon on 17 March and they were ready to start digging. The engineers originally tasked the divisions to provide 1,800 men to dig the trenches and another 2,000 for the covering party.[21] The Light Division supplied 500 men for the trenches and 500 men for the covering party. The 43rd Foot worked the trenches for the first twelve hours and were relieved the next morning at 7:00 a.m. They rotated the men every six hours. The 52nd Foot provided men to the covering party and were on duty for twelve hours without a relief.[22]

---

18. Lamare, Jean, *An Account of the Second Defense of the Fortress of Badajoz by the French in 1812*, pp.8–10.
19. Booth, Charles, *Redcoats of Wellington's Light Division: Unpublished & Rare Memoirs of the 52nd (Oxfordshire) Regiment of Foot*, p.115.
20. Barlow, George Ulrich, *A Light Infantryman With Wellington: The Letters of Captain George Ulrich Barlow, 52nd and 69th Foot, 1808–1815*, p.141.
21. Jones, John, *Journal of the Sieges Carried on by the Army Under the Duke of Wellington Between the Years 1811 & 1814*, Vol.1, p.158.
22. Oglander, Henry, *The Journals of Captain Henry Oglander of the 43rd & 47*th *Foot*, p.138, and Ewart, John, *Peninsular War Diary of Captain John Frederick Ewart, 52nd Light Infantry, 1811–1812*, p.77.

After being tasked, the men waited on the engineers to show them where to dig. At dusk, (about 6:30 p.m.), the engineers moved to the Sierra de San Miguel, a hill that was about 150m from Fort Picurina and about 25m higher. There they began tracing the lines that would overlook the fort. It took almost three hours for them to do so. As the troops waited, about 6:00 p.m. 'rain began to fall in torrents, and continued the whole night.'[23]

Bugler William Green, 3rd Company 1st Battalion 95th Rifles described what it was like to work in the trenches.

> We worked hard, and by daylight in the morning we were safe under cover; we were relieved off duty and other troops took our place. Next day we had to break ground in open daylight; each man had to carry a skip [a gabion] and a spade; we set our skips about three paces apart, and began to fill them with earth to make a cover for us from the enemies fire; their musket balls reached us, we had two or three men wounded and one officer but no one killed. Other skips were brought to fill up the intervals and set one upon another and filled with earth, so that we soon had a good shelter from the enemies balls…the weather was so bad with the heavy rain that the men had to work up to their knees in mud.[24]

The first parallel was to be dug about 150m from Fort Picurina. They were too close to the fort to deploy the covering party between it and the place to be dug. So, the covering parties were placed in low areas on the side. The engineers were concerned that the noise of the digging would alert the defenders so 'only 600 men instead of 1,000 were found disposable for the parallel. They were placed at 3 feet apart, and opened 600 yards of it…at daylight the approaches and parallel were generally 3 feet deep, and 3 feet 6 inches wide, and the relief was employed to improve them.'[25]

The plan worked. The heavy rains masked the sound of the digging and it was not until dawn that the defenders discovered them. They immediately opened with artillery and musket fire. The Light Division had no men killed that day; however, the 4th Division was not so lucky. Lieutenant John Cooke, 43rd Foot, was part of the covering party during the day and

> saw the first shot; it was fired from the Fort Picurina, and killed two poor fellows in the covering party of the fourth division, which was formed

23. Cooke, John, *A True Soldier Gentleman: The Memoirs of Lt. John Cooke 1791–1813*, pp.114–115.
24. Green, William, *Where Duty Calls Me: The Experiences of William Green of Lutterworth in the Napoleonic Wars*, p.34.
25. Jones, John, *Journal of the Sieges Carried on by the Army Under the Duke of Wellington Between the Years 1811 & 1814*, Vol. 1, pp.158–159.

> under the slope of a hill. In a few minutes the round shot came up the road quite often enough to put our blood into circulation; and we immediately took our station under a small natural rise of ground, where we remained covering the workmen for twelve hours. The cannonade was regular during the day, both from the town and from Fort Picurina.[26]

The officers and men not working that night, spent a miserable twelve hours outside in the rain trying to stay warm. Plans had been made by the quartermaster general department to have 1,400 Portuguese Army tents[27] delivered to the 4 divisions building the siege works, however they had not arrived in time. Captain William Balvaird, 1st Battalion 95th Rifles, had the foresight to bring his own tent and he shared it with every officer who was not on duty.[28] Much to the delight of the soldiers the next day the tents arrived and had been set up by the evening. Cooke wrote that when he

> returned to camp an hour after dark, and I was surprised to find the division had been supplied with Portuguese tents. I found my friend waiting in one for me, and the canteens laid out with all the affection of a youthful soldier. I had been exposed in the rain for twenty-five hours, and this was one of the happiest moments of my life.[29]

These tents helped, but as one officer found they 'are by no means proof against the descending torrents at the moment I am now watching. My baggage during the day is covered with oilskin, which at night is substituted for a counter-pane and is indeed absolutely necessary.'[30]

The poor weather also had an impact when it was not raining. The heavy rain caused the Calamon and Rivillas streams that were between the bivouac area and the siege works to become high. The troops would have to wade through freezing water and would arrive wet before their six-hour tour of duty began and then return to their tents with no way of drying their boots.

The heavy rain continued through the next day (18 March) and work continued on expanding the parallels and constructing Battery 1. The 43rd Foot was in the trenches during the day, while the 52nd Foot provided the covering

---

26. Cooke, John, *A True Soldier Gentleman: The Memoirs of Lt. John Cooke 1791–1813*, p.115.
27. They included 1,200 tents for the troops, 65 tents for captains, 80 tents for subalterns, and 4 tents for generals. Source: AHM-DIV-1-14-320-26 M-0005.
28. Gairdner, James, *The American Sharpe: The Adventures of an American Officer of the 95th Rifles in the Peninsula & Waterloo Campaigns*, p.23.
29. Cooke, John, *A True Soldier Gentleman: The Memoirs of Lt. John Cooke 1791–1813*, p.115.
30. Barlow, George Ulrich, *A Light Infantryman with Wellington: The Letters of Captain George Ulrich Barlow, 52nd and 69th Foot, 1808–1815*, pp.142–143.

party. The French continued to fire on the trenches and Rifleman William Pallentine, 3rd Battalion 95th Rifles was seriously wounded. That night the Left Wing of the 1st Battalion 95th Foot formed part of the covering party. The 43rd Foot was back in the trenches the next morning while the 52nd Foot was in the covering party. At 1:00 p.m. the garrison conducted a sortie with 1,400 infantry and 40 cavalry. They used the covered way to mask their approach and they were close to the trenches before they were noticed. In a brilliant use of intelligence gleaned by observing the Allies' work schedule, the enemy's attack was timed to hit at the end of the shift and before the relieving party entered the trenches. At the approached of the enemy, the men of the 43rd Foot, who were without their weapons and accoutrements, quickly fled. Instead of chasing them the French infantry started filling in the trenches. Captain Duffy, 43rd Foot, who was on duty in the trenches, said the enemy's real mission was to collect the shovels and picks the working party had dropped. Rumors abound that 'a *Louis d'Or* (a gold coin) was offered for every entrenching tool taken into the general, we lost 200 of them in this business.'[31]

The French cavalry crossed the trench line and galloped to the engineer camp about 800m on the other side of the hill. There they wreaked havoc, sabred a few soldiers in the camp, made a nuisance of themselves by knocking over tents and tables, and when the covering party was sighted, the cavalry returned to city.[32] While the sortie was underway, the defenders' artillery on the walls of the city kept the rest of the siege lines under fire, including grape shot. Rifleman Martin O'Brian, 3rd Battalion 95th Rifles, was killed, and Lieutenant Richard Freer, 1st Battalion 95th Rifles was seriously wounded. About ninety men were killed or wounded in the other divisions.[33] The most notable casualty was Captain Robert Cuthbert, Lieutenant General Picton's aide-de-camp, who died of his wounds. The heavy rain continued through the afternoon and night. The roads to the division's cantonments had turned into a sea of mud and it took the 43rd Foot almost two hours to march the 4km back to their camp.

On 20 March, the 43rd Foot had the morning shift in the trenches. It was relieved by troops from the 52nd Foot. It had been raining all day and little progress was being made. Lieutenant Barlow, 52nd Foot, wrote home that,

> some of the showers being the hardest I have ever beheld. The trenches are full of mud and water up to the knees and was not the soil of a most

31. Duffy, John, *Journals of Majors John Duffy and John Maxwell Tylden of the 43rd Foot*, p.149.
32. Oglander, Henry, *The Journals of Captain Henry Oglander of the 43rd & 47th Foot*, p.139.
33. Ewart, John, *Peninsular War Diary of Captain John Frederick Ewart, 52nd Light Infantry, 1811–1812*, p.78.

> favourable nature, it would be impossible to drag up the heavy artillery. The matter at present is one of great difficulty, sixteen bullocks, together with the manual assistance being required to draw such pieces and even then, the opening of our trenches has been delayed nearly two days. We indeed have of late been living in an amphibious state, oftener wet than dry...[34]

Captain Ewart noted in his diary that the trenches

> very far advanced on each side of the Fort Picurina, from which the enemy could not fire, except some musketry which was sharply returned by our covering parties, which were stationed in parties of 300 each in regular trenches ready to advance against any other sortie, in the evening of which the working parties were ordered to take their arms, to lay down their tools and positively to keep the trenches, which are made so as to enable the soldiers to fire over the banks with ease.[35]

The rain continued throughout the night and the next day, 21 March, found the Right Wing of the 1st Battalion 95th Rifles in the trenches. Despite the rain, the city's defenders continued to fire on the work parties in the trenches. When their relief came about noon time, some of the riflemen were too impatient to wind their way through the trenches to the top of the hill and thus be out of sight of the enemy's guns. It became a game to see who could get up there the quickest. This led to tragic consequences. Riflemen Edward Costello, James Brooks, and Thomas Tracey, all from the 3rd Company, 1st Battalion 95th Rifles would wait for a pause in the firing and them jump out of the trench race up the hill to the next parallel. Brooks had a premonition of his own death several days before. Every night he dreamt that he saw a headless rifleman. When their relief arrived the three riflemen

> jumped out of the trench, exposing ourselves to a fire from the walls of the town while we ran to the next parallel. In executing this feat I was a little ahead of my comrades, when I heard the rush of a cannon-ball, and feeling my jacket splashed by something, as soon as I had jumped into the next parallel...I turned round and beheld the body of Brooks headless, which actually stood quivering with life for a few seconds before it fell. His dream, poor fellow, had singularly augured the conclusion of his own career. The shot had smashed and carried away the whole of his head, bespattering

34. Barlow, George Ulrich, *A Light Infantryman with Wellington: The Letters of Captain George Ulrich Barlow, 52nd and 69th Foot, 1808–1815*, p.142.
35. Ewart, John, *Peninsular War Diary of Captain John Frederick Ewart, 52nd Light Infantry, 1811–1812*, p.78.

> my jacket with the brains, while Tracey was materially injured by having a splinter of the skull driven deep through the skin behind his ear.[36]

Tracey's wound was not considered serious enough to warrant hospitalisation. Also among the wounded was Captain George Johnston, 43rd Foot, who was slightly wounded in the groin. The 43rd Foot and 52nd Foot formed part of the covering party that night. Captain Duffy commanded the troops from the 43rd Foot in the covering party.

Fort Picurina also posed a problem for the troops in the trenches. Lieutenant Cooke wrote that,

> the left of our lines, previously to the escalade of Picurina, ran within about a hundred yards parallel to it. One hundred of our regiment were employed one night on the delightful job of carrying the trenches across the Seville road. We commenced at the distance of one hundred and fifty yards from the fort. The instant the enemy heard the pickaxes striking on the hard road, they opened, when, strange to relate, eleven rounds of grape were poured on us, and yet only one officer was hit. The gunners could not depress their artillery so as to cover the spot we were on.[37]

Captain Fergusson, 43rd Foot, was the officer who was wounded 'in the side by the splinter of a shell'.[38] He had been severely wounded at Ciudad Rodrigo on 19 January and chose to return to duty, despite having a musket ball embedded in his body close to his spine.

The weather worsened on 22 March. Not much was accomplished during the morning other than bailing out the flooded trenches. They had to line the bottom of the parallels with sandbags and fascines to make it easier for the troops to move through them. During the morning Ensign George Hall, 52nd Foot, was severely wounded by the splinter from a shell.[39] The 43rd Foot was back in the trenches that night and was responsible for carrying platforms from the engineer's camp to Batteries 4 and 5 that had been constructed to the right of the Talavera Road. Their work took them most of the night, but they were back in their camp by 4:00 a.m. the next morning.[40] At 4:00 p.m. the skies opened up. The heaviest rain since the start of the siege began and soon the

---

36. Costello, Edward, *Adventures of a Soldier*, pp.162–163.
37. Cooke, John, *A True Soldier Gentleman: The Memoirs of Lt. John Cooke 1791–1813*, p.117.
38. Fergusson, James, *Men of Wellington's Light Division: Unpublished Memoirs of the 43rd (Monmouthshire) Regiment in the Peninsular War*, p.78.
39. Dawson, Charles, *Redcoats of Wellington's Light Division: Unpublished & Rare Memoirs of the 52nd (Oxfordshire) Regiment of Foot*, p.161.
40. Oglander, Henry, *The Journals of Captain Henry Oglander of the 43rd & 47th Foot*, p.140.

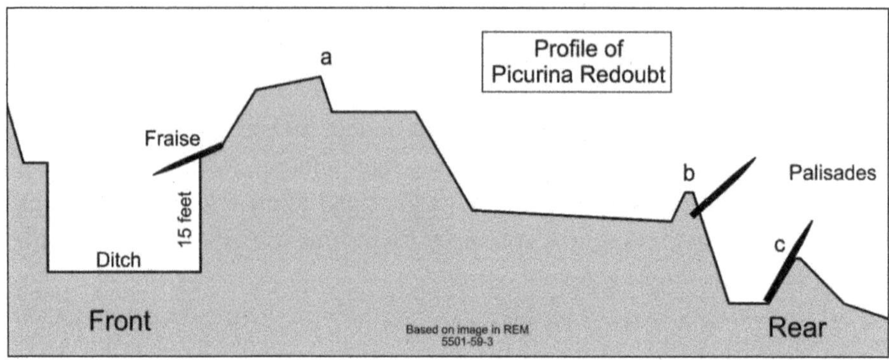

trenches were flooded again. A near disaster struck the whole operation when the rains caused the Guadiana River to become a raging torrent. Eleven of the twenty pontoons that formed the bridge south of Badajoz were sunk, while the flying bridge nearby was damaged. The army was stuck on the far side of an impassable river. If the bridge was not repaired quickly, it would be difficult to maintain the army in the vicinity of Badajoz. Artillery fire would have to be curtailed due to a shortage of ammunition and food would have to be rationed. Even the evacuation of the wounded to the hospital at Elvas had come to a halt. There was some talk about abandoning the siege.[41] The Light Division was responsible for the covering party that night.

The miserable weather continued into 23 March. There were showers in the morning and 'about 1 pm when a most furious rain commenced, which continued with little intermission till midnight.'[42] The rain was 'so exceptionally severe that the firing from the enemy ceased entirely and the working parties gave up work excepting making drains to carry off the water from the trenches which were knee deep.'[43] The engineers' brigade major, Captain Jones, was extremely frustrated 'the ground had become so completely saturated with wet [*sic*] as to lose its consistency and it was found impossible to put it into any shape, it falling back into the ditch as fast as it could be thrown up.'[44] Fortunately for most of the Light Division, only the 52nd Foot was tasked to provide troops. They went on duty at 6:00 p.m. and were relieved at midnight.[45]

The rain finally stopped on 24 March and the sun came out. The division had much of the day off, but had responsibility for the covering party beginning

41. Jones, John, *Journal of the Sieges Carried on by the Army under the Duke of Wellington between the Years 1811 & 1814*, Vol. 1, pp.167–168.
42. Oglander, Henry, *The Journals of Captain Henry Oglander of the 43rd & 47th Foot*, p.140.
43. Duffy, John, *Journals of Majors John Duffy and John Maxwell Tylden of the 43rd Foot*, p.150.
44. Jones, John, Unpublished Journal.
45. Ewart, John, *Peninsular War Diary of Captain John Frederick Ewart, 52nd Light Infantry, 1811–1812*, p.79.

95th Rifle Officer 1812. (*Courtesy of the Anne S.K. Brown Military Collection*)

View of Ciudad Rodrigo from the Great Teson. The site of the Lesser Breach is on the far left. (*Author's Collection*)

View of Ciudad Rodrigo from the Fausse Braie. (*Author's Collection*)

View of Ciudad Rodrigo's Ravelin from Fausse Braie. (*Author's Collection*)

Memorial Plaque at the Site of the Lesser Breach in Ciudad Rodrigo's Wall. (*Author's Collection*)

View of the Ditch between the Fausse Braie and Ciudad Rodrigo's Wall. (*Author's Collection*)

Sketch of Cuidad Rodrigo by John Luard drawn on 20 January 1812. (*Gareth Glover Collection*)

Storming of Ciudad Rodrigo by John Heaviside Clark. (*Courtesy of the Anne S.K. Brown Military Collection*)

Sketch of Badajoz from the South by Lieutenant John Luard drawn in April 1812. (*Gareth Glover Collection*)

View of the Walls Near La Trinidad Bastion at Badajoz. (*Courtesy of Dr. Mark Thompson*)

A Close Up View of the Walls Near La Trinidad Bastion at Badajoz. (*Courtesy of Dr. Mark Thompson*)

Badajoz Castle Walls near where the 3rd Division Attacked. (*Courtesy of Dr. Mark Thompson*)

Sketch of the Assault on Badajoz by Lieutenant John Cooke, 43rd Foot. Drawn in 1825. (*Courtesy of the Bodleian Library*)

Lieutenant John Bell circa 1860. (*Courtesy of the King's Own Royal Regiment Museum Trust. Accession number KO0427-32*)

Brevet Major William Napier. (*Author's Collection*)

Captain Charles Beckwith, 95th Rifles, Brigade Major 1st Brigade, the Light Division, circa 1830. (*Author's Collection*)

Lieutenant Colonel John Colborne, circa 1852. (*Author's Collection*)

Ensign George Gawler, 52nd Foot, in 1865. (*Courtesy of the State Library of South Australia's Collection*)

Captain George Napier, 43rd Foot, circa 1834. (*Author's Collection*)

Captain Harry Smith, 95th Rifles, Brigade Major 2nd Brigade, circa 1847. (*Courtesy of the Anne S.K. Brown Military Collection*)

at 6:00 p.m. The six batteries were finished and that night twenty-eight guns were moved into them.[46] The pontoon bridge had been repaired the previous day and some officers took the opportunity to ride to Elvas.[47]

The Assault on Fort Picurina

At 11:00 a.m. the next day (25 March) the guns opened on Fort Picurina and continued firing for the rest of the day. The fort was a five-sided bastion with two 50m long walls forming the salient angle facing northwest. The walls then angled inward at about 120° and continued for another 20m where they connected to the back wall that faced the city. The walls had a ditch in front of them and were 10m high from the bottom of the ditch to the top of the wall. The first 4m of the wall were perpendicular and then sloped inward to the top. About halfway up the wall was a line of fraises, sharpened pieces of wood that formed an obstacle to anyone attempting to climb it. The fort was protected by a counterscarp of about 3m, which left 7m exposed to artillery fire. The fort had seven guns.[48] Mines were placed in the walls at the three angles closest to the siege lines and the ramparts were lined with howitzer shells and combustibles to drop over walls onto any assaulting troops in the ditch. Two hundred muskets were placed along the interior walls to provide each defender with multiple guns to fire. The commander of the fort was Colonel Gaspard Thierry. According to Colonel Lamare, the weakest part of the defence was its garrison. Instead of assigning troops from one battalion to defend it, the 200 men were taken from all the battalions in the city, including from the Hessian Regiment. There was no real unity of command and all the troops did not speak the same language.[49]

The Allied bombardment had little effect on Fort Picurina except for damaging some of the palisades along the covered way. In the late afternoon, Wellington ordered it to be stormed after dark. Major General Kempt was given command of the assault.

> Two detachments of 200 men each to be formed, one on the left of the parallel, the other near the spot where the great Talavera Road crosses the parallel. Each detachment to be preceded by six carpenters with cutting

46. Jones, John, *Journal of the Sieges Carried on by the Army Under the Duke of Wellington Between the Years 1811 & 1814*, Vol. 1, p.171.
47. Ewart, John, *Peninsular War Diary of Captain John Frederick Ewart, 52nd Light Infantry, 1811–1812*, p.79.
48. Jones, John, *Journal of the Sieges Carried on by the Army Under the Duke of Wellington Between the Years 1811 & 1814*, Vol. 1, p.173.
49. Lamare, Jean, *An Account of the Second Defense of the Fortress of Badajoz by the French in 1812*, pp.14 and 18.

> tools, six miners with crowbars and 12 sappers carrying ladders under the command of an officer of engineers who is likewise to lead each of the columns. Both columns to quit the parallel at the same time the signal being two guns fired quick from number two battery. The detachment from the left of the parallel to march round the right flank of the work and to endeavour to force in at the gorge. The detachment from the right to march direct upon the communication from the town to the work, there to leave 100 men posted to prevent any succours being sent from the town to the work and the other hundred men to mount upon the work to assist the first attachment in forcing it, or to prevent the escape of the garrison...A party of 100 men under the directions of Captain Holloway, Royal Engineers, was assembled in No.2 battery in readiness to assist by a third attack should the others find much difficulty.[50]

This third party was to be formed by the Light Division and be the assault's reserve.

The companies from the 43rd and 52nd Foot that formed the covering party during the day were relieved from their duties at 6:00 p.m. and returned to their bivouacs. Their reliefs were also from the 43rd and 52nd Foot because the division was also tasked to provide working parties for the batteries starting at 6:00 p.m. Upon arriving at the trenches, they were met by Captain William Jones, who was acting as the field officer in charge of the division's soldiers serving in the work party. He informed Captain Ewart of the impending assault and that he would serve as the commander of the reserve.

This reserve force was made up of volunteers from the 52nd Foot and the 1st Battalion 95th Rifles. An analysis of those killed in action showed that they came from the 1st, 3rd, 8th, 9th, and 10th Companies of the 52nd Foot, and the Right Wing (1st, 3rd, and 8th Companies) of the 1st Battalion 95th Rifles. Although only 100 were required, 140 sergeants, corporals, and privates/riflemen volunteered. Captain Ewart had two of his company officers, Lieutenant Charles Dawson and Ensign William Nixon, to assist him, while Lieutenant James Stokes, led the riflemen.

After forming up, the reserve force moved to the engineer depot on the far side of the hill, where they collected fascines to help break their jump into the ditch, ladders to climb the wall from the bottom of the ditch, and axes to break down the palisades. They then returned to the trenches near Battery 2. The attack started at 10:00 p.m. and the two assault columns from the 3rd Division made it to the ditch in front of the fort unnoticed by the defenders. The right column moved through the ditch to the right while the left column went to the left. They were quickly discovered by the defenders and neither were able

50. Jones, John, Unpublished Journal.

to gain a foothold on the walls. The right column continued along the ditch and came to a part of the wall that was only lightly defended. It was able to get its ladders up and soon they had men at the ramparts. The French commander moved part of his defenders to that place to retake the wall. By doing so, he weakened his forces that were holding the wall against the left column.

Major General Kempt noticed that the left column had made no progress and ordered Captain Ewart to take his reserve force and reinforce them. Lieutenant Dawson left one of the accounts of the reserve force's assault.

> I had charge of the ladders with orders to place them against the fort as soon as we arrived; we moved forward down the trench and got into the high road leading to Badajoz under cover of low ground, until we got in a line with the fort, we then made a strait [*sic*] cut to gain the road between the fort & the town, receiving all this time the fire both of the town & fort & here we were impeded by a trench 7 or 8 feet deep, which however we crossed with little difficulty, the fire here became exceedingly hot. We ran forward to the fort and found a very strong palisading, which effectually stopped us, for a short time, the men with hatchets not being there to cut them down, the palisades so high, the ladder got entangled in them & only half over, too heavy for the men who brought them to get them quite over, we remained a few minutes in that state, our men got one of them clear and took it round to another part of the fort, planted it and got up with others who soon followed with cheers.[51]

Captain Harry Smith, the brigade major of the 2nd Brigade, confirmed that rifleman from the 1st Battalion were with Lieutenant Dawson carrying ladders. One of the carriers was Corporal William Brotherwood, of the 1st Battalion's 2nd Company, who told Smith after the attack, that when they got to the ditch 'the boys of the 3rd Division said to our fellows, "Come, stand out of the way"; to which our fellows replied, "Damn your eyes, do you think we Light Division fetch ladders for such chaps as you to climb up? Follow us" springing on the ladders, and many of them were knocked over.'[52] Lieutenant Simmons, who was part of the work force that occupied the fort after it was captured, backs up this story in his diary. He wrote that Lieutenant James Stokes 'was ordered to carry the ladders to mount the walls. He was, after placing the ladders, the first in the place.' The force waited upon the fraises until 'till some twenty or thirty

51. Dawson, Charles, *Redcoats of Wellington's Light Division: Unpublished & Rare Memoirs of the 52nd (Oxfordshire) Regiment of Foot*, pp.161–162.
52. Smith, Harry, *The Autobiography of Sir Harry Smith*, p.62.

were assembled; when they pushed up the parapet, but were so firmly received by the defenders that many were shot or bayoneted back.'[53]

The reserve force's timing was impeccable. They hit the wall shortly after part of the defenders there were withdrawn to support the defenders on the wall that was being attacked by the right column. The engineer's brigade major, Captain Jones, was present during the assault, and wrote that 'some of the garrison continued to resist even after the assailants were in possession of the rampart, and were consequently bayoneted; and many were drowned in the inundation in attempting to escape.'[54] By 11:30 p.m. the fort had surrender[55] and 'a colonel, two other officers, and 80 men, were made prisoners.'[56]

One of the most peculiar incidents during the assault involved an officer in the 52nd Foot. Captain William Madden had spent his day off hunting. Upon arriving in the bivouac area, he heard that the attack on the fort was about to begin. Not wanting to miss it, he rushed through the trenches and arrived at Battery 2 shortly after the reserve force moved towards the fort. In his hurry he never bothered to change out of his hunting clothes and was still wearing his shooting jacket when he arrived in the trenches. He made it to the ditch and climbed the wall while the fighting was still going on. Neither the attackers nor the defenders recognised him and both sides fired at him. Lucky for him, he escaped unscathed.[57]

The next morning Lieutenant Simmons returned to the fort because

> curiosity led me to see the fort and obstacles the men who stormed it had to encounter. Upon the parapet were pointed palisades, and live shells all round, ready to be lighted and thrown into the ditch. There were also numbers of other shells and powder for the purpose of injuring the assailants, but the determined and spirited manner in which the men stormed the work prevented the enemy from doing the mischief they had premeditated.[58]

Casualties among the reserve force show how determined the defenders were. Half the Light Division officers were either seriously wounded or died of

53. Jones, John, *Journal of the Sieges Carried on by the Army Under the Duke of Wellington Between the Years 1811 & 1814*, Vol. 1, p.175.
54. Ibid, p.176.
55. Simmons, George, *A British Rifleman: Journals and Correspondence During the Peninsular War and the Campaign of Wellington*, p.226.
56. Jones, John, *Journal of the Sieges Carried on by the Army Under the Duke of Wellington Between the Years 1811 & 1814*, Vol. 1, p.176.
57. Dobbs, John, *Recollections of an Old 52nd Man*, p.23.
58. Simmons, George, *A British Rifleman: Journals and Correspondence During the Peninsular War and the Campaign of Wellington*, pp.226–227.

their wounds. Captain Ewart was wounded in his right upper arm and was evacuated to the general hospital at Elvas via the flying bridge.[59] Lieutenant Nixon was shot three times and his friends did not think he would survive. He was evacuated to England in early June.[60] The 52nd Foot had two corporals (Edward Davis and Roger Fishlock) and six privates (John Antoins, Thomas Burns, Patrick Garty, Richard Hanlon, James Shea, and John Toole) killed. The 1st Battalion 95th Rifles lost one sergeant (William Kenderine) and three Riflemen (Edward Evans, Joseph Gibbons, and Peter Lavasey). It is impossible to determine how many riflemen were wounded, since the records do not list the date the soldier was wounded. It was likely another twelve to fifteen men. Total casualties in the 143 men of the reserve force were 64: 14 killed in action and 50 wounded…a staggering 45 per cent casualties taking an outlying fort.[61] It was a portend for the future.

As soon as the fort was taken, Major General Kempt sent work parties into it to start digging new trenches on the side that faced the city. The men had to work fast before the defenders on the city's walls started firing. Lieutenant Simmons 'knew well, as soon as the enemy were aware of the place being in our possession, that they would commence a fire of grape, so that I made my men work hard to cover themselves. About midnight a most furious fire of shot, shell, and grape went over us, and did us no harm. Before daylight our trench was perfect.'[62]

Life in the Trenches

Lieutenant John Kincaid, 1st Battalion 95th Rifles[63] said, 'One day's trench-work is as like another as the days themselves; and like nothing better than serving an apprenticeship to the double calling of grave-digger and game-keeper, for we found ample employment both for the spade and the rifle…'

For the rest of the month the soldiers were in the trenches at least six hours a day. The weather continued to be good. The closer the trenches got to the walls of the city, the more intense the defenders fire became. Corporal Thomas

59. Ewart, John, *Peninsular War Diary of Captain John Frederick Ewart, 52nd Light Infantry, 1811–1812*, p.79.
60. Hall, John, *Biographical Dictionary of British Officers Killed and Wounded, 1808–1814*, pp.195 & 438–439, and Dawson, Henry, *Redcoats of Wellington's Light Division: Unpublished & Rare Memoirs of the 52nd (Oxfordshire) Regiment of Foot*, p.143.
61. Total casualties among all the assaulters were 54 killed and 265 wounded.
62. Simmons, George, *A British Rifleman: Journals and Correspondence During the Peninsular War and the Campaign of Wellington*, p.226.
63. Kincaid, John, *Adventures in the Rifle Brigade in the Peninsula, France, and the Netherlands from 1809–1815*, p.126.

Garretty, 7th Company 43rd Foot, recalled what it was like to be on the receiving end of their guns.

> Directions, I remember, were given on one occasion to fill a quantity of sand-bags. Poor Woollams,[64] a private in the regiment, and myself, worked together; he held the mouth of the sack open, while I threw in the sand with a shovel: before we had been long thus engaged, a shell struck his knee, and in an instant severed his leg, which dropt on the ground: he fell backwards, while the shell, which lodged in the earth at a few feet distance, had burnt nearly to the exploding point. Aware of the approaching danger, I threw myself on my face; and I had scarcely taken the precaution when the shell burst with ruinous effect. Stones, dust, and fragments of timber were scattered in all directions; and among other substances whirled into the air, was the lost limb of my comrade. I knew it while descending by the pattern of the gaiter. As the leg was useless, I ran to the sufferer to whom it had belonged, tied my coat-strap round his thigh to check the effusion of blood, and, after placing him in a blanket, carried him to the nearest hospital, where surgical assistance was promptly afforded. On my return to the trenches, another friend [who] was borne off greatly hurt a comrade was loading his musket, and while the ramrod was in the barrel, the piece was accidentally discharged. The ramrod pierced through his body, and so firmly was the worm-end fixed near the backbone, that the strongest man among us was unable to move it. He was conveyed to the infirmary, and things went on as usual, as no calamity of this sort could be allowed to interfere with the duties then before us…another time, during a violent cannonade from the besieged, I had been conversing with a man on the trenches, when our discussion was closed by a round shot, which took away the head of the respondent, as smoothly as if it had been sabred.[65]

Casualties continued to mount from the defensive fire and one of the deadliest days was 30 March. Battery 9 was in the ditch of Fort Picurina and about 300m from the city's walls. It had just begun firing for the first time when a shell hit the magazine where the battery's powder cartridges were stored. About 300 18-pounder cartridges were blown up killing 4 artillerymen and 4 soldiers from the Light Division: Privates John Lee and Francis Murralls, 52nd Foot, and Riflemen Joseph Ennis and John Gibson both from the 5th Company 3rd Battalion 95th Rifles.

By 1 April, most of the siege work had been dug and seven batteries with a total of thirty-eight guns began firing on the walls. The division was still tasked

64. We have not been able to identify this soldier.
65. Garretty, Thomas, *Memoirs of a Sergeant Late in the Forty-Third Light Infantry Regiment*, pp.148–149.

to help expand the trenches and repair damaged batteries, but compared to the previous weeks there was little to do. Some officers in the trenches would carry a book to read while they waited on duty.[66] Captain James Stewart, who was serving as a DAQMG, Adjutant Charles Eeles, and Captain Harry Smith took the day off and went coursing for hares. Smith was knocked unconscious when his horse tripped in a hole and landed on him.[67]

The 95th Rifles were tasked to send men forward of the batteries to snipe at the defending gunners. To some it was a great sport. On the morning of 4 April, Lieutenant Simmons, who was part of the covering party, took ten men while it was still dark to dig rifle pits forward of the battery they had been stationed behind.

> I was with a party of men behind the advanced sap, and had an opportunity of doing some mischief. Three or four heavy cannon that the enemy were working were doing frightful execution amongst our artillerymen in their advanced batteries. I selected several good shots and fired into the embrasures. In half an hour I found the guns did not go off so frequently as before I commenced this practice, and soon after, gabions were stuffed into each embrasure to prevent our rifle balls from entering. They then withdrew them to fire, which was my signal for firing steadily at the embrasures. The gabions were replaced without firing the shot. I was so delighted with the good practice I was making against Johnny that I kept it up from daylight till dark with forty as prime fellows as ever pulled trigger. These guns were literally silenced. A French officer (I suppose a marksman), who hid himself in some long grass, first placed his cocked hat some little distance from him for us to fire at. Several of his men handed him loaded muskets in order that he might fire more frequently. I was leaning half over the trench watching his movements. I observed his head, and being exceedingly anxious that the man who was going to fire should see him, I directed him to lay his rifle over my left shoulder as a more elevated rest for him. He fired. Through my eagerness, I had entirely overlooked his pan, so that it was in close contact with my left ear; and a pretty example it made of it and the side of my head, which was singed and the ear cut and burnt. The poor fellow was very sorry for the accident. We soon put the Frenchman out of that. He left his cocked hat, which remained until dark, so that we had either killed or wounded him. My friends in camp joked me a good deal the next morning, observing, 'Pray, what's the matter with your ear? How did the injury happen?' and so on.[68]

66. Cooke, John, *A True Soldier Gentleman: The Memoirs of Lt. John Cooke 1791–1813*, p.117.
67. Smith, Harry, *The Autobiography of Sir Harry Smith*, p.63.
68. Simmons, George, *A British Rifleman: Journals and Correspondence During the Peninsular War and the Campaign of Wellington*, pp.227–228.

Rifleman Costello was less enthusiastic about being in the covering party.

> A very disagreeable duty, that usually fell upon a few of the best shots of the battalion, consisted in being obliged to run out, in independent files, to occupy a number of holes, that had been dug at night between our batteries and the walls of the town. From these pits, of which each man had one to himself, our particular business was to pick off any of the enemy who exposed themselves at their guns, on the walls through the embrasures. Many a Frenchman was thus knocked off by us. But it often occurred also that our own men were killed or wounded in their holes, which made it doubly dangerous for the man of the relieving party, who, instead of finding a ready covering, perceived it occupied by a wounded or dead man. Before he could get a shelter therefore or remove the body, there was a great chance of his being shot.[69]

Costello also mentioned an issue that could have a long-term effect on the hearing of the riflemen in the fire pits. 'While employed in this duty in front of our batteries, the tremendous noise made by artillery in both front and rear was attended at first by a most unpleasant effect, as it destroyed the sense of hearing for some hours after leaving the trenches.'[70]

None of the Light Division sources mention the employment of the 1st and 3rd Caçadores in the siege. Several mention Portuguese helping to resupply the guns, but none identify which units they were from. A review of the casualty returns for the two caçadore battalions show that they took casualties every day from 28 March to 5 April. Whether they were part of the working parties or the covering force is unknown.[71]

As the siege continued and breaches were made in the walls, Wellington realised that something needed to be done to reduce the flooded area in front of the walls. Two dams had been built to block the flow of the Rivillas stream. The plan was 'to apply a *petard* to the masonry and blow it in. With that intent, five barrels of powder were emptied into two cases and 20 sandbags filled with earth to place on top of them as soon as the cases shall be laid against the wall.'[72]

On 2 April, the sun set at 6:37 p.m. and it was completely dark by 7:40 p.m. It was a waning moon and it would not rise until close to midnight. The 52nd Foot provided fifty-four men to assist the engineers in destroying the dams. Lieutenant Robert Blackwood was in command of these men.[73]

69. Costello, Edward, *Adventures of a Soldier*, pp.166–167.
70. Ibid, p.167.
71. AHM 1-14-256-04 M-13 to AHM 1-14-256-04 M-17; AHM 1-14-256-04 M-20 to AHM 1-14-256-04 M-20 to AHM 1-14-256-04 M-23.
72. Jones, John, Unpublished Journal.
73. Moorsom, William, *Historical Record of the Fifty-Second Regiment*, p.165.

> As soon as it was thoroughly dark, Lieutenant [Frank] Stanway, Royal Engineers marched out of the right of the parallel with four men carrying each of the boxes of powder and 20 men carrying the sandbags. He was followed by an armed [escort] of 30 men. Lieutenant Stanway marched directly forward to the bed of the river Rivillas under the castle; he then turned to his left and having marched about 100 yards, according to orders he halted his covering party and proceeded on with the powder. He was challenged twice by the sentries on the bridge, and once fired upon, but remaining quiet a minute or two under cover of the noise of the water running over the sluice. He reached the proper spot and deposited the boxes of powder against the wall, but did not think it of any consequence to put the sandbags over them. He then applied the lighted [*sic*] slow match and retired. The explosion not taking place as he expected, he returned to the boxes and found that the water had extinguished the slow match. He then applied another piece to the *saucisson* and in due time the powder exploded. On the explosion more than 50 men opened their fire on the spot.[74]

The explosion damaged the dam, but not enough to lower the water enough in the flooded area to make it passable to troops.

By 4:00 p.m. on 6 April two breaches had been determined to be practical for assault. One was between Bastions 8 and 9, and the other between Bastions 6 and 7. Wellington ordered the assault to take place that night. This was none too soon for the soldiers of the Light Division. Lieutenant Kincaid said the closer the date of the assault came 'the anxiety of the soldiers increased; not on account of any doubt or dread as to the result, but for fear that the place should be surrendered without standing an assault.'[75] Kincaid said this anxiety was fueled by a desire for glory, for

> singular as it may appear, although there was a certainty of about one man out of every three being knocked down, there were, perhaps, not three men, in the three divisions, who would not rather have braved all the chances than receive it tamely from the hands of the enemy. So great was the rage for passports into eternity, in our battalion, on that occasion, that even the officers' servants insisted on taking their places in the ranks; and I was obliged to leave my baggage in charge of a man who had been wounded some days before.[76]

Kincaid may be correct, but could it be more of a desire to seek revenge for having to work in the trenches for hours and to return to their miserable bivouacs knowing they would have to do it again the next day?

---

74. Jones, John, Unpublished Journal.
75. Kincaid, John, *Adventures in the Rifle Brigade in the Peninsula, France, and the Netherlands from 1809–1815*, p.129.
76. Ibid.

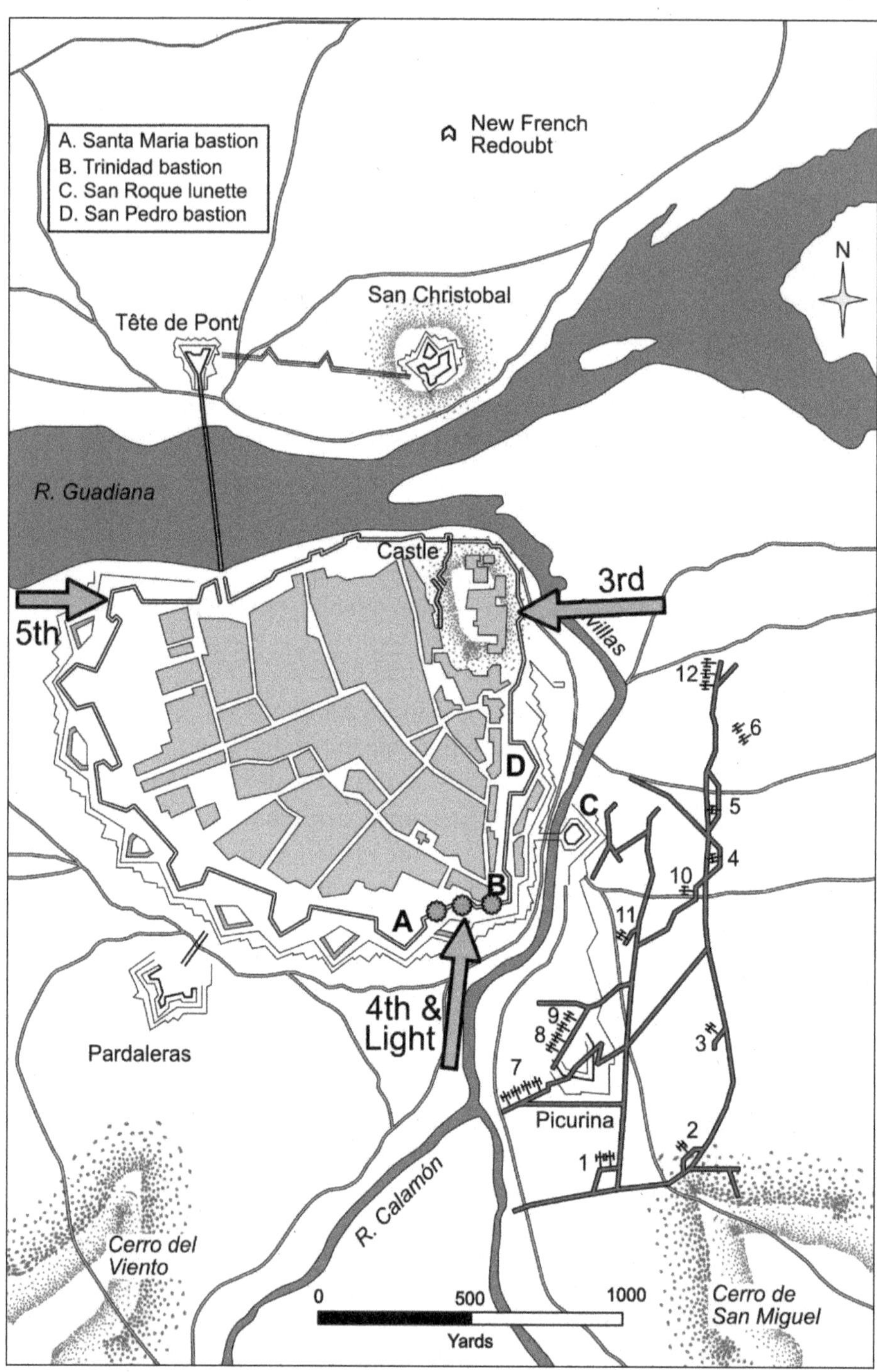

Assault of Badajoz 6 April 1812

Chapter 9

The Taking of Badajoz 5 April–7 April 1812

> I never feared nor saw danger till this night. As I walked at the head of the column, the thought struck me very forcibly 'You will be in hell before daylight!' Such a feeling of horror I never experienced before!
>
> Bugler William Green,
> Right Wing 1st Battalion 95th Rifles[1]

By 5 April, two breaches had been made in the walls of Badajoz, and the plan was to attack them that night. The order was given; the forlorn hopes and storming parties were organised and the troops made themselves ready for the assault.

> The officers commanding corps & those of the forlorn hope & storming party, with the men of the forlorn hope attended at 3 pm on the hill above the 48th [Foot] camp & received directions from Colonel Barnard. In short, everything appeared quite settled and the hour was anxiously expected by every individual, when by a last effort their toils were to be at once ended & rewarded. But to the surprise of every person about 4 pm, an order was received declaring the storm of the fortress to be postponed.[2]

That afternoon, Lieutenant Colonel Richard Fletcher, the senior Royal Engineer during the siege, conducted a reconnaissance of the breaches and felt that the defenses were too formidable and that they should delay the assault by a day 'and turn all the guns of the batteries on the old wall of the curtain between the two breaches, so as in one day's firing to obtain an opening into the place which should turn the retrenchment of the bastions, and which opening being assaulted as soon as made, could have no interior defence.'[3] Wellington concurred and

---

1. Green, William, *Where Duty Calls Me: The Experiences of William Green of Lutterworth in the Napoleonic Wars*, p.35.
2. Oglander, Henry, *The Journals of Captain Henry Oglander of the 43rd & 47th Foot,* p.144.
3. Jones, John, *Journal of the Sieges Carried on by the Army Under the Duke of Wellington Between the Years 1811 & 1814*, p.193.

cancelled the attack. He also ordered the guns sweep the breaches at night with grape shot to make it difficult for the defenders to repair them.

The guns battered the walls through the night and in the afternoon a third breach had been formed. One was on the southern side of the La Trinidad Bastion 7, and the second was on the eastern flank of the Santa Maria Bastion 6. The third breach was on the wall between the two bastions, but close to the La Trinidad Bastion. The three breaches were within 200m of each other. Badajoz's walls in this area were about 6.5m (20ft) high. The wall between the two bastions, also known as a curtain, was protected by a ravelin, but it left the upper 3m (10ft) exposed. Between the ravelin and the walls was a 3m deep ditch that was about 6m wide. In front of the ravelin was the glacis, sloping ground that led to the ravelin and the bastions. Like at Ciudad Rodrigo, the glacis ended at a 3m drop into a 6m wide ditch. By following this ditch to either the left or the right, the assaulters could avoid the ravelin. The walls were further protected by the flooding of the Rivillas stream, which made a direct approach from the siege lines to the breaches impossible. The attackers would have to move several hundred metres parallel to the walls between the stream and the glacis to reach the breaches.

Unlike the accounts of the breaches at Ciudad Rodrigo, few sources state how wide the breaches were at the top. Lieutenant Barlow, 52nd Foot, wrote that the 'breach would not admit of more than 13 or 15 men abreast.'[4] Colonel Lamare said that by 'the 5th, the breaches had become so completely practicable, that a squadron of Cavalry might have marched up any of them.'[5] Based on their descriptions, the top of the breach was about 12m (40ft) wide.

The defenders attempted to clear the debris from the bottom of the breach at night, however the Allies' guns began to sweep the breach with grapeshot at night. This caused heavy casualties among the work crews trying to remove the rubble.[6] By the night of the assault,

> the breach in the face of La Trinidad, of which 10 feet from the bottom of the escarp was covered by a low earthen counterguard, was steep, although the line of fire at which the artillery commenced to batter was as low as is recommended for making breaches, where a choice exists; but the breach in the flank of Santa Maria (and also that in the curtain), the escarps of which being totally exposed were battered from the level of the ditch, were remarkably easy and good.[7]

---

4. Barlow, George Ulrich, *A Light Infantryman With Wellington: The Letters of Captain George Ulrich Barlow, 52nd and 69th Foot, 1808–1815*, p.146.
5. Lamare, Jean, *An Account of the Second Defense of the Fortress of Badajoz by the French in 1812*, p.27.
6. Ibid, p.28.
7. Jones, John, *Journal of the Sieges Carried on by the Army Under the Duke of Wellington Between the Years 1811 & 1814*, p.409.

To protect themselves on the walls, the defenders replaced the destroyed parapets with 'fascines, sandbags and wool-packs.'[8] Retrenchments were dug behind the breaches so if a breach was captured the attacker would have another, intact wall to assault before gaining access to the city. Between the parapets and the retrenchments were 'ditches and pits fifteen feet deep cut everywhere, into which our people might fall like traps during the darkness of the night.'[9] At the bottom of these ditches were 'placed swords and bayonets fixed upon pieces of wood to wound those who fell upon them. Holes were made in the ramparts big enough for a man to sit in, with a deep groove to lay his musket in and fire.'[10] Artillery pieces were placed so that they could fire at the enemy climbing the breaches.

The defenders were ingenious in creating obstacles to make it difficult to climb the breach. At the very top of each one was a chevaux-de-frise that covered the width of the breach. Embedded in the wooden beam were sharpened sword blades that prevented an attacker from moving past it. It was chained to the wall to keep it from being pulled down by a grappling hook. On the slope of the breach, were long wooden planks that were filled with nails, spikes, and hooks. These were not anchored in place but tied by a rope to the top of the breach. They were designed to be slippery and shift if anyone placed his weight on it. The movement would throw the attacker off balance and either fall on the spikes or tumble down the slope, bowling over the men below, and possibly being impaled by the bayonets of their friends.[11]

The defenders also placed mines that could be detonated from above. Colonel Lamare wrote later that 'we had arranged at the foot of the counterscarp immediately in front of the breaches sixty 14-inch shells, at the distance of about four yards apart in a circular form and covered them with about four inches of earth. Powder hoses, placed between tiles arranged in the form of mine tubes, were designed to communicate the fire to this species of defensive mines.'[12]

To enhance the firepower of the infantry,

> shells and grenades were placed in rows along the parapet to be hurled down on the heads of our poor fellows and a new species of destruction fired out of their muskets, called by us *musket grape*, being a number of slugs

8. Ibid, p.28.
9. Barlow, George Ulrich, *A Light Infantryman With Wellington: The Letters of Captain George Ulrich Barlow, 52nd and 69th Foot, 1808–1815*, p.146.
10. Simmons, George, *A British Rifleman: Journals and Correspondence During the Peninsular War and the Campaign of Wellington*, p.231.
11. Garretty, Thomas, *Memoirs of a Sergeant Late in the Forty-Third Light Infantry Regiment*, p.165.
12. Lamare, Jean, *An Account of the Second Defense of the Fortress of Badajoz by the French in 1812*, p.30.

> bound together, and resembling that sort of cannon shot in miniature; in a word every obstacle which the engineer's art or invention could devise.[13]

One imaginative defensive arrangement was the placing of a large boat in the flooded area near La Trinidad Bastion. About fifty soldiers would be stationed on it so they could fire on the flank of any force attacking the breach. The deep water would keep the attackers from capturing the boat.[14]

The Defenders

There were about 5,000 French and their allies in Badajoz at the beginning of March. By the night of the assault 'there still remained about 3,000 determined men; the love of country, and the sentiment of deep national hatred, increased the desire of coming to a decisive action.'[15] The sixteen grenadier and light infantry companies of the French and Hessian battalions were given the mission of defending the three breaches. Major Gottfried Meister, the Hessian Regiment's senior major, was responsible for the breach in the Santa Maria Bastion and the wall between it and the La Trinidad Bastion. Among the troops under Meister's command were the 2nd Grenadier Company, commanded by Captain Graf von Eugen Lehrbach and the 2nd Voltigeur Company, commanded by Captain Johann Grübel. Both companies were from the 2nd Battalion Hesse Darmstadt Crown Prince Regiment.[16] Meister also had six French companies under his command. Chief of Battalion Elie Barbot, commander of the 3rd Battalion 88th Line Infantry, commanded the forces in the La Trinidad Bastion. With him were six French companies, and the 1st Grenadier Company 2nd Battalion Hesse Darmstadt Crown Prince Regiment, commanded by Captain Wilhelm Gran. Major Christian Weber, the commander of the 1st Battalion of the Hesse Darmstadt Crown Prince Regiment, was responsible for defending the walls between the La Trinidad Bastion to the castle with four fusilier companies from his battalion. The length of the walls he defended was about 200m long (including the two bastions), but they had not been battered by the besiegers, so his force of about 400 men was thought adequate to defend it. In reserve, behind the breaches were the 3rd Battalions of the 88th and 103rd French Line Regiments. Both were under the command of Chief of Battalion

13. Barlow, George Ulrich, *A Light Infantryman With Wellington: The Letters of Captain George Ulrich Barlow, 52nd and 69th Foot, 1808–1815*, p.146.
14. Ibid, p.28.
15. Ibid, p.29.
16. Keim, A., *Geschichte des 4. Großherzoglich Hessischen Infanterie-Regiments (Prinz Karl) Nr. 118*, pp.214–215.

Durand Lurat, commander of the 3rd Battalion 103rd Regiment. Intermixed with the infantry were artillerymen and engineers. The defenders on the walls were armed with three muskets each, as well as artillery shells and barrels of combustibles to light and throw onto the enemy below.[17]

The Attack Order

Once the breach was deemed practical, Wellington ordered the assault. A twenty-seven paragraph order was issued to the divisions. Eighteen of the paragraphs were relevant to the Light Division.

1. The fort of Badajos [*sic*] is to be attacked at 10 o'clock this night.
2. The attack must be made on three points; the castle, the face of the bastion of La Trinidad, and the flank of the bastion of Sta. Maria.
8. The 4th division, with the exception of the covering party in the trenches, must make the attack on the face of the bastion of La Trinidad, and the light division on the flank of the bastion of Sta. Maria.
9. These two divisions must parade in close columns of divisions at 9 o'clock. The light division, with the left in front; the 4th division with its advanced guard, with the left in front; the remainder with the right in front. The 4th division must be on the right of the little stream, near the picket of the 4th division, and the light division must have the river on their right.
10. The light division must throw 100 men forward into the quarries, close to the covered-way of the bastion of Sta. Maria, who, as soon as the garrison are disturbed, must keep down by their fire the fire from the face of the bastion of Sta. Maria, and that from the covered-way.
11. The advance of both divisions must consist of 500 men from each, attended by twelve ladders; and the men of the storming party should carry sacks filled with light materials, to be thrown into the ditch, to enable the troops to descend into it. Care must be taken that these bags are not thrown into the covered way.
12. The advance of the light division must precede that of the 4th division; and both must keep as near the inundation as they possibly can.
13. The advance of both divisions must be formed into firing parties and storming parties. The firing parties must be spread along the crest of the glacis to keep down the fire of the enemy; while the men of the storming party who carry bags will enter the covered-way at the

17. Lamare, Jean, *An Account of the Second Defense of the Fortress of Badajoz by the French in 1812*, pp.25–26 and 28, and Keim, A., *Geschichte des 4. Großherzoglich Hessischen Infanterie-Regiments (Prinz Karl) Nr. 118*, pp.214–-215.

place d'armes, those of the light division, at the place d'armes on the left, looking from camp, of the unfinished ravelin; those of the 4th division, on the right of that ravelin, at the place d'armes under the breached face of the bastion of La Trinidad.

14. The storming party of the advance of the light division will then descend into the ditch, and turning to its left, storm the breach in the flank of the bastion of Sta. Maria, while the storming party of the 4th division will likewise descend into the ditch, and storm the breach in the face of the bastion of La Trinidad. The firing parties are to follow immediately in the rear of their respective storming parties.
15. The heads of the two divisions will follow their advanced guards, nearly together, but they will not advance beyond the shelter afforded by the quarries on the left of the road till they will have seen the heads of the advanced guards ascend the breaches: they will then move forward to the storm in double quick time.
16. If the light division should find the bastion of Sta. Maria intrenched, they will turn the right of the intrenchment by moving along the parapet of the bastion. The 4th division will do the same by an intrenchment which appears in the left face, looking from the trenches of the bastion of La Trinidad.
17. The light division, as soon as they are in possession of the rampart of Sta. Maria, are to turn to their left, and to proceed along the rampart to their left, keeping always a reserve at the breach.
19. Each (the 4th and light) division must leave 1,000 men in reserve in the quarries. It will be necessary for the commanding officer of the light division to attend to the ditch on his left as he will make his attack. He should post a detachment in the ditch towards the salient angle of the bastion of Santa Maria, so as to be covered by the angle from the fire of the next bastion on its left, looking from the trenches.
20. The 4th division must endeavour to get open the gate of La Trinidad; the light division must do the same by the gate called Puerto del Pillar.
21. The soldiers must leave their knapsacks in camp.
24. The remainder of the covering party to be a reserve in the trenches. The working parties in the trenches are to join their regiments at half-past seven o'clock. Twelve carpenters with axes, and ten miners with crowbars, must be with each (the 4th and light) division. A party of one officer and 20 artillerymen must be with each division.
26. The pickets of the brigades on the Sierra del Viento, and that in the low grounds towards the Guadiana, should endeavour to alarm the enemy during the attack by firing at the Pardaleras, and at the men in the covered way of the works towards the Guadiana. The commanding officer of the light division will attend to this.

27. The Commander of the Forces particularly requests the General Officers commanding divisions and brigades, and the Commanding Officers of regiments, and the Officers commanding companies, to impress upon their men the necessity of their keeping together, and formed as a military body after the storm, and during the night. Not only the success of the operation, and the honour of the army, but their own individual safety, depend upon their being in a situation to repel any attack by the enemy, and to overcome all resistance which they may be inclined to make, till the garrison have been completely subdued.[18]

Preparing for the Assault

On paper, the Light Division had about 3,900 officers, non-commissioned officers, musicians, and privates available for the assault.

Table 9.1: Light Division Troops Available for the Assault on 6 April 1812[19]

	Officers						NCOs		MUS	Privates	
	LTC	Maj	Cpt	LT	Ens	Adj	Sgt	Cpl	MUS	Fit for Duty	Total
43rd Foot	1	1	6	21	2	-	35	NA	23	844[20]	**933**
52nd Foot	-	1	8	12	7	1	53	30	22	865	**999**
1st Bn 95th	-	1	6	14	8	1	41	39	19	530	**659**
2nd Bn 95th	-	-	2	2	-	-	8	10	2	133	**157**
3rd Bn 95th	-	-	4	10	3	-	16	20	6	233	**292**
1st Caç	1	1	5	6	5	1	31	NA	12	358	**420**
3rd Caç	1	1	5	6	5	1	31	NA	12	388	**450**
	3	5	36	71	30	4	215	99	96	3,351	**3,910**

The above figures are based on the 24 March 1812 strength returns, plus the reported casualties that the division took from 25 March–5 April. For the British units, the numbers reflect the officers killed or wounded, but only the NCOs, musicians, and men killed in action. The Portuguese numbers include everyone in the unit. These numbers do not reflect the soldiers who fell sick during the twelve days since the 24 March report was written. The total number of troops was no more than 3,900.

18. Jones, John, *Journal of the Sieges Carried on by the Army Under the Duke of Wellington Between the Years 1811 & 1814*, pp.195–201.
19. These numbers do not include the officers assigned to the division staff.
20. Includes corporals and privates.

The division would be organised into five parts: the covering party, the forlorn hope, the storming party, the main body, and the reserve.

The covering party consisted of the four companies that composed the Left Wing of the 1st Battalion 95th Rifles. Brevet Major Alexander Cameron commanded it. Its mission was to line the glacis protecting the breaches while the forlorn hope and the storming party moved forward.[21]

The mission of the forlorn hope was to be the first to reach the breach and by doing so cause the defenders to set off any mines or explosives that they had planted. It was considered a suicide mission, but the rewards for surviving were great. Its commander would be awarded a substantive promotion. Command of the forlorn hope was usually offered to the senior lieutenant. For the assault Lieutenant Horatio Harvest, 43rd Foot, was chosen. Why he was selected is not known. Harvest was the senior lieutenant in his battalion, but there were three lieutenants in the 52nd Foot who were senior to him. It might have been because the 52nd Foot provided the commander of the forlorn hope at Ciudad Rodrigo. In addition to Lieutenant Harvest, the forlorn hope consisted of two sergeants and twenty-five other privates from the 52nd Foot. Also assigned to the forlorn hope were several men with axes and crowbars.[22] Additionally, First Lieutenant William Johnston, 1st Battalion 95th Rifles, 'was to precede the forlorn hope, in command of a party carrying ropes, prepared with nooses, to throw over the sword blades, as the most likely method of displacing, by dragging them down the breach.'[23]

The storming party was to move before the main body 'and were provided ladders, hatchets, planks & bags of grass to fill the ditch'[24] to make it easier for the main body to clear the walls of the enemy. Each of the British battalions were to provide 100 men as well as an appropriate number of officers, sergeants, corporals, and 2 buglers. The commanders of the storming party were Major Peter O'Hare, 1st Battalion 95th Rifles, while Captain William Jones, 52nd Foot, was second in command.

All members of the party were volunteers, and little is known as to how they were selected. In the 43rd Foot, each company was to provide ten men.[25] Corporal Thomas Garretty, 43rd Foot, was among those chosen. He believed that 'the difficulty was, not to procure men enough, but how to refuse applications,

21. Kincaid, John, *Adventures in the Rifle Brigade in the Peninsula, France, and the Netherlands from 1809–1815*, p.130.
22. Oglander, Henry, *The Journals of Captain Henry Oglander of the 43rd & 47th Foot*, p.144.
23. Kincaid, John, *Random Shots from a Rifleman*, p.159.
24. Duffy, John, *Journals of Majors John Duffy and John Maxwell Tylden of the 43rd Foot*, p.153.
25. Hamilton, Anthony, *Hamilton's Campaign With Moore and Wellington During the Peninsular War*, pp.121–122.

for all were ready.'[26] Competition to be named to the storming party was stiff and, in some cases, bribes were paid to the sergeant doing the selection. Bugler Green, 1st Battalion 95th Rifles, wanted to go and the

> bugle major [Kelly Dennis] made us cast lots which two of us should go on this momentous errand; the lot fell on me and another young lad. But one of our buglers who had been on the forlorn hope at Ciudad Rodrigo offered the bugle major two dollars to let him go in my stead. On my being apprised of it, he came to me, and said '[Henry] West will go on the forlorn hope instead of you,' I said 'I shall go where my duty calls me.' He threatened to confine me to the guard tent. I went to the adjutant [Lieutenant Charles Eeles], and reported him; the adjutant sent for him, and said, 'So you are in the habit of taking bribes;' and told him 'He would take the stripes off his arm if he did the like again!' He then asked me 'If I wished to go?' I said 'Yes, sir.' He said 'Very good,' and dismissed me.[27]

A complete list of the officers and men who volunteer does not exist. From the 43rd Foot were Captain James Fergusson, who had been seriously wounded at Ciudad Rodrigo, and Lieutenant Charles Taggart. From the 52nd Foot, were Lieutenants James McNair and Charles Booth, while Ensign George Gawler led one of the ladder parties.[28] Among the rifle volunteers were Captains Jeremiah Crampton 1st Battalion, John Hart 2nd Battalion, and Thomas Diggle 3rd Battalion; and Lieutenants Edward Coxen and Henry Manners from the 2nd Battalion. Some sources state that Lieutenants Walter Bedell and Alexander McGregor, both from the 2nd Battalion were also part of it. However both had been seriously wounded at Ciudad Rodrigo and McGregor had been seconded to the Portuguese Army in January, so they probably were not part of the storming party.[29] Sergeant Patrick Fleming, Rifleman Edward Costello, and Bugler William Green were from the 3rd Company 1st Battalion; and Rifleman John Lowe, the 3rd Company 3rd Battalion were members of the storming party. Fleming was highly regarded in the battalion, having been promoted from corporal only seventeen days before. Costello had been hospitalised on 24 March but still managed to volunteer.

The main body would be commanded by Lieutenant Colonel Barnard, the acting division commander. He would have his two ADCs, Lieutenants James Shaw and Willliam Armstrong, as well Major Charles Rowan, AAG, and

26. Garretty, Thomas, *Memoirs of a Sergeant Late in the Forty-Third Light Infantry Regiment*, p.160.
27. Green, William, *Where Duty Calls Me: The Experiences of William Green of Lutterworth in the Napoleonic Wars*, p.35.
28. C.W.N., *George Gawler, K.H., 52nd Light Infantry: A Life Sketch*, p.11.
29. Verner, Willoughby, *History & Campaigns of the Rifle Brigade: 1800–1813*, Vol. 2, p.375.

Lieutenant John Bell,[30] DAQMG, to assist him. Two Royal Engineers, Captain John Williams and Lieutenant Edward de Salaberry, were attached to the division to ensure they attacked the correct breach. The main body consisted of the 43rd Foot, the 52nd Foot, the Right Wing of the 1st Battalion 95th Rifles, the two companies of the 2nd Battalion 95th Rifles, and the five companies of the 3rd Battalion 95th Rifles. Its mission was to assault the breach in the Santa Maria Bastion.

In the reserve were the 1st and 3rd Caçadore Battalions and the Left Wing of the 1st Battalion 95th Rifles. The reserve was commanded by Lieutenant Colonel George Elder, the commander of the 3rd Caçadores. He 'was directed to follow the leading brigade at a respectable distance, and not to advance until the rear of the 43rd Regiment entered the ditch.'[31] According to the Portuguese Army Archives, Captain Powell Morphew's 1st Company of the 3rd Caçadores was on detached duty, likely with the storming party.

Waiting to Begin the Assault

After being ordered to stand down, the division returned to its bivouac. Those companies that were originally tasked to be on the covering force resumed their places in the trenches. The company that Lieutenant James Gairdner, 1st Battalion 95th Rifles, belonged to was ordered to relieve a company of the 52nd Foot, which was stationed near the river, about noon. They waited there until 6:00 p.m. when they returned to their bivouacs and joined the reserve force.[32] The soldiers who had volunteered for the storming party were given the day off. Many spent the day cleaning themselves, their kit, and uniforms, as if they were going on parade.[33] Bugler Green took the opportunity to go to 'the river, and had a good bathe; I thought I would have a clean skin whether killed or wounded, for all who go on this errand expect one or the other.'[34]

Many of the officers, knowing how formidable the defenses were, sought out friends and made arrangements in case they were killed. Lieutenant Cooke, 43rd Foot, found Lieutenant Harvest about 2:00 p.m. 'He was sucking an orange, and walking on a rising ground, alone, and very thoughtful. It gave me pain,

30. John Bell was promoted to captain in the 4th Foot on 12 March 1812, but word had not reached him yet.
31. Elder, George, 'Memorandum of the Siege and the Assault of Badajoz on the Evening of the 6th of April, 1812', *United Services Journal*, p.55.
32. Gairdner, James, *The American Sharpe: The Adventures of an American Officer of the 95th Rifles in the Peninsula & Waterloo Campaigns*, p.25.
33. Cooke, John, *A True Soldier Gentleman: The Memoirs of Lt. John Cooke 1791–1813*, p.119.
34. Green, William, *Where Duty Calls Me: The Experiences of William Green of Lutterworth in the Napoleonic Wars*, p.35.

as I knew he was to lead the forlorn hope. He observed, "My mind is made up; I am sure to be killed."'[35] Lieutenant Dobbs, who lost his brother at Ciudad Rodrigo, found Captain Jones, who was second in command of the storming party about 2:00 p.m. Jones had a premonition of his death, and Dobbs and him spent the time 'chatting together a few hours before the storming. He was a Welshman, and had a gruff way of speaking, in addition to his native accent. Speaking of the assault, he said, "I'll be a man or a mouse tonight."'[36]

One group of officers from the 3rd Battalion 95th Rifles got together for a final meal. William Surtees, the battalion's quartermaster, was a member of the same mess as the senior captain, Captain William Percival. The

> other messmates were poor little [First Lieutenant Christopher] Croudace [age 22] and [First Lieutenant Arthur] Cary, [age 27] both lieutenants, the latter acting adjutant, and another. We had taken a farewell glass before we got up from dinner, not knowing which of them would survive the bloody fray that was likely soon to commence. Poor Croudace, a native of the county of Durham, and consequently a near countryman, put into my hand a small leather purse, containing half a doubloon, and requested me to take care of it for him, as he did not know whose fate it might be to fall or to survive. I took it according to his wish, and put it into my pocket, and, after a little more conversation, and another glass, for the poor little fellow liked his wine, we parted, and they moved off.[37]

Lieutenant Colonel Elder held a dinner party that evening in his tent. He invited five friends to the party, including Captain Powell Morphew, another British officer seconded to the 3rd Caçadores.

> During dinner and after, not a single word was mentioned on the subject of the attack which was to take place that night. About eight o'clock, the orderly serjeant came into the tent to report that the parade was ready–formed. We immediately stood up, and I proposed a bumper to our success; and as my old friend Major O'Hare of the Rifle Corps was named to command the forlorn hope, I shook him by the hand and said, that I hoped we should meet the next day, when I should have the pleasure to congratulate him on his promotion to a lieutenant-colonelcy. The poor fellow thanked me and said, 'By Jove, Elder, we have seen a great deal of service together, and we have had our share of hard knocks, and I sincerely hope that we shall meet tomorrow.'[38]

35. Cooke, John, *A True Soldier Gentleman: The Memoirs of Lt. John Cooke 1791–1813*, p.119.
36. Dobbs, John, *Recollections of an Old 52nd Man*, pp.24–25.
37. Surtees, William, *Twenty Five Years in the Rifle Brigade*, p.138.
38. Elder, George, 'Memorandum of the Siege and the Assault of Badajoz on the Evening of the 6th of April, 1812', *United Services Journal*, pp.55–56.

Forming for the Assault

The division was ordered to begin the assault at 10:00 p.m. To do this, each battalion had to form up and the men detailed to the covering party, forlorn hope, and the storming party were sent to the spot where they would be formed. The soldiers of the 43rd Foot were in formation at 8:30 p.m.

> and the roll called in an under-tone. Lieutenant-Colonel M'Leod spoke long and earnestly to the regiment before it joined the division, expressing the utmost confidence in the result of the attack, and finished by repeating, that he left it to the honour of all persons to preserve discipline, and not to commit any cruelty on the poor inhabitants of the town.[39]

The rifles issued a half pound of bread and a gill of rum, about 4 ounces, to each man.[40]

Rifleman Costello was in the right front section of the storming party when his old captain

> Major O'Hare, who commanded the wing to which my company belonged, came up with Captain Jones of the 52nd Regiment, both in command of the storming party. A pair of uglier men never walked together, but a brace of better soldiers never stood before the muzzle of a Frenchman's gun.
>
> 'Well, O'Hare,' said the Captain, 'what do you think of to-night's work?'
>
> 'I don't know,' replied the Major, who seemed, as I thought, in rather low spirits. 'Tonight, I think, will be my last.'
>
> 'Tut, tut, man! I have the same sort of feeling, but I keep it down with a drop of the cratur [whiskey],' answered the Captain, as he handed his calabash to the Major.

While they waited, Sergeant Fleming, who was also in Costello's company, was told they needed men to carry ladders. Much to Costello's chagrin, Major O'Hare ordered the sergeant to 'Take the right files of the leading sections,'

> no sooner said than done. I and my front-rank men were immediately tapped on the shoulder for the ladder-party. I now gave up all hope of ever returning. At Rodrigo, as before stated, we had fatigue-parties for the ladders, but now the case was altered; besides which the ladders, now in preparation, were much longer than those employed at that fortress.[41]

39. Cooke, John, *A True Soldier Gentleman: The Memoirs of Lt. John Cooke 1791–1813*, p.119.
40. Green, William, *Where Duty Calls Me: The Experiences of William Green of Lutterworth in the Napoleonic Wars*, p.35.
41. Costello, Edward, *Adventures of a Soldier*, pp.169–170.

Major O'Hare told the storming party when the order came to begin the assault, they were 'to go as still as possible,' and every word of command was given in a whisper.[42]

The division moved out about 9:30 p.m. and waited near the quarry for the assault to begin. For some soldiers, the wait became unbearable. Corporal Garretty recalled,

> here and there a soldier might be perceived stealing from the trenches, with a little refreshment in his canteen for the friend with whom he was to part; and in return, more than one message, the last to be delivered on earth, was sent from many a brave man to mother, wife, or some other valued relative, with directions that, if killed, the knapsack of a certain number, with its contents, should be duly forwarded. The night was dry but clouded; the air thick with watery exhalations from the river; the ramparts and the trenches were unusually still, yet a low murmur pervaded the latter, and in the former, lights were seen to flit here and there; while the deep voices of the sentinels at times proclaimed that all was well in Badajos [*sic*].[43]

For most part, the troops sat quietly, however, there was an incident that nearly announced their presence to the defenders. Near where the division waited was the 4th Division.

> Suddenly, a voice was heard from that direction, giving orders about ladders so loud, that it might be heard by the enemy on the ramparts. It was horrid. It was the only voice that broke on the stillness of the moment; everybody was indignant, and Colonel M'Leod sent an officer to say that he would report the circumstance to the General-in-Chief. I looked up the side of the quarry, fully expecting to see the enemy come forth, and derange the plan of attack. It was at half-past nine this happened, but at a quarter before ten the ill-timed noise ceased, and nothing could be heard but the loud croaking of the frogs.[44]

The Assault

The division could not have asked for better conditions. The sun had set at 6:41 p.m. and by 7:00 p.m. it was dark. The quarter moon would not rise until 2:21 a.m. the next morning. The pitch dark would mask their movement.

42. Green, William, *Where Duty Calls Me: The Experiences of William Green of Lutterworth in the Napoleonic Wars*, p.35.
43. Garretty, Thomas, *Memoirs of a Sergeant Late in the Forty-Third Light Infantry Regiment*, pp.160–161.
44. Cooke, John, *A True Soldier Gentleman: The Memoirs of Lt. John Cooke 1791–1813*, p.119-120.

Shortly before 10:00 p.m. the division moved out from the quarry. The covering party went first, followed by the forlorn hope, and then the storming party. The main body was formed with the 43rd Foot in front and then the 52nd Foot behind them. Following the 52nd Foot was the reserve led by the Left Wing of the 1st Battalion 95th Rifles, then the 1st and 3rd Caçadores.

Lieutenant John Kincaid was the acting adjutant of the Left Wing of the 1st Battalion 95th Rifles when the order came to begin the assault.

> The enemy seemed aware of our intentions. The fire of artillery and musketry, which, for three weeks before, had been incessant, both from the town and trenches, had now entirely ceased, as if by mutual consent, and a deathlike silence, of nearly an hour, preceded the awful scene of carnage…our four companies led the way. Colonel Cameron and myself had reconnoitred the ground so accurately by day-light, that we succeeded in bringing the head of our column to the very spot agreed on, opposite to the left breach, and then formed line to the left, without a word being spoken, each man lying down as he got into line, with the muzzle of his rifle over the edge of the ditch, between the palisades [*sic*], all ready to open. It was tolerably clear above, and we distinctly saw their heads lining the ramparts; but there was a sort of haze on the ground which, with the colour of our dress, prevented them from seeing us, although only a few yards asunder. One of their sentries, however, challenged us twice, '*qui vive*,' and, receiving no reply, he fired off his musket, which was followed by their drums beating to arms; but we still remained perfectly quiet, and all was silence again for the space of five or ten minutes, when the head of the forlorn hope at length came up, and we took advantage of the first fire, while the enemy's heads were yet visible.[45]

Captain Harry Smith, the brigade major of the 2nd Brigade, was with Lieutenant Colonel Barnard, the division commander, when

> Old Alister [Alexander] Cameron, who was in command of four Companies of the 95th Regiment, extended along the counterscape to attract the enemy's fire, while the [storming party] column planted their ladders and descended, came up to Barnard and said, 'Now my men are ready; shall I begin?'
>
> 'No, certainly not,' says Barnard. The breach and the works were full of the enemy, looking quietly at us, but not fifty yards off and most prepared, although not firing a shot. So soon as our ladders were all ready posted,

45. Kincaid, John, *Adventures in the Rifle Brigade in the Peninsula, France, and the Netherlands from 1809–1815*, pp.130–131.

> and the column in the very act to move and rush down the ladders, Barnard called out, 'Now, Cameron!' and the first shot from us brought down such a hail of fire as I shall never forget, nor ever saw before or since. It was most murderous.[46]

This was the last time there was any control over the assault. The storming party rushed forward and soon came to the edge of the glacis that fell 3m to the ditch below. Some ladders were placed and the troops climbed down them, but the surge of the mass of men from behind them pushed many of them over the side. Private Anthony Hamilton, 43rd Foot, was one of those pushed. 'Nearly half our party, myself among the number, were precipitated into the ditch below. Much bruised by the fall I lay a few minutes insensible, till on the arrival of the main body, the ladders were fixed down the counterscarp, and the descent into the ditch was quickly effected [*sic*].'[47]

Ensign George Gawler, aged 16, led the 52nd Foot's ladder party and described the confusion that existed in the storming party. He

> was ordered to take charge of the six ladders at the extreme head of the stormers. We moved on rather rapidly, and saw no other parties on the way. The town clock loudly and heartily tolled ten just after the breaching batteries had suddenly ceased. A sharp fire of musketry was sounding far away to the right, but besides this all was still. I planted the leading ladder, and went down it; the other ladders followed very quickly. The last ladder was not steady when the enemy's fire opened. The light was most brilliant. I saw distinctly all the ditch to the Bastion of Santa Maria on the left, and along a good part of the counterscarp of the proper left face of the ravelin. I scrambled immediately to the top of the ravelin to look for the way to the centre breach, having had no orders to attack any in particular.[48]

Rifleman Costello had been detailed to carry a ladder and a grass bag. This bag was about 2 by 1m and was filled with grass and hay. Its purpose was to break the fall of anyone who jumped instead of using a ladder to get down to the ditch. A secondary purpose was as a make shift shield to protect the carrier from the defenders' fire. As the storming party advanced, Costello was

> accompanied at each side by two men with hatchets to cut down any obstacle that might oppose them, such as chevaux de frise. There were

46. Smith, Harry, *The Autobiography of Sir Harry Smith*, p.64.
47. Hamilton, Anthony, *Hamilton's Campaign With Moore and Wellington During the Peninsular War*, p.122.
48. C.W.N., *George Gawler, K.H., 52nd Light Infantry: A Life Sketch*, pp.11–12.

> six of us supporting the ladder allotted to me, and I contrived to carry my grassbag before me. We had proceeded but a short distance when we heard the sound of voices on our right, upon which we halted, and supposing they might be enemies, I disengaged myself from the ladder, and cocking my rifle, prepared for action. Luckily we soon discovered our mistake, as one of our party cried – 'Take care! 'Tis the stormers of the 4th division coming to join us.' This proved to be the case. This brief alarm over, we continued advancing towards the walls the Rifles, as before, keeping in front. We had to pass Fort St. Roche on our left, near to the town, and as we approached it the French sentry challenged. This was instantly followed by a shot from the fort and another from the walls of the town. A moment afterwards, a fire-ball was thrown out, which threw a bright red glare of light around us, and instantly a volley of grape shot, canister, and small arms poured in among us, as we stood on the glacis, at a distance of about thirty yards from the walls. Three of the men carrying the ladder with me, were shot dead in a breath, and its weight falling upon me, I fell backward with the grass-bag on my breast. The remainder of the stormers rushed up, regardless of my cries or those of the wounded men around me, for by this time our men were falling fast. Many in passing were shot and fell upon me, so that I was actually drenched in blood. The weight I had to sustain became intolerable, and had it not been for the grass bag which in some measure protected me, I must have been suffocated. At length, by a strong effort, I managed to extricate myself, in doing which I left my rifle behind me, and drawing my sword, rushed towards the breach. There I found four men putting a ladder down the ditch; and, not daring to pause, fresh lights being still thrown out of the town, with a continual discharge of musketry, I slid quickly down the ladder, but before I could recover my footing, was knocked down again by the bodies of men who were shot in attempting the descent. I, however, succeeded in extricating myself from underneath the dead, and rushing forward to the right, to my surprise and fear I found myself nearly up to my neck in water. Until then I was tolerably composed, but now all reflection left me, and diving through the water, being a good swimmer, I attempted to make to the breach. In doing this I lost my sword.[49]

Bugler Green was also carrying a grass bag and was

> in the act of throwing my bag, when a ball went through the thick part of my thigh, and having my bugle in my left hand, it entered my left wrist and I dropped, so I did not get into the ditch. I scarcely felt the ball go through my thigh, but when it entered my wrist, it was more like a 6-pounder than a musket-ball! It smashed the bone and cut the guides, and the blood was

49. Costello, Edward, *Adventures of a Soldier*, pp.171–173.

> pouring from both wounds, I began to feel very faint. Our men were in the ditch, while the enemy had shells loaded on the top of the wall about two yards apart. As they were fired they rolled into the ditch, and when they burst, 10 or 12 men were blown up in every direction! However, some of them arrived at the breach, but a great many both killed and wounded lay around me; the balls came very thick about us, and we were not able to move. At length the whole of the light division came past me; my comrade, a sergeant, seeing me (for there was plenty of light!) said 'Bill, are you wounded?' I said 'Yes, and cannot get up!' He said 'Here is a little rum in my flask, drink it, but I cannot assist to carry you out of the reach of shot.' His name was Robert Fairfoot. Shortly afterwards a musket balls struck him, went through the peak of his cap, and lodged in his forehead; the ball was extracted, he recovered… The whole of the division made for the breach; and a tremendous fire was going on. I heard our bugle-major sound the advance and double-quick. I rolled on my back (for I fell on my side) and repeated the sound; this was the last time I blew the bugle. As another division came past me an officer with his sword drawn stepped up to me and said 'Desist blowing that bugle, you are drawing all the fire on my men!' I said 'I was only doing my duty!'[50]

The forlorn hope and the storming party quickly went through the ditch and over the ravelin. By mistake they attacked the breach in the La Trinidad Bastion, instead of the one in the Santa Maria Bastion. They almost made it to the breach when disaster struck. Lieutenant Maillet, a French miner, had orders to blow the sixty artillery shells upon the approach of the British. He did so when

> the assailants were crossing the ditch to reach the breaches. The explosion took place with the most tremendous noise; the fire which darted from the shells and the barrels, with a noise like that of thunder, illuminated the horizon and presented the most awful spectacle. During this appalling scene 6 or 700 of our men, each furnished with three muskets, fired at the English at their very muzzles, many of whom could not again mount the counterscarp to retire.[51]

It was likely here, that Lieutenant Harvest, the commander of the forlorn hope, and the leaders of the storming party, Major O'Hare and Captain Jones, were killed.

---

50. Green, William, *Where Duty Calls Me: The Experiences of William Green of Lutterworth in the Napoleonic Wars*, pp.35–36.
51. Lamare, Jean, *An Account of the Second Defense of the Fortress of Badajoz by the French in 1812*, p.30.

The shortage of ladders created a huge traffic jam that exposed the troops to both musket and artillery fire. Lieutenant George Barlow, 52nd Foot, was in the main body and described the slaughter on the glacis in a letter home a few weeks later.

> This great body of men had to descend a steep counterscarp by five or six ladders only, which as you may suppose, took some time, as four only could go down at once on each. We had then to drive them out of a demi-lune, and all this close under the noses of between 2 and 3,000 men the greater part of whom had *three* spare muskets each, with people to load them in their rear, and kept up one of the most rapid and murderous fires, such as our oldest veterans affirm they never before experienced. Aim was unnecessary, we stood so thick and crowded on the glacis, and in the ditch, besides the enemy threw amongst us a number of fire balls which enabled them to see our movements as clear as at noon day.[52]

It was not long before the assault columns on the glacis turned into a mob and fights broke out among the troops about who could go first. Lieutenant Cooke was accosted by 'a soldier of the 52nd in the hurry growled out a hearty curse, and was very angry at my preceding him, and furious blows were exchanged amongst the troops in their eagerness to get forward; while the grape-shot and musketry tore open their ranks.'[53] Corporal Garretty threatened to shoot the soldier in front of him if he did not move forward. As Hamilton found out falling over the wall could be quite dangerous. The ditch was flooded in places and soldiers who were knocked unconscious stood a good chance of drowning.[54]

The dark night added to the confusion, because either the Light or the 4th Division got lost as they approached the walls, and both ended up in the ditch in front of the ravelin. There was no stopping the men. Most were able to climb out of the ditch onto the ravelin without using ladders. Lieutenant Bell, the DAQMG assigned to the division, was with his friends in the 52nd Foot when they rushed towards the breach. They

> pushed on over the bodies of those that fell and quickly filled the ditch and swarmed towards the breach. Some mistook an unfinished ravelin for the breach and climbed to the top in triumph, only to be swept away by a cannon on a bastion firing grape shot at point blank range. The carnage

52. Barlow, George Ulrich, *A Light Infantryman With Wellington: The Letters of Captain George Ulrich Barlow, 52nd and 69th Foot, 1808–1815*, pp.145–146.
53. Cooke, John, *A True Soldier Gentleman: The Memoirs of Lt. John Cooke 1791–1813*, pp.120–121.
54. Garretty, Thomas, *Memoirs of a Sergeant Late in the Forty-Third Light Infantry Regiment*, pp.163–164.

> was already horrendous as Charles [Kinloch] and his troops slipped on the blood and gore of those blasted into eternity by the constant flow of burning shells and powder barrels rolled into the ditch by the French.[55]

The huge number of men from the two divisions pouring into area less than 200m wide gave them an impetus that was impossible to stop. It was 'deep and broad, were coming on like streams of burning lava.'[56] The main body reached the breach and stopped momentarily. When Lieutenant Cooke, 43rd Foot,

> arrived at the foot of the centre breach, eighty or ninety men were formed. One cried out, 'Who will lead?' This was the work of a moment. Death, and the most dreadful sounds and cries, encompassed us. It was a volcano! Up we went, some killed, and others impaled on the bayonets of their own comrades, or hurled headlong amongst the outrageous crowd. The chevaux-de-frise looked like innumerable bayonets. When within a yard of the top, my sensations were most extraordinary; I felt half strangled, and fell from a blow that deprived me of sensation. I only recollect feeling a soldier pulling me out of the water, where so many men were drowned. I lost my cap, but still held my sword; on recovering, I looked towards the breach. It was shining and empty! fire-balls were in plenty, and the French troops standing upon the walls, taunting, and inviting our men to try it again. What a crisis! what a military misery! Some of the finest troops in the world prostrate-humbled to the dust.[57]

Corporal Garretty described the sheer terror and impossibility of trying to get up the breach.

> The enemy's shouts were also loud and terrible, and the bursting of shells and of grenades, the roaring of the guns from the flanks, answered by the iron howitzers from the battery of the parallel, the heavy rolls and explosion of the powder barrels, the flight of the blazing splinters, the loud exhortations of the officers, and the continued clatter of the muskets, made a maddening din. Impatient of delay, a heavy column now bounded up the great breach; but across the top glittered a range of sword-blades, sharp pointed, keen edged on both sides, and firmly fixed in ponderous beams, which were chained together and set deep in the ruins; and for ten feet in front the ascent was covered with loose planks studded with sharp iron points, on which, the feet of the foremost being set, the planks moved,

55. Bell, John, 'Letter dated 7 April 1812', Kinloch, Charles, *A Hellish Business: The Letters of Captain Charles Kinloch 52nd Light Infantry 1806–1816*, p.94.
56. Garretty, Thomas, *Memoirs of a Sergeant Late in the Forty-Third Light Infantry Regiment*, p.163.
57. Cooke, John, *A True Soldier Gentleman: The Memoirs of Lt. John Cooke 1791–1813*, p.121.

> and the unhappy soldiers, falling forward on the spikes, rolled down upon the ranks behind. Then the Frenchmen, exulting at the success of their stratagem, and leaping forward, plied their shot with terrible rapidity; for every man had several muskets, and each musket, in addition to its ordinary charge, contained a small cylinder of wood, stuck full of leaden slugs, which scattered like hail when they were discharged.[58]

Lieutenant Colonel McLeod led one of the assaults on the breach. He was 'killed while trying to force the left corner of the large breach. He received his mortal wound within three yards of the enemy, just at the bottom of some nine feet planks, studded with nails, and hanging down the breach from under the chevaux-de-frise.'[59]

In the frenzy of the assault, Rifleman Costello, had lost his rifle and sword bayonet, but

> succeeded in clambering up a part of the breach, and came near to a chevaux de frise consisting of a piece of heavy timber studded with sword blades, turning on an axis: but just before reaching it I received a stroke on the breast, whether from a grenade or a stone, or by the butt-end of a musket, I cannot say, but down I rolled senseless, and drenched with water, and human gore. I could not have laid long in this plight, for when my senses had in some measure returned, I perceived our gallant fellows still rushing forward, each seeming to share a fate more deadly than my own. The fire continued in one horrible and incessant peal, as if the mouth of the infernal regions had opened to vomit forth destruction upon all around us, and this was rendered still more appalling by the fearful shouts of the combatants and cries of the wounded that mingled in the uproar.[60]

About 11:45 p.m. Lieutenant James Shaw, Lieutenant Colonel Barnard's ADC, realised that the left breach, which the division was supposed to assault, had not been attacked. He gathered

> about seventy men of different regiments, and with great difficulty, as you may suppose, after such a milling for two hours, made a desperate effort to gain the top; but when half-way up, as if by enchantment, he stood alone. Two rounds of grape and the musketry prevented any more trouble, for almost the whole of the party lay stretched in various attitudes! This attack was very daring. It was a forlorn hope under accumulated dangers;

58. Garretty, Thomas, *Memoirs of a Sergeant Late in the Forty-Third Light Infantry Regiment*, pp.164–165.
59. Cooke, John, *A True Soldier Gentleman: The Memoirs of Lt. John Cooke 1791–1813*, p.121.
60. Costello, Edward, *Adventures of a Soldier*, p.173.

> almost all the troops had retired, and a few moments before a great alarm was excited by a cry from the heaps of wounded, that the French were descending into the ditch.[61]

The division's reserve under the command of Lieutenant Colonel Elder was originally ordered to

> follow the leading brigade at a respectable distance, and not to advance until the rear of the 43rd Regiment entered the ditch. I therefore remained under cover until an officer of the Rifle Regiment (who very handsomely volunteered for those services) followed the 43rd Regiment, and in a short time returned, and reported that he had seen the troops into the ditch. I then advanced, and on my reaching the glacis, I was astonished when I observed the frightful confusion among the troops in the ditch; and in order to ascertain the particulars, I immediately descended the ladders, at the bottom of which I met Major Broke, (now Colonel Sir Charles Broke Vere,) who was severely wounded. I understood from him, that nearly all the field – officers were either killed or wounded; and that the attack on the great breach, La Trinidad, had failed; and that he was going back to report the particulars to the Commander-in-Chief, Lord Wellington. I immediately pushed forward; and as I was endeavouring to form some of the troops near me, in order to lead them to the small breach on my left, Santa Maria, I was at that moment severely wounded.[62]

The division's Portuguese troops advanced to the breach in the Santa Maria Bastion, but they too failed to take it.

For about two hours the division continued to try to take the breaches. Despite knowing that it was suicidal the officers, including Lieutenant Barlow, 52nd Foot,

> led on repeatedly their men up to the very muzzles of the enemies [*sic*] pieces, so as to feel the wadding as well as the ball; when one fell, another supplied his place. It is impossible to describe their feelings on beholding all efforts so vain, this struck them the more as they have been hitherto so invariably successful, the division never having failed at any single object during a long course of service. Excepting myself and one or two others, they all were killed and wounded on the very breach one after another, and in this awful crisis persevered in using their utmost personal exertion.[63]

61. Cooke, John, *A True Soldier Gentleman: The Memoirs of Lt. John Cooke 1791–1813*, p.122.
62. Elder, George, 'Memorandum of the Siege and the Assault of Badajoz on the Evening of the 6th of April, 1812', *United Services Journal*, p.55.
63. Barlow, George Ulrich, *A Light Infantryman With Wellington: The Letters of Captain George Ulrich Barlow, 52nd and 69th Foot, 1808–1815*, p.146.

Eventually the troops had had enough. There were

> small groups of soldiers seeking shelter from the cartwheels, pieces of timber, fire-balls, and other missiles hurled down upon them; the wounded crawling past the fire-balls, many of them scorched and perfectly black, and covered with mud, from having fallen into the lunette, where three hundred were suffocated or drowned; and all this time the French on the top of the parapets, jeering and cracking their jokes, and deliberately picking off whom they chose…[64]

Around midnight, Lieutenant Colonel Barnard received orders from Wellington to withdraw. Lieutenant Kincaid, said he was near the division's commander when the order was received and that Barnard was reluctant to 'order a retreat while yet a chance remained; but, after heading repeated attempts himself, he saw that it was hopeless, and the order was reluctantly given…'[65] Kincaid said it was about 2:00 a.m. before Barnard gave the order to withdraw, but he was probably wrong about the time. Barnard may not have liked the order, but it was unlikely he would have ignored it.

The division's retreat was seen by the defenders who kept up their fire. Corporal Garretty described it as a combination of

> carnage and confusion; from the French fire never slackened, and a cry arose that the French were making a sally from the distant flanks, which caused a rush towards the ladders. Then the groans and lamentations of the wounded, who could not move, and expected to be slain, increased; many officers, who had not heard of the order, endeavoured to stop the soldiers from going back, and some would even have removed the ladders, but were unable to break through the crowd.[66]

After the division withdrew, the defenders began to shift their troops towards the castle. The ferocious attacks by the Light and 4th Divisions had caused the French to move his reserves from the castle and other walls. Once they were weakened the 3rd Division was able to scale the castle walls and capture it, while the 5th Division was able to penetrate the city near Bastion 1 on the southwest side of the city. This movement of many of the defenders away from the three breaches where the Light and 4th Divisions had shed so much blood went unnoticed by the men of the Light Division.

---

64. Cooke, John, *A True Soldier Gentleman: The Memoirs of Lt. John Cooke 1791–1813*, p.123.
65. Kincaid, John, *Adventures in the Rifle Brigade in the Peninsula, France, and the Netherlands from 1809–1815*, p.133.
66. Garretty, Thomas, *Memoirs of a Sergeant Late in the Forty-Third Light Infantry Regiment*, p.166.

About 12:30 a.m. Wellington sent orders for the Light and 4th Divisions to assault the breaches again. Major Lord Fitzroy Somerset, Wellington's military secretary, carried the order to the Light Division. Captain Harry Smith was the first staff officer he found, and he could not believe the news that Somerset carried.

> 'Where is Barnard?'
>
> I didn't know, but I assured his Lordship he was neither killed nor wounded.
>
> A few minutes after his Lordship said that the Duke desired the Light and 4th Divisions to storm again. 'The devil!' says I. 'Why, we have had enough; we are all knocked to pieces.'
>
> Lord Fitzroy says, 'I dare say, but you must try again.'
>
> I smiled and said, 'If we could not succeed with two whole fresh and unscathed Divisions, we are likely to make a poor show of it now. But we will try again with all our might.'
>
> Scarcely had this conversation occurred when a bugle sounded within the breach, indicating what had occurred at the citadel and Puerto de Olivença; and here ended all the fighting. Our fellows would have gone at it again when collected and put into shape, but we were just as well pleased that our attempt had so attracted the attention of enemy as greatly to facilitate that success which assured the prize contended for.[67]

The division was reformed as best as possible and once again they moved to the breaches. Their march took them past hundreds of their dead and wounded comrades. They soon reached the foot of the breach and much to their surprise only 'a few random shots were now fired, and we entered [the city] without opposition.'[68]

---

67. Smith, Harry, *The Autobiography of Sir Harry Smith*, p.66.
68. Simmons, George, *A British Rifleman: Journals and Correspondence During the Peninsular War and the Campaign of Wellington*, p.230.

Chapter 10

The Aftermath of the Assault 7 April–9 April 1812

> I have to add with sorrow that the conquest of Badajos [*sic*] was attended with excesses that tend to tarnish the soldier's character. All, indeed, were not alike, for hundreds risked and many lost their lives in striving to stop the violence; but the madness of ungovernable licentiousness generally prevailed; and as the worst men were leaders here, all the dreadful passions of human nature were displayed: shameless rapacity, brutal intemperance, savage lust, cruelty and murder, shrieks and piteous lamentations, groans, shouts, curses, the hissing of fires bursting from the houses, the crashing of doors and windows, and the reports of muskets used in violence, resounded for two days and nights in the devoted town.
>
> Corporal Thomas Garretty, 43rd Foot[1]

Once the men of the Light Division climbed the breach into the city, all discipline broke down and the men scattered to plunder the city. The one exception was the Left Wing of the 1st Battalion 95th Rifles, under the command of Brevet Major Alexander Cameron, the senior surviving officer in the battalion. He knew that the city had not been secured and based on what happened after Ciudad Rodrigo fell, that if he lost control of his men, disaster could strike. He was determined to keep them together until the enemy garrison had surrendered and left the city. Lieutenant John Kincaid, his acting adjutant, sent out 'piquets [*sic*] into the different streets and lanes leading from the breach, and kept the remainder in hand until day should throw some light on our situation'.[2] While posting one of the picquets

> a man of ours brought me a prisoner, telling me that he was the governor; but the other immediately said that he had only called himself so, the better to ensure his protection; and then added, that he was the colonel of one of the French regiments, and that all his surviving officers were assembled

1. Garretty, Thomas, *Memoirs of a Sergeant Late in the Forty-Third Light Infantry Regiment*, pp.170–171.
2. Kincaid, John, *Adventures in the Rifle Brigade in the Peninsula, France, and the Netherlands from 1809–1815*, p.134.

> at his quarters, in a street close by, and would surrender themselves to any officer who would go with him for that purpose. I accordingly took two or three men with me, and, accompanying him there, found fifteen or sixteen of them assembled, and all seeming very much surprised at the unexpected termination of the siege. They could not comprehend under what circumstances the town had been lost, and repeatedly asked me how I had got in; but I did not choose to explain further than simply telling them that I had entered at the breach…They were all very much dejected, excepting their major, who was a big jolly-looking Dutchman, with medals enough, on his left breast, to have furnished the window of a tolerable toy-shop…When I had allowed their chief a reasonable time to secure what valuables he wished, about his person, he told me that he had two horses in the stable, which, as he would no longer be permitted to keep, he recommended me to take; and, as a horse is the only thing on such occasions that an officer can permit himself to consider a legal prize, I caused one of them to be saddled, and his handsome black mare thereby became my charger during the remainder of the war.[3]

At this point Lieutenant Kincaid made an error that almost got him killed by friendly fire.

> In proceeding with my prisoners towards the breach, I took, by mistake, a different road to that I came; and, as numbers of Frenchmen were lurking about for a safe opportunity of surrendering themselves, about a hundred additional ones added themselves to my column, as we moved along, jabbering their native dialect so loudly, as nearly to occasion a dire catastrophe, as it prevented me from hearing some one challenge in my front; but, fortunately, it was repeated, and I instantly answered; for Colonel Barnard and [Brevet Lieutenant Colonel] Sir Colin Campbell [AAG] had a piquet of our men, drawn across the street, on the point of sending a volley into us, thinking that we were a rallied body of the enemy.[4]

While the riflemen were still listening to their officers, Brevet Major Cameron put them in formation and talked to them. He

> promised that they should have the same indulgence as others, and that he should not insist upon keeping them together longer than was absolutely necessary; but he assured them that if any man quitted the ranks until he gave permission, he would cause him to be put to death on the spot; That had the desired effect until between nine and ten o'clock in the morning,

3. Ibid, pp.135–136.
4. Ibid, p.137.

> when, seeing that the whole of the late garrison had been secured and marched off to Elvas, he again addressed his battalion, and thanked them for their conduct throughout; he concluded with, 'Now, my men, you may fall out and enjoy yourselves for the remainder of the day, but I shall expect to see you all in camp at the usual roll, call in the evening!'[5]

Major Cameron was overly optimistic. During the evening roll call, not one soldier was present.[6]

The Sack of Badajoz

There are few accounts from soldiers of the Light Division on the sacking of Badajoz. Rifleman Costello, who was in the Right Wing of the 1st Battalion 95th Rifles was slightly wounded by a graze to his head, but he did not let that stop him.

> Leaning upon my comrade, and using his rifle as a crutch, accompanied by a few of our riflemen, I entered the town that had been so gloriously won…Angry and irritated from the pain occasioned by the wound, we had just turned the corner of a street, when we observed some men, and, from the light that shone from a window opposite, we could see from their uniforms they were evidently Frenchmen. The moment they saw us they disappeared, with the exception of one man, who seemed to make a rush at us with his musket. [Rifleman Patrick] O'Brien sprang forward and wrested the firelock from his grasp. A feeling of revenge, prompted by the suffering I endured from my wounds, actuated my feelings, and I exclaimed, 'O'Brien, let me have the pleasure of shooting this rascal, for he may be the man who has brought me to the state I am now in!' I then presented my rifle close to his breast, with the full intention of shooting him through the body, but as my finger was about to press the trigger he fell upon his knees and implored mercy. The next moment the rifle dropped from my hand, and I felt a degree of shame that a feeling of irritation should have nearly betrayed me into the commission of a crime for which I could never have forgiven myself.
>
> The Frenchman, as soon as he perceived me desist, immediately started from his knees, on which he had fallen trembling, and, by way of showing his gratitude, threw his arms round my neck, and wanted to kiss my cheek. He instantly followed me, and I forthwith for the time took him under my protection.

5. Kincaid, John, *Random Shots from a Rifleman*, p.161.
6. Ibid, p.162.

We looked anxiously around for a house where we could obtain refreshment, and, if truth must be told, a little money at the same time. For even wounded as I was, I had made up my mind to be a gainer by our victory. At the first house we knocked at, no notice was taken of the summons, we fired a rifle at the key-hole, which sent the door flying open. This, indeed, was our usual method of forcing locks. As soon as we entered the house we found a young Spanish woman crying bitterly, and praying for mercy. She informed us she was the wife of a Frenchman; and to the demand of my companion O'Brien for refreshment, replied there was nothing but her poor self in the house. She, however, produced some spirits and chocolate, the latter of which, being very hungry and faint, I partook of with much relish.

As the house looked poor we soon quitted it in quest of a better. Supported by O'Brien and the Frenchman, we proceeded in the direction of the market-place. It was a dark night, and the confusion and uproar that prevailed in the town may be better imagined than described. The shouts and oaths of drunken soldiers in quest of more liquor, the reports of fire-arms and crashing in of doors, together with the appalling shrieks of hapless women might have induced any one to have believed himself in the regions of the damned.

When we arrived at the market-place we found a number of Spanish prisoners rushing out of a gaol they appeared like a set of savages suddenly let loose, many still bearing the chains they had not had time to free themselves from, and among these were men of the 5th and 88th Regiments holding lighted candles. We then turned down a street opposite to the foregoing scene, and entered a house which was occupied by a number of men of the 3rd Division. One of them immediately, on perceiving me wounded, struck off the neck of a bottle of wine with his bayonet, and presented some of it to me, which relieved me for a time from the faintness I had previously felt. The scenes of wickedness that soldiers are guilty of on capturing a besieged town are oftentimes truly diabolical, and I now, in the reflections this subject gives rise to, shudder at the past. I had not long been seated at the fire which was blazing up the chimney, fed by mahogany chairs, broken up for the purpose, when I heard screams for mercy from an from an adjoining room. On hobbling in, I found an old man, the proprietor of the house, on his knees, imploring mercy of a soldier who had levelled his musket at him. I with difficulty prevented the soldier from shooting him, as he complained that the Spaniard would not give up his money. I immediately informed the wretched landlord in Spanish, which I spoke tolerably well, that he could only save his life by surrendering his cash. Upon this he brought out with trembling hands a large bag of dollars from under the mattress of the bed. These by common consent were immediately

> divided among the men present; and I must confess I participated in the plunder, getting sixteen dollars for my share.
>
> After this I resumed my seat at the fire, when a number of Portuguese soldiers entered, one of whom, taking me for a Frenchman, for I had the French soldier's jacket on, my own being wet, snapped his piece at me, which luckily hung fire. I instantly rushed at him as well as I was able, when a scuffle ensued, and one of the Portuguese being stabbed by a bayonet, they retired, dragging the wounded man with them. After ejecting the Portuguese, our men, who had by this time got tolerably drunk, proceeded to ransack the house. Unhappily they discovered the two daughters of the old man of the house, who had concealed themselves upstairs. They were both young and pretty. The mother, too, was shortly afterwards dragged from her hiding-place. I refrain from describing the scene which followed.[7]

What the Officers Did to Stop the Plundering

Other than Brevet Major Cameron on the first night, there is no evidence that the officers were able to keep their soldiers from going on a rampage. Lieutenant Colonel Barnard had originally stood at the top of the breach and almost lost his life trying to stop the men from entering the city. He used his

> personal and bodily strength to the entrance of the plunderers, but in vain. They rushed in, in spite of all opposition; and in wrenching a musket from one of the soldiers of the 52d, who was forcing past him, he fell, and was nigh precipitated into the ditch. He, however, finding resistance here in vain, set off, accompanied by several other officers, into the town, to endeavour to restrain, as much as lay in his power, the licentiousness of those inside, whose bad passions, it was but too evident, would be let loose upon the defenceless inhabitants.[8]

Individually or in small groups, some officer 'did all they could to repress these outrages, but the soldiers were now so completely dispersed that one quarter of them could not be found; and indeed the only benefit almost that the officers could render was, by each placing himself in a house, which generally secured it from being broken open and plundered.'[9] Others thought that there was nothing they could do and returned to their encampments, until the drunken soldiers stopped from exhaustion and finally sobered up.[10] Captain Harry Smith

---

7. Costello, Edward, *Adventures of a Soldier*, pp. 175-179.
8. Surtees, William, *Twenty-Five Years in the Rifle Brigade*, p.144.
9. Ibid, p.148.
10. Kincaid, John, *Adventures in the Rifle Brigade in the Peninsula, France, and the Netherlands from 1809–1815*, p.138.

wrote that 'though the officers exerted themselves to the utmost to repress it, many who had escaped the enemy being wounded in their merciful attempts!'[11]

On the morning of the second day, Lieutenant Kincaid organised a group of officers to go into the town

> to collect our men, but only succeeded in part, as the same extraordinary scene of plunder and rioting still continued. Wherever there was any thing to eat or drink, the only saleable commodities, the soldiers had turned the shopkeepers out of doors, and placed themselves regularly behind the counter, selling off the contents of the shop. By and bye, another and a stronger party would kick those out in their turn, and there was no end to the succession of self-elected shopkeepers.[12]

The officers were shown little respect from the drunken soldiers, even by their own troops.

> One man of our first battalion…had got a hogshead of brandy into the streets, and, getting his mess tin, and filling it from the cask, and seating himself astride like Bacchus, swore that every person who came past should drink, be who he may. His commanding-officer [Brevet Major Cameron] happened to be one who came that way, and he was compelled to take the tin and drink, for, had he refused, it is not improbable the wretch would have shot him, for his rifle was loaded by his side, and the soldiers had by this time become quite past all control.[13]

Even Wellington was accosted by drunken soldiers when he went into the town on the second day. He was quickly 'surrounded by a number of British soldiers, who, holding up bottles with the heads knocked off, containing wine and spirits, cried out to him, a phrase then familiarly applied to him by the men of the army, "Old boy! will you drink? The town's our own-hurrah!"'[14]

Wellington had enough. On 9 April, he ordered 'a Portuguese brigade to be marched in, and kept standing to their arms, in the great square, where the Provost Marshal erected a gallows, and proceeded to suspend a few of the delinquents, which very quickly cleared the town of the remainder.'[15]

---

11. Smith, Harry, *The Autobiography of Sir Harry Smith*, p.68.
12. Kincaid, John, *Adventures in the Rifle Brigade in the Peninsula, France, and the Netherlands from 1809–1815*, p.138.
13. Surtees, William, *Twenty-Five Years in the Rifle Brigade*, p.148.
14. Costello, Edward, *Adventures of a Soldier*, p.181.
15. Kincaid, John, *Adventures in the Rifle Brigade in the Peninsula, France, and the Netherlands from 1809–1815*, pp.138-139

Rifleman Costello was still in the town on 9 April and he

> observed a sort of gallows erected with three nooses hanging from them, ready for service. Johnny [John] Castles, a man of our company, and as quiet and inoffensive a little fellow as could be, but rather fond of a drop, but not that distilled by Jack Ketch & Co., had a near escape. He was actually brought under the gallows in a cart and the rope placed round his neck, but his life was spared. Whether this was done to frighten him or not I cannot say; but the circumstance had such an effect on him, that he took ill, and was a little deranged for some time after.[16]

The soldiers filtered out of the city with their loot during the three days and soon the cantonments took on the look of an open-air market. 'The different camps of our army were for several days after more like rag-fairs than military encampments, such quantities of wearing-apparel of all kinds were disposing of by one set of plunderers to the other.'[17] Before long, word spread throughout the area and the markets were crowded with the local farmers who were bartering for the 'clothes and other articles…[eventually] the men were made to throw away a quantity of things, and to prevent them secreting any of the articles, their packs were examined, and the plunder that had not been made away with was collected into heaps and burnt.'[18]

A Love Story

From savage pillaging and terror came a love story. On 10 April, Lieutenant Kincaid was standing outside a friend's tent when he saw two ladies in the distance.

> They seemed both young, and when they came near, the elder of the two threw back her mantilla to address us, showing a remarkably handsome figure, with fine features; but her sallow, sun-burnt, and care-worn, though still youthful countenance, showed that in her, 'The time for tender thoughts and soft endearments had fled away and gone.' She at once addressed us in that confident heroic manner so characteristic of the high-bred Spanish maiden, told us who they were, the last of an ancient and honourable house, and referred to an officer high in rank in our army, who had been quartered there in the days of her prosperity, for the truth of her tale. Her husband, she said, was a Spanish officer in a distant part of the kingdom; he might or he

16. Costello, Edward, *Adventures of a Solider*, pp.180–181.
17. Surtees, William, *Twenty-Five Years in the Rifle Brigade*, p.148.
18. Simmons, George, *A British Rifleman: Journals and Correspondence During the Peninsular War and the Campaign of Wellington*, p.233.

> might not still be living. But yesterday, she and her young sister were able to live in affluence and in a handsome house today, they knew not where to lay their heads-where to get a change of raiment, or a morsel of bread. Her house, she said, was a wreck, and, to show the indignities to which they had been subjected, she pointed to where the blood was still trickling down their necks, caused by the wrenching of their earrings through the flesh, by the hands of worse than savages, who would not take the trouble to unclasp them!
>
> For herself, she said, she cared not; but for the agitated, and almost unconscious maiden by her side, whom she had but lately received over from the hands of her conventual instructresses, she was despair, and knew not what to do; and that in the rapine and ruin which was at that moment desolating the city, she saw no security for her but the seemingly indelicate one she had adopted, of coming to the camp and throwing themselves upon the protection of any British officer who would afford it; and so great, she said, was her faith in our national character, that she knew the appeal would not be made in vain, nor the confidence abused. Nor was it made in vain! nor could it be abused, for she stood by the side of an angel! A being more transcendently lovely I had never before seen-one more amiable I have never yet known! Fourteen summers had not yet passed over her youthful countenance, which was of a delicate freshness , more English than Spanish-her face, though not perhaps rigidly beautiful, was nevertheless so remarkably handsome, and so irresistibly attractive, surmounting a figure cast in nature's fairest mould [*sic*], that to look at her was to love her and I did love her; but I never told my love, and in the mean time another, and a more impudent fellow stepped in and won her! but yet I was happy for in him she found such a one as her loveliness and her misfortunes claimed-a man of honour, and a husband in every way worthy of her![19]

The girl was Juana María de los Dolores de León. The person who stole her from Lieutenant Kincaid was Captain Harry Smith. Juana married Harry a few days later and she would follow him throughout the Peninsular War, to India, and then to South Africa. Harry was appointed the governor of the Cape Colony in South Africa in 1847. The town of Ladysmith, South Africa is named after her. Harry died in 1860. They were married for forty-eight years.

Searching for the Wounded

Unable to stop the rampage, the few unscathed surviving officers went looking for their friends. Lieutenant Cooke climbed the breach and found 'One man

19. Kincaid, John, *Random Shots From a Rifleman*, pp.165–166.

only was at the top of the left breach – the heaps of dead had, as a matter of course, rolled to the bottom – and that was one of the Rifle Corps, who had succeeded in getting under the chevaux-de-frise. His head was battered to pieces, and his arms and shoulders torn asunder with bayonet wounds.'[20]

Lieutenant Kincaid went at the

> glimpse of daylight permitted I went to take a look at the breach, and there saw a solitary figure, with a drawn sword, stalking over the ruins and the slain, which, in the gray dawn of morning, appeared to my astonished eyes like a headless trunk, and concluded that it was the ghost of one of the departed one in search of his earthly remains. I cautiously approached to take a nearer survey, when I found that it was Captain [Lieutenant James] McNair, of the 52d, with his head wrapped in a red handkerchief. He told me that he was looking for his cap and his scabbard, both of which had parted company from him in the storm, about that particular spot; but his search proved a forlorn hope. I congratulated him that his head had not gone in the cap, as had been the case with but too many of our mutual companions on that fatal night.[21]

Quartermaster Surtees was with Captain William Percival, the acting commander of the five companies of the 3rd Battalion 95th Rifles, the next morning and they tried to evacuate as many of the wounded as possible from where they laid for the past ten hours. They could hear

> the heart-piercing and afflicting groans which arose from the numbers of wounded still lying in the ditch, set to work to get as many of these poor fellows removed as was in our power. This we found a most arduous and difficult undertaking, as we could not do it without the aid of a considerable number of men; and it was a work of danger to attempt to force the now lawless soldiers to obey, and stop with us till this work of necessity and humanity was accomplished.
>
> All thought of what they owed their wounded comrades, and of the probability that ere long a similar fate might be their own, was swallowed up in their abominable rage for drink and plunder; however, by perseverance, and by occasionally using his stick, my commandant at length compelled a few fellows to lend their assistance in removing what we could into the town, where it was intended that hospitals should be established. But this was a most heartrending duty, for, from the innumerable cries of, 'Oh! for God's sake, come and remove me!' it was difficult to select the most proper

20. Cooke, John, *A True Soldier Gentleman: The Memoirs of Lt. John Cooke 1791–1813*, pp.125–126.
21. Kincaid, John, *Random Shots From a Rifleman,* p.162.

> objects for such care. Those who appeared likely to die, of course it would have been but cruelty to put them to the pain of a removal; and many who, from the nature of their wounds, required great care and attention in carrying them, the half-drunken brutes whom we were forced to employ exceedingly tortured and injured; nay, in carrying one man out of the ditch they very frequently kicked or trode upon several others, whom to touch was like death to them, and which produced the most agonizing cries imaginable.
>
> ...it soon began to grow excessively hot, and what with the toil and the heat of the sun, and the very unpleasant effluvia which now arose from the numerous dead and wounded, we were both compelled, about mid-day, to desist from our distressing though gratifying labours.
>
> It was now between twelve and one o'clock, and though we had had a great many removed, a much greater number lay groaning in the ditch; but our strength was exhausted, for he was lame and unable to move much, and I had been obliged to assist in carrying many myself, the drunken scoundrels whom we had pressed into the service seldom making more than one or two trips till they deserted us.[22]

Many wounded soldiers did not wait for help, but made their own way back to the aid stations. Corporal Garretty, 43rd Foot was shot in the left thigh as he rushed to the breach. At first, he ignored his wound but felt himself

> getting weak and feverish...In this condition, faint with loss of blood, I contrived to descend into the ditch with the help of my musket. Meanwhile the depth of water by some added inundation had been increased, and no ladder was to be discovered for my ascent on the opposite side. Unwilling to die there, I made another effort, and at length observed a ladder standing in front of the ditch. Unable to get up with my musket, I reluctantly left that behind, and scrambled up with extreme difficulty. Numerous shots were fired at me while ascending, and I perceived bullets whistling through the rounds of the ladder, but not one of them struck me...I found, to my surprise, a young man belonging to the gallant [Captain William] Napier's company, who kindly offered his arm, and supported me to the field hospital...with so large an influx of patients it will be supposed that the hospital attentions were not very prompt: I was placed on the ground, with many others in a worse condition than myself, to await my turn for surgical assistance. After some hours I found that unless my wound ceased bleeding I should not long survive: this, with a little contrivance, I managed to effect. But the most intolerable sensation was that of raging thirst: all my worldly substance, ten times valued, would have been no price at all

22. Surtees, William, *Twenty-Five Years in the Rifle Brigade*, pp.144–146.

> for a draught of water. Meantime the frost was so severe, that my limbs appeared to be deprived of flexibility and motion…In the course of a day or two we were placed in military spring waggons, and conveyed to Elvas. We were afterwards transferred to bullock-carts: a mode of conveyance not remarkable either for comfort or speed; the carriages were clumsily constructed, and ensured very little in the way of easy riding; added to which, we moved only at the rate of about one mile an hour…On alighting from our vehicles at Elvas, we were at first placed in a dark, uncomfortable apartment, adjoining the fortifications; the roof was of arched masonry, and so damp on the inner side, that water fell on us in large drops. Our attendants were also nothing to boast of; for under pretence of bringing our haversacks containing provisions, they walked away with them altogether, an evil against which we knew no remedy, being unable, through weakness, to search for the depredators, or procure more food. The confusion in this unhappy lazar-house was extreme. Every man naturally thought his own case the most serious, and that it demanded care before all others. We were not, however, destined to remain. long in these unsuitable quarters: orders were received directing our removal to Estramores [Estramoz], and our journey thither was commenced the same night. The procession was rather melancholy several times we had to halt in order to bury some poor creature, who, exhausted by suffering, had fled away. On our arrival at Estramores, we found accommodation more suited to the exigencies of the invalided guests: a convent, sufficiently spacious, had been fitted up as a military hospital, and was well adapted for the purpose. When able to look around, I discovered several of my former associates. Here lay the man through whose body a ramrod had forced its way. On another couch reposed Patrick Marr, a daring fellow, but of bad character. He, with others, had led on the forlorn hope, and was violently struck with a musket bullet. Then there was a young man, named Forbes,[23] who volunteered with myself into the 43d; in a short period he died.[24]

Bugler William Green, 1st Battalion 95th Rifles, was also wounded during the assault.

> In a short time the firing from the wall slackened on us poor fellows that lay killed and wounded at the first onset, and those that could move got up. I was enabled through mercy to hobble to the rear, holding my left hand with my right on, as the ball had entered the joint to my wrist. I thought I was safe and out of the reach of shot from the enemy, but it did not prove

23. We have not been able to identify this soldier.
24. Garretty, Thomas, *Memoirs of a Sergeant Late in the Forty-Third Light Infantry Regiment*, pp.169–173.

so, for soon a shower of grape shot came over my head and just missed my cap; I had moved a short distance from where I was at first, and had sat up a short time, but through loss of blood from my wounds, I was glad to lay myself down again. In a short time, four men, belonging to the band of some regiment came up to me and asked if I [was] wounded? I said 'Yes'.

They had what we called a stretcher, two slant poles with a piece of sacking nailed to them for the wounded to lay on and carried me to the doctor. These band-men were employed in this work, as they are not required to go into action. I asked them 'if they could give me a drink of water?'

They replied 'They had none.' One of them said 'There is some a little way off, but there are both dead men and horses in it, you cannot drink it.'

I replied 'my good fellow, run and fill your canteen.' It held about three pints; I drank it off. He ran and filled it again; I then got into the stretcher, they carried me shoulder high, and at the distance of about a mile we reached the tents, where were about 50 staff and regimental doctors. I was so thirsty that I had emptied the three other pints before they set me down; I hobbled into the tent, there was a doctor standing by the tent-pole, with his coat off, a pair of blue sleeves on, and a blue apron; a large wax taper was burning and there was a box of instruments laying by his side. The tent was full of wounded, all laying with their feet towards the pole; it was an awful sight to see, and to hear their groans was truly heart-rending.

I stepped up to the doctor, he saw blood trickling down my leg, and tore off a piece of my trousers to get at the wound, which left my leg and part of my thigh bare. He then made his finger and thumb meet in the hole the ball had made, and said 'the ball is out my lad!' He put in some lint and covered the wound with some strapping and bid me lay down and make myself as comfortable as I could, saying 'there are others who need dressing worse than you!'

I said 'I have another wound in my wrist,' so he cut the back part of my wrist, about an inch and half, put in an instrument and pulled out a piece of the thumb bone, about half an inch long, which had been broken off by the ball, and driven to the back of the wrist. The ball could not be extracted. He then dressed the wound, and bid me lay down outside the tent as there was no room inside. When I was out, a corporal of my company who had got a musket-ball in his shoulder, bid me try to walk with him to our own tents, about a mile off. I was willing to go with him as there was no shelter or cover we could get under. I made the attempt, but before we had walked 20 paces, my thigh being bare of covering, the bleeding had parted the lint and the strapping from the wound. The night was very cold, so that every step I took was like a penknife in the wound, and I was two hours going the mile…Mercy having so far restored me as to be enabled to go about, after two days and nights being at my regiment tents, I was ordered to join the camp where the whole of wounded were stationed. When I arrived there the sight was sickening in the extreme, some without arms, some without legs, and others wounded in different parts, some sitting and lying down, but none walking. Lord Wellington was there, going from one to another, with his arms folded and asking several where they were wounded. He came to me and put the same question. I said, 'Through the right thigh and the left wrist.'

He shook his head and said 'Poor fellow!' I think he cried to see so many fine young men so disabled. The sight was enough to melt the hardest heart to show 'bowels of mercy,' and to compassionate with sympathetic feelings.

On the 10th all the wounded were put into carts drawn by oxen, six in each cart, to be conveyed to Elvas in Portugal, about 12 miles distant. Here we were put into convents; there was a bed for each man. This was the first night I had lain on a bed since May 24th, 1809, nearly three years; and though I had a bed there was no sleep for me. The pain of my wound (for I was not so far recovered as to be free from pain), and the groans of my wounded comrades, prevented sleep for several nights. I was well attended by the doctor, but I could eat very little. I was nine days without anything passing my bowels.

On the twelfth day from my being wounded the ball was extracted from my hand, which looked more like a soldier's three-cocked hat than a musket ball. My hand was in a bad state, and I begged the doctor to take it off. He promised me he would the next day. He was an Italian gentleman, and could only speak broken English. I was in a room with eleven others, who had either a leg or an arm taken off, and he was said to be clever in amputating a limb. After three weeks the general doctor looked into my ward, I beckoned him with my hand, when he came and asked me what I wanted. I said 'Do sir, if you please, take my hand off; I cannot live, it is so painful.'

He bid the nurse undo the bandage and take off the splints. He looked me in the face and said, 'If I were to take your hand off now you would not live two days; it is not in a fit state to be taken off.' My arm was swelled up to the shoulder nearly as thick as my thigh. He ordered brandy and bark, which being applied the swelling went down in a few days. My doctor came to me one night and said, 'Bugler, I shall take your hand off tomorrow morning at 9 o'clock.'

I said, 'You have told me so many times, don't tell be so any more.'

He replied, 'I have spoken to two English gentlemen to assist me.' I felt pleased that at this time I could put confidence in him, at least I thought I might.

The nurse dressed my wound but I was in such pain that I said 'You must undo my arm, you have left some of the old poultice in the wound.'

She untied the bandage, and replied, 'It is all right;' but in rubbing the wound with some light a large piece of bone from the joint fell upon the floor, I remarked 'It was that which pained me.'

I afterwards had a good night's sleep. In the morning some of the men said, 'Have it cut off;' others said, 'Let it be on;' at length the three doctors came. A servant came into the ward and bid me throw the bed rug over me, as I was wanted in the operation room where the doctors were waiting. I had made up my mind to keep my hand on, and bid the man tell the doctor to come to me.

He came and was shown the piece of bone; he then flew in a passion, and exclaimed 'You are making a fool of me, and the other two gentlemen I have brought to assist me;' and then added 'You will never be worth a farthing to you king or your country any more!'

I answered, 'I have done my duty as a British soldier, and do not owe either to king or country;' (I was told that for every limb that was taken off this doctor had five pounds extra above his daily pay, whether the patient lived or died.)

He said, 'If you have it off you will be entitled to what is called blood money, and you will never be able to earn a penny with that hand.'

I felt sorry that I had ruffled his mind by not consenting to have it off; so I said 'Well, Sir, take it off if you think it will not get well.'

He then again looked at the piece of bone, turned it over with his fingers, and said in a cooler tone, 'We will let it be a day or two.' I had another good night's sleep; when he came to dress our wounds next morning I was out of bed.

The doctor looked towards my bed, and seeing I was not there, he exclaimed in a loud voice, 'Where's the bugler?'

As I stood behind him taking off the bandage I replied, 'Here, sir.'

He looked and said 'Let it alone, sir, I shall make you wait until I have dressed all the others, your turn will be last this morning.'

When he had done with the others he took me in hand, and putting on the bandage said, 'How is your thing?'

I replied 'It is quite well, sir,' and skinned over.

He then said 'You may go tomorrow with some more on the way to Lisbon, you will there get on board of a ship, for England, and get three days' provisions and if you cannot walk, you can ride, as there will be spring waggons and I shall be glad to get rid of you!'

At night an English woman brought a shirt she had from me to wash, I was in bed; she said, I have sewed the other mens' shirts and yours is the last; there are shot holes in the left sleeve. I told her that it was not mine as there were no shot holes in the one I gave her to wash, mine was almost a new one.

> 'Well,' said the woman, 'Let me see your jacket?' She took it off the bed, and on examination we found two shot holes in the sleeve, although on my person no marks of this kind had been discovered.[25]

Evacuation of the Wounded to Elvas

Lieutenant John Dobbs, 52nd Foot, one of the twelve officers in his regiment to survive the siege without a wound, was ordered to escort the division's wounded to the hospital in Elvas on 8 April.

> On going to take charge I found the surgeon still busily employed in cutting off legs and arms, of which there was an immense heap close to the hospital tents. My orders were to deliver my charge at the hospital, formed at Elvas, and to return at once to the regiment, from which I could not be spared. I arrived late in the day, placed my charge in safety, and returned to my regiment, having escaped an attack from some brigands whom I passed in the dark. They gave me a few shots to hasten my return.[26]

25. Green, William, *Where Duty Calls Me: The Experiences of William Green of Lutterworth in the Napoleonic Wars*, pp.36–43.
26. Dobbs, John, *Recollections of an Old 52nd Man*, p.26.

Chapter 11

Light Division Casualties at Badajoz

Badajoz was a victory for Wellington and his army, but for the Light Division it was an absolute disaster. During the 21 days of the siege, the division lost almost 1,350 men a staggering 34 per cent of its strength! One man in three were killed or wounded and many more were hospitalised due to the horrific living conditions.

Table 11.1: Light Division Casualties During the Siege of Badajoz 17 March–6 April 1812

	Killed or Died of Wounds			Wounded			Total
Unit	Officers	Sergeants	Men	Officers	Sergeants	Men	
43rd Foot	4	3	90	16	18	239	**370**
52nd Foot	5	4	60	18	24	305	**416**
1st Bn 95th Rifles	3	4	41	9	16	157	**230**
2nd Bn 95th Rifles	1	-	20	1	2	35	**59**
3rd Bn 95th Rifles	5	2	28	2	6	75	**118**
1st Caç	2	1	11	2	2	37	**55**
3rd Caç	1	-	49	7	2	41	**100**
Total	**21**	**14**	**299**	**55**	**70**	**889**	**1,348**

The casualties among the leaders were even higher. Of the 299 sergeants 39 per cent were killed or wounded. But this number was light compared to officer casualties. At the beginning of the siege 145 officers were present for duty.[1] The day after the assault eighty of them (55 per cent) were dead or wounded. Its already weakened senior leadership was down to one man. On 17 March, there were three lieutenant colonels, and five majors present with the colours. On 7 April, only the division commander, Lieutenant Colonel Barnard, was unscathed. Of its thirty-seven company commanders, i.e. captains, twenty-one (57 per cent) were killed or wounded. Fifty-three (52 per cent) of the subalterns were also casualties.

1. This number does not include the staff officers, such as the battalion's quartermaster and surgeons, but does include its adjutant. Nor does it include the officers assigned to the division staff.

Table 11.2: Light Division Officer Casualties During the Siege of Badajoz 17 March–6 April 1812

	Killed or Died of Wounds					Wounded					
Unit	LTC	Maj	Cpt	LT	Ens	LTC	Maj	Cpt	LT	Ens	Total
43rd Foot	1	-	-	3	-	-	1	3	12	-	20
52nd Foot	-	-	3	2	-	-	1	5	9	3	23
1st Bn 95th Rifles	-	1	-	2	-	-	-	4	5	1	13
2nd Bn 95th Rifles	-	-	1	-	-	-	-	-	1	-	2
3rd Bn 95th Rifles	-	-	-	5	-	-	-	1	2	2	10
1st Caç	-	-	1	1	-	-	1	-	-	1	4
3rd Caç	-	-	1	-	-	1	1	2	2	1	8
Total	1	1	6	13	-	1	4	15	31	8	80

The above table only tells part of the story. It does not differentiate between the severely wounded and the slightly wounded, which were often unreported. There was a tradition among the British officers that unless an individual was hospitalised, he was not reported as being wounded. However, many of the contemporary sources list officers who were slightly wounded. For example, Lieutenant John Cooke, 43rd Foot, was not listed in the returns as being wounded, however he was wounded in the head during the assault.

Although data is available for the number of severely wounded among both the British and Portuguese units of the division, how long the officer was hospitalised is only known for the British units. Their wounds varied from the loss of an eye or an amputation of a limb to being shot in the body. Those with the most serious wounds were treated and once stabilised were usually sent back to England by July to recover. However, two officers from the 1st Battalion 95th Rifles, Lieutenants Jonathan Forster and Richard Freer, were hospitalised for six months, before returning to England in October. Captain Robert Campbell, 52nd Foot, was so badly wounded, he could not be sent back to England until November. The average length of stay in a hospital for a severely wounded officer, before he was healthy enough to rejoin his unit, was two and a half months.

Table 11.3: Status of the Light Division's Severely Wounded Officers in the British Battalions

Rank	Total	Months Hospitalised			Returned to England
		1	2	3	
Lieutenant Colonel	1	-	-	-	1
Major	2	-	-	-	2
Captain	8	2	2	2	2
Lieutenant	23	1	6	4	12
Ensign / Second Lieutenant	6	-	2	1	3
Total	40	3	10	7	20

Table 11.4: British Regiments Officers Killed or Severely Wounded and Returned to England (RTE)

	LTC		Maj		Cpt		LT		Ens/2LT		Total	Total of Officers on 17 March	Per Cent of Officers Lost
	KIA	RTE	KIA	RTE	KIA	RTE	KIA	RTE	KIA	RTE			
43rd Foot	1	-	-	1	-	-	3	5	-	-	10	31	32%
52nd Foot	-	-	-	1	4	2	2	3	-	2	14	29	48%
1st Bn 95th	-	-	1	-	1	-	2	4	-	-	8	30	27%
2nd Bn 95th	-	-	-	-	1	-	-	1	-	-	2	4	50%
3rd Bn 95th	-	-	-	-	-	-	5	-	-	-	5	17	29%
Total	1	-	1	2	6	2	12	13	-	2	39	111	35%

Those who went to England were the most seriously wounded. There was little hope that any of the twenty would return within the year. When added to the nineteen killed or died of wounds, the regiments lost 35 per cent of its officers for the foreseeable future. Over the next twenty-three months, thirteen came back to their regiment in the Peninsula. The average length they were on convalescent leave, from the time they were wounded in April 1812, was fourteen months. Two of the officers did not return until 1814.

The following is the list of casualties in each regiment. Some regiments separated the casualties by date while others reported them at the end of the siege and did not show when they occurred.

The 43rd Foot

The date a soldier who was killed was noted in the regimental muster rolls. If a soldier was not available for duty because he was in the hospital, he was listed as being sick. There is no way of determining if he was sick or wounded by examining the muster rolls. At the end of the siege, the regiment provided its HQ with the number of killed and wounded, but not when they became a casualty. An examination of the muster rolls show that five privates were killed in the trenches. All others were killed or died of wounds from the assault on 6 April.

Table 11.5: The 43rd Foot Casualties 17 March–6 April 1812

Killed or Died of Wounds			Wounded			Total
Officers	Sergeants	Men	Officers	Sergeants	Men	
4	3	90	16	18	239	370

Table 11.6: The 43rd Foot Officer Casualties 17 March–6 April 1812

Killed or Died of Wounds					Wounded					
LTC	Maj	Cpt	LT	Ens	LTC	Maj	Cpt	LT	Ens	Total
1	-	-	3	-	-	1	3	12	-	20

The officer casualties were:

Lieutenant Colonel Charles McLeod

McLeod twice led the attack on the breach. During the second attempt he

> was killed while trying to force the left corner of the large breach. He received his mortal wound within three yards of the enemy, just at the bottom of some nine feet planks, studded with nails, and hanging down

> the breach from under the chevaux-de-frise. A few moments before he fell, he had been wounded in the back by a bayonet of one of our soldiers, who slipped.[2]

Private Anthony Hamilton was asked to dig the grave for him and with another soldier buried him on a hill about 800m from the south walls of the town.[3]

> We did not like to take him to the miserable breach, where, from the warmth of the weather, the dead soldiers had begun to turn, and their blackened bodies had swollen enormously; we, therefore, laid him amongst some young springing corn; and, with sorrowful hearts, six of us (all that remained of the officers able to stand) saw him covered in the earth. His cap, all muddy, was handed to me, I being without one.[4]

Major Joseph Wells

Wells was severely wounded during the assault and was sent to England in June to recover.

Captain James Fergusson

Fergusson was severely wounded by a shell splinter in the side on 29 March but had recovered enough to volunteer for the storming party. He was wounded in the head during the assault on the breach. Before long he was hospitalised in Castelo Branco due to the wound he received at Ciudad Rodrigo. The musket ball that was lodged close to his spine incapacitated him and it was eventually removed. Despite the seriousness of his wound, he rejoined the regiment at Fuenteguinaldo by the end of May.[5]

Captain George Johnston

Johnston was slightly wounded in the groin.

Captain Thomas Strode

Strode was slightly wounded but not hospitalised.

---

2. Cooke, John, 'The Storming of Badajoz', *Stories of the Peninsular War*, p.145.
3. Hamilton, Anthony, *Hamilton's Campaign With Moore and Wellington During the Peninsular War*, p.126.
4. Cooke, John, 'The Storming of Badajoz', *Stories of the Peninsular War*, p.154.
5. Hall, John, *Biographical Dictionary of British Officers Killed and Wounded, 1808–1814*, p.202, and Fergusson, James, *Men of Wellington's Light Division: Unpublished Memoirs of the 43rd (Monmouthshire) Regiment in the Peninsular War*, p.79.

Lieutenant Mackay Baillie

Baillie was severely wounded and hospitalised in Castelo Branco. He was back with his regiment by the end of May.

Lieutenant Thomas Capel

Capel was severely wounded and went to England in July. He did not return until April 1813.

Lieutenant James Considine

Considine was severely wounded but back with the regiment by the end of June.

Lieutenant John Cooke

Cooke was slightly wounded in the head that caused one of his eyes to swell shut and in the leg. He bandaged himself with a handkerchief and never sought treatment for either wound.[6]

Lieutenant Edward Freer

Freer was seriously wounded by a musket ball in the right testicle. He was also slightly wounded in the left arm by a musket ball.[7] He was hospitalised at Estremoz, but was back with the regiment by the end of June.

Lieutenant William Freer

Freer was wounded three times. The most serious was by a musket ball in the right arm which shattered the bone. His arm was amputated above the elbow. He was also shot in the buttock; the musket ball being removed a few days after his amputation. He also received a severe contusion in his knee by a rock.[8] He was evacuated to England on 16 May and did not rejoin the regiment until February 1813.

Lieutenant Horatio Harvest

Harvest was killed in action.

Lieutenant Augustus Hodgson

Hodgson was seriously wounded and died of his wounds on 8 April 1812.

6. Cooke, John, 'The Storming of Badajoz', *Stories of the Peninsular War*, p.154.
7. Freer, Edward, *With the 43rd in the Peninsula: The Letters of William Freer, Edward Freer and Daniel Gardner of the 43rd Foot (1808–15)*, p.104.
8. Freer, William, *With the 43rd in the Peninsula: The Letters of William Freer, Edward Freer and Daniel Gardner of the 43rd Foot (1808–15)*, pp.103 and 105.

Lieutenant Wyndham Madden

Madden was severely wounded by a musket ball. The day after the assault he was found by Lieutenant Cooke 'lying in a tent with his trowsers [*sic*] on and his shirt off, covered with blood, bandaged across the body to support his broken shoulder, laid on his back, and unable to move.'[9] His healing was slow and he could not write, so he had Lieutenant Considine write a letter to his parents on 18 May saying he was could sleep almost all the night long without the aid of opium &c. A week later he wrote home again that the 'swelling on my shoulder has at last come to a head and today they are going to let it out, by which means they will be able in a day or two to put my arm into splints, oh, how happy I shall be when I can tell you I am on my way to Lisbon.'[10] He was overly optimistic about getting home leave in June, and it was not until September that he was allowed to go home to recover. He returned to the regiment in October 1813. Lieutenant Madden was fortunate to be under the care of one of the foremost surgeons in the army, Staff Surgeon George Guthrie, who performed the surgery. He found that the musket ball 'fractured the head of the [right] humerus, and lodged in it. The broken pieces were from time to time removed by incisions, together with the ball and he ultimately preserved a very serviceable arm.'[11]

Lieutenant John O'Connell

O'Connell was slightly wounded but never hospitalised.

Lieutenant Henry Oglander

Oglander was severely wounded in his left arm which had to be amputated. He was also wounded in the thigh.[12] He was very sick for the first six weeks after the surgery and came down with lockjaw. He finally continued writing in his diary on 19 May

> I have been speedily regaining my health & strength; had not a most violent attack of spasms in my limbs & sometimes even in my stomach thrown me back and reduced me to a dreadful state of languor & debility. This most dangerous disorder was however fortunately conquered by the application of large doses of laudanum, taken both exteriorly & interiorly. To regain lost strength was also a work of difficulty & time & I was only supported

9. Cooke, John, 'The Storming of Badajoz', *Stories of the Peninsular War*, p.156.
10. Madden, Wyndham, *Men of Wellington's Light Division: Unpublished Memoirs of the 43rd (Monmouthshire) Regiment in the Peninsular War*, p.182.
11. Crumplin, Michael, *Guthrie's War: A Surgeon of the Peninsula & Waterloo*, p.85.
12. Hall, John, *Biographical Dictionary of British Officers Killed and Wounded, 1808–1814*, p.449.

> by high living. I was ordered to take a bottle & even a bottle and a half of Madeira in the course of a day; besides jellies and any other nourishing thing I could procure. A weakness in my jaws, nearly amounting to a lock jaw, prevents me from using any food but such as could be given in a liquid or very soft state, so that I was precluded from the use of many sources of nourishment.[13]

Oglander was promoted to captain in the 47th Foot on 2 April and on 7 July he went home to England to recover his health.

Lieutenant Samuel Pollock

Pollock was severely wounded in the foot during the assault.[14] According to regimental lore, he

> lay suffering in his tent, a private of his company brought him an offering of three fine fowls, remarking that they would make good broth. This man had been rather a disorderly character, and Pollock had on many occasions administered punishments. He was therefore surprised by the act, and said, 'you are the last man in the company from whom I should expect such attention.'
>
> 'Sir,' replied Howard, 'I have gratitude. You might have had me flogged twenty times; but, Sir, you always punished me yourself, and I have gratitude.'[15]

He went to England on 16 May and never returned to the Peninsula.

Lieutenant George Ridout

Ridout was severely wounded and hospitalised in Estremoz. Despite his wounds he rejoined his regiment by the beginning of July.

Lieutenant Charles Taggart

Taggart was killed in action on 6 April 1812.

Lieutenant Thomas Wilkinson

Wilkinson was severely wounded on 26 March and was hospitalised in Estremoz. He rejoined his regiment in June.

---

13. Oglander, Henry, *The Journals of Captain Henry Oglander of the 43rd & 47th Foot*, p.145.
14. Hall, John, *Biographical Dictionary of British Officers Killed and Wounded, 1808–1814*, p.471.
15. Levinge, Richard, *Historical Records of the Forty-Third Regiment Monmouthshire Light Infantry 1739 to 1867*, p.165.

The 52nd Foot

The 52nd Foot kept records of their casualties during the siege and the assault.

Table 11.7: The 52nd Foot Casualties 17 March–5 April 1812

	Killed or Died of Wounds			Wounded			Total
	Officers	Sergeants	Men	Officers	Sergeants	Men	
19–21 March	-	-	1	-	-	2	3
23–24 March	-	1	1	-	1	3	6
25 March	-	-	8	2	3	34	47
5 April	-	-	-	-	1	4	5
Total	-	1	10	2	5	43	61

Table 11.8: The 52nd Foot Casualties 6 April 1812

	Killed or Died of Wounds			Wounded			Total
	Officers	Sergeants	Men	Officers	Sergeants	Men	
6 April	5	3	50	16	19	262	355

Table 11.9: The 52nd Foot Casualties 17 March–6 April 1812

Killed or Died of Wounds			Wounded			Total
Officers	Sergeants	Men	Officers	Sergeants	Men	
5	4	60	18	24	305	416

Table 11.10: The 52nd Foot Officer Casualties 17 March–6 April 1812

Killed or Died of Wounds					Wounded					
LTC	Maj	Cpt	LT	Ens	LTC	Maj	Cpt	LT	Ens	Total
-	-	3	2	-	-	1	5	9	3	23

The officer casualties were:

Brevet Lieutenant Colonel Edward Gibbs

Gibbs lost an eye in the assault and returned to England on 13 May. He would not rejoin the regiment for a year.

Captain Robert Campbell

Campbell was severely wounded by a shot in his arm.[16] He was hospitalised until November when he was sent back to England.

16. Dawson, Henry, *Redcoats of Wellington's Light Division: Unpublished & Rare Memoirs of the 52nd (Oxfordshire) Regiment of Foot*, p.145.

Captain John Ewart

Ewart was severely wounded in the right arm near the shoulder on 25 March and spent the next seven weeks in the hospital in Estremoz. On 12 May, he was ordered to escort 200 of the division's convalescents north to join the division near Ciudad Rodrigo.[17] He would receive a year's additional pay because of his wound.

Captain William Jones

Jones was killed in the assault. After his body was recovered, it was discovered he had been shot fifteen times.[18]

Captain William Madden

Madden was killed in action on 6 April 1812.

Captain William Mein

Mein was shot through the left thigh at Ciudad Rodrigo, and was sent to a hospital in the rear. He had recovered enough to be at Badajoz. During the assault he was severely wounded by a shot in the right thigh.[19] He was hospitalised at Estremoz until July.

Captain Augustus Merry

Merry's leg was splintered by a cannonball, and he refused to have it amputated.[20] He died on 9 April 1812.

Captain Clement Poole

Poole was killed in action on 6 April 1812.

Lieutenant George Barlow

> was first hit in the thigh when the column approached the glacis; the ball carried away a canteen hanging down my back by cutting in two the leather strap to which it was affixed, and taking a downward direction lodged a little below the right hip bone…The pain in a few moments decreased

---

17. Dawson, Henry, *Redcoats of Wellington's Light Division: Unpublished & Rare Memoirs of the 52nd (Oxfordshire) Regiment of Foot*, p.143, and Hall, John, *Biographical Dictionary of British Officers Killed and Wounded, 1808–1814*, p.195.
18. Napier, *At War With Wellington: The Peninsular War Letters of William, George and Charles Napier*, p.114.
19. Hall, John, *Biographical Dictionary of British Officers Killed and Wounded, 1808–1814*, p.402.
20. Napier, *At War With Wellington: The Peninsular War Letters of William, George and Charles Napier*, p.145, and Cooke, John, 'The Storming of Badajoz', *Stories of the Peninsular War*, p.148.

> however and about a quarter of an hour afterwards as the column moved forwards, I got over the palisades of the ditch, was shown some ladders a little on the left. I turned half round to the men telling them to follow me thither and waving my cap when the second shot struck my right arm, chapeau dropt quick enough as you may suppose and I not being able to hold out any longer, with great difficulty persuaded a couple of soldiers (Portuguese) to help me off. They wanted me to lay flat on the glacis in company with them till the fire which was very heavy should abate a little. To this I would not agree, feeling myself growing fainter every instant from loss of blood. A British soldier coming past with a bearer at that moment, lifted me into it and carried me to the surgeons.[21]

Lieutenant Barlow went before a medical board and was sent to England on 16 May. He did not return for a year.

Lieutenant Robert Blackwood

Blackwood was severely wounded in the arm and his friends thought he would lose it. In June he went to England to recuperate.[22]

Lieutenant Charles Booth

Booth was killed in action on 6 April 1812.

Lieutenant Francis Davies

Davies was shot just as he got into the ditch.

> I lay on the ground for a few minutes, when I found myself so well that I got up and went on to the breach, there I found a great crowd, the men could not get on, I stayed there for about ten minutes when I turned so sick with the loss of blood that I layed [*sic*] down at the bottom of the breach. That soon went off and I went on again, I was in the breach about a quarter of an hour longer, when the men finding that they could not get on, began to fall back. In going back I got a shot through my cap, which I felt graze my hair, another shot carried away the hook which is attached to the belt for fastening up the sword and another hit my scabbard. I lost my cap getting out of the ditch. When I got to the place where the regiment were forming, I found myself so stiff that I made the best of my way to the hospital.[23]

Although listed as slightly wounded, he would spend the next two months in the hospital.

---

21. Barlow, George Ulrich, *A Light Infantryman With Wellington: The Letters of Captain George Ulrich Barlow, 52nd and 69th Foot, 1808–1815*, p.147.
22. Dawson, Henry, *Redcoats of Wellington's Light Division: Unpublished & Rare Memoirs of the 52nd (Oxfordshire) Regiment of Foot*, p.58.
23. Davies, Francis, *Redcoats of Wellington's Light Division: Unpublished & Rare Memoirs of the 52nd (Oxfordshire) Regiment of Foot*, p.168.

Lieutenant Charles Dawson

Dawson was shot in the left calf trying to rally his men, who

> not liking to be under such a heavy fire ran to the ladders to ascend the counterscarp. I ran up also to get to the top in order to stop them, just as I arrived at the top, the shot struck me, I hobbled away as fast as I could until I got to the bottom of the glacis, where I found the most part of the division assembling ready to make another attack, from thence I was carried to the hospital where I soon got dressed. My leg contracted directly after the blood began to get cool & has been so ever since, but I think it will get straight again whenever I can begin to walk.[24]

Two days later the ball still had not been removed. He arrived at the hospital at Elvas on 15 April and expected

> to move on a spring waggon tomorrow to Estremoz. The ball bring [*sic*] still on occasions very severe pain, having as it is supposed bruised the muscle of the leg and remaining near the nerve, which it occasionally touches, it went in in the inner part of the left leg, 6 inches below the knee, and the leg is so swelled, the ball cannot be felt.[25]

He returned to England in June to recuperate.

Lieutenant Henry Dawson

Dawson was slightly wounded in the leg, but it did not prevent him from marching with his regiment when it moved north in mid-April. By 27 April it 'had put on such an ugly appearance as to alarm me & my doctor, but by good care & paying proper attention to his advice, I have been able to walk about a little and to ride for an hour today, and do not find my leg the worse for it.'[26] His wound did not heal and he had to stay behind in Portalegre when the regiment marched north. On 5 May, he returned to the hospital in Estremoz where he remained until July.

Lieutenant Charles Kinloch

Kinloch was shot by 'a musket ball [that] entered my left shoulder but without damaging the bone & was extracted from my back…besides my wound I was

---

24. Dawson, Charles, *Redcoats of Wellington's Light Division: Unpublished & Rare Memoirs of the 52nd (Oxfordshire) Regiment of Foot*, p.163.
25. Ibid, p.162.
26. Dawson, Henry, *Redcoats of Wellington's Light Division: Unpublished & Rare Memoirs of the 52nd (Oxfordshire) Regiment of Foot*, pp.146–147.

absolutely bruised by stones etc from top to toe & my cap shot through into the bargain.'[27] He was listed as only being slightly wounded but it was serious enough for him to be sent to England in May. He would not rejoin the regiment for nineteen months.

Lieutenant James McNair

McNair was seriously wounded in the head and spent the next two months recovering.[28]

Lieutenant William Royds

Royds was slightly wounded during the assault but was not hospitalised.

Lieutenant Job Royle

Royle was killed in action on 6 April 1812.

Lieutenant Charles Yorke

Yorke was slightly wounded and was hospitalised until July when he rejoined the regiment.

Ensign George Gawler

Gawler was

> struck by a musket ball on the bone of the right knee, and rolled over the left face of the ravelin into three or four feet of water. Just as I fell, the discharge of a field piece from the flank of Santa Maria passed close to me…Holding on to the bank, I got out of the water a yard or two from the salient angle of the unfinished ravelin, and was in the ditch until after the bugles had concluded sounding the retreat.[29]

A soldier of the 52nd Foot found him and made the young ensign grab his accoutrements so that he could 'drag him up' a ladder, 'or,' said he, 'the enemy will come out and bayonet you.'[30] Ensign Gawler survived the assault, but his rescuer was killed helping him. His medical certificate described the wound as a musket ball that 'entered about two inches below the patella of the right knee, passed over the head of the tibia, and came out about two inches from

27. Kinloch, Charles, *A Hellish Business: The Letters of Captain Charles Kinloch, 52nd Light Infantry 1806–1816*, p.96.
28. Hall, John, *Biographical Dictionary of British Officers Killed and Wounded,1808–1814*, p.381.
29. C.W.N., *George Gawler, K.H., 52nd Light Infantry: A Life Sketch*, p.12.
30. Moorsom, William, *Historical Record of the Fifty-Second Regiment*, p.170.

the place it entered, injuring the part so much that he was incapacitated from performing military duty for three months.'[31] Gawler was hospitalised until July when he returned to the regiment.

Ensign George Hall

Hall was severely wounded on 22 March. At first it was thought to not be very serious, but he was eventually hospitalised and evacuated to England on 16 May.[32]

Ensign William Nixon

Nixon was severely wounded on 25 March and was evacuated to England on 11 June.

Adjutant John Winterbottom

Winterbottom was wounded slightly in the head during the assault. He was never listed as being hospitalised.

The 1st Battalion 95th Rifles

Like the 43rd Foot, the 1st Battalion only the date a soldier who was killed was noted in the regimental muster rolls. If a soldier was not available for duty because he was in the hospital, he was listed as being sick. There is no way of determining if he was sick or wounded by examining the muster rolls. At the end of the siege, the regiment provided its HQ with the number of killed and wounded, but not when they became a casualty. An examination of the muster rolls show that one sergeant and seven privates were killed in the trenches. All others were killed or died of wounds from the assault on 6 April.

Table 11.11: The 1st Battalion 95th Rifles Officer Casualties 17 March–6 April 1812

Killed or Died of Wounds					Wounded					
LTC	Maj	Cpt	LT	Ens	LTC	Maj	Cpt	LT	Ens	Total
-	1	-	2	-	-	-	4	5	-	12

31. C.W.N., *George Gawler, K.H., 52nd Light Infantry: A Life Sketch*, p.13.
32. Dawson, Charles, *Redcoats of Wellington's Light Division: Unpublished & Rare Memoirs of the 52nd (Oxfordshire) Regiment of Foot*, p.161, and theatre returns May 1812.

The officer casualties were:

Major Peter O'Hare
O'Hare was killed in action on 6 April 1812. He was found by Lieutenant Simmons who saw 'two or three musket balls had passed through his breast. A gallant fellow, Sergeant [Patrick] Flemming, was also dead by his side, a man who had always been with him…I was now gazing upon his body lying stretched and naked amongst thousands more.'[33]

Captain William Balvaird
Balvaird was severely wounded and was hospitalised in Elvas for two months. He rejoined the battalion in early July.

Captain Jeremiah Crampton
Crampton was severely wounded and was hospitalised in Elvas until 5 July when he was sent back to England. He died from his wounds on 18 September 1812.

Captain Loftus Gray
Gray was severely wounded in the mouth during[34] the assault and spent two months in the hospital at Elvas. He was back with the battalion by late June.

Captain John McDiarmid
McDiarmid was slightly wounded in the assault but never hospitalised.

First Lieutenant Jonathan Forster
Forster was shot four times[35] and spent the next six months hospitalised. He was sent back to England on 13 October.

First Lieutenant Richard Freer
Freer was severely wounded during the French sortie on 20 March. He was originally hospitalised in Elvas but was moved to Estremoz in May. He stayed there until 13 October when he was sent back to England.

First Lieutenant James Gairdner
Gairdner was severely wounded in the assault where he

33. Simmons, George, *A British Rifleman: Journals and Correspondence During the Peninsular War and the Campaign of Wellington*, pp.231–232.
34. Ibid, p.229.
35. Boyle, Gerald, *Rifle Brigade Century: An Alphabetical List of the Officers of the Rifle Brigade (The Prince Consort's Own) (Regular Battalions) from 1800 to 1905*, p.64.

> received three wounds early in the attack, viz. one in the right leg, very slight, one in the left arm and one in the chin. and after lying on the ground was at last helped off by a sergeant of our company and with the assistance of some of the 52nd band who were coming with bearers carried to the hospital tent where my wounds were dressed and I was then put into a tent for the reception of wounded officers.[36]

Lieutenant Gairdner initially shared a house in Badajoz with Lieutenants Fitzmaurice and Johnston but was moved to Elvas on 16 April and then to Estremoz two days later. On 20 April, he went before a medical board and was found that his wounds were not serious enough to warrant sending him back to England. He rejoined the battalion on 24 June.

First Lieutenant William Johnston

Johnston was severely wounded in the arm. Lieutenant Kincaid found him in a tent with a 'shattered arm bandaged; he was lying on his boat cloak fast asleep; and, coupling his appearance with the recollection of the daring duty he had been called on to perform but a few hours before, in front of the forlorn hope, I thought that I had never set my eyes on a nobler picture of a soldier.'[37] He was sent to England in June to recover and would not return to the battalion until March 1814.

First Lieutenant Donald McPherson

McPherson died of his wounds on 7 May 1812.

First Lieutenant James Stokes

Stokes was killed in action on 6 April 1812.

Second Lieutenant John Fitzmaurice

Fitzmaurice was shot in the right leg, which broke it. He was initially kept in a house in Badajoz but then sent by a bullock cart to Elvas and eventually by boat to Lisbon. In June he was evacuated to England and did not return until March 1813.[38]

The 2nd Battalion 95th Rifles

The 2nd Battalion 95th Rifles had one rifleman killed during the siege and nineteen during the assault.

36. Gairdner, James, *The American Sharpe: The Adventures of an American Officer of the 95th Rifles in the Peninsula & Waterloo Campaigns*, p.45.
37. Kincaid, John, *Random Shots from a Rifleman*, p.162.
38. Fitzmaurice, John, *A Biographical Sketch of Major General John Fitzmaurice*, p.30.

Table 11.12: The 2nd Battalion 95th Rifles Casualties 17 March–6 April 1812

Killed or Died of Wounds			Wounded			Total
Officers	Sergeants	Men	Officers	Sergeants	Men	
1	-	20	2	2	35	**60**

Officer casualties included:

Captain Thomas Diggle
Diggle was killed in action on 6 April 1812.

First Lieutenant Henry Manners
Manners was severely wounded by a shot in the knee. He was hospitalised in Elvas until June when he was sent to England. He never returned to the Peninsula.

The 3rd Battalion 95th Rifles

The 3rd Battalion 95th Rifles had one sergeant, and ten riflemen killed, and two sergeants wounded during the siege. How many riflemen were wounded during the siege is unknown. Total casualties during the siege and assault were:

Table 11.13: The 3rd Battalion 95th Rifles Casualties 17 March–6 April 1812

Killed or Died of Wounds			Wounded			Total
Officers	Sergeants	Men	Officers	Sergeants	Men	
5	2	28	3	6	75	**119**

Table 11.14: The 3rd Battalion 95th Rifles Officer Casualties 17 March–6 April 1812

Killed or Died of Wounds					Wounded					
LTC	Maj	Cpt	LT	Ens	LTC	Maj	Cpt	LT	Ens	Total
-	-	-	5	-	-	-	1	4	-	**10**

Officer casualties included:

First Lieutenant William Allix
Allix was killed in action on 6 April 1812.

First Lieutenant Arthur Carey
Carey was severely wounded during the assault on 6 April and died of his wounds on 7 April. Quartermaster Surtees found him

> beneath one of the ladders by which they had descended into the ditch. He was shot through the head, and I doubt not received his death-wound on the ladder, from which in all probability he fell. He was stripped completely naked, save a flannel waistcoat which he wore next his skin. I had him taken up and placed upon a shutter, (he still breathed a little, though quite insensible,) and carried him to the camp. A sergeant and some men, whom we had pressed to carry him, were so drunk that they let him fall from off their shoulders, and his body fell with great force to the ground. I shuddered, but poor Cary, I believe, was past all feeling, or the fall would have greatly injured him. We laid him in bed in his tent, but it was not long ere my kind, esteemed, and lamented friend breathed his last...Cary was buried [the] next day behind the tents.[39]

First Lieutenant Christopher Croudace

Croudace was shot through the body and carried to the rear. He had just reached the aid station where he died.[40]

First Lieutenant Tarleton Hovenden

Hovenden was killed in action on 6 April 1812.

First Lieutenant Alexander MacDonnell

MacDonnell was severely wounded in the assault and died of his wounds on 7 August 1812.

First Lieutenant Duncan Stewart

Stewart was severely wounded during the assault but was able to rejoin his battalion by the middle of June.

Second Lieutenant Walter Firman

Firman was severely wounded during the assault and was unable to join his battalion until July.

Second Lieutenant Thomas Worsley

Worsley had just turned 18 years old two days before when he was severely wounded in the assault by a musket ball 'in the right ear, which came out at the back of the neck, and though after a painful illness, he recovered, yet his head got a twist, and he was compelled to wear it, looking over the right shoulder.'[41]

39. Surtees, William. *Twenty-Five Years in the Rifle Brigade,* p.146.
40. Ibid.
41. Kincaid, John, *Random Shots from a Rifleman,* p.173.

Second Lieutenant Worsley spent the next two months in the hospital but by late June had recovered enough to rejoin his battalion.

The 1st Caçadores and 3rd Caçadores

Unlike the British battalions, the division's Portuguese battalions provided daily casualty reports during the siege.

Table 11.15: The 1st and 3rd Caçadores Casualties During the Siege of Badajoz 17 March–5 April 1812[42]

	Killed or Died of Wounds			Wounded			Total
	Officers	Sergeants	Men	Officers	Sergeants	Men	
1st Caç	-	-	1	-	-	14	15
3rd Caç	-	-	15	-	-	11	26
Total	-	-	16	-	-	25	41

Despite losing their battalion commanders during the assault, the two battalions still provided casualty returns for the assault.

Table 11.16: The 1st and 3rd Caçadores Casualties During the Assault on Badajoz 6 April 1812[43]

	Killed or Died of Wounds			Wounded			Total
	Officers	Sergeants	Men	Officers	Sergeants	Men	
1st Caç	2	1	10	2	2	23	40
3rd Caç	1	-	34	7	2	30	74
Total	3	1	44	9	4	53	114

The total casualties for the two caçadore battalions were:

Table 11.17: Total Casualties the 1st and 3rd Caçadores Casualties at Badajoz 17 March–6 April 1812[44]

	Killed or Died of Wounds			Wounded			Total
	Officers	Sergeants	Men	Officers	Sergeants	Men	
1st Caç	2	1	11	2	2	37	55
3rd Caç[45]	1	-	49	7	2	41	100
Total	3	1	60	9	4	78	155

42. PT-AHM-DIV-1-14-057-05 M0003.
43. PT-AHM-DIV-1-14-057-05 M0001.
44. PT-AHM-DIV-1-14-057-05 M0004.
45. The 1st Company, 3rd Caçadores was detached, probably with the storming party. All three of its officers were casualties. Its commander, Captain Powell Morphew, was killed, while

The officer casualties included:

The 1st Caçadores

Major John Henry Algeo
Algeo was slightly wounded.

Captain Donald MacDonald
MacDonald died from his wounds on 9 April 1812.

Lieutenant José Maria Velez Juzarte
Juzarte was killed during the assault.

Ensign Feliciano Rebelo
Rebelo was severely wounded during the assault.

The 3rd Caçadores

Lieutenant Colonel George Elder
Elder passed out from his wounds and his troops thought he was dead. He was trampled by troops moving forward, which revived him. He saw that they were riflemen and he 'had just strength enough to exclaim, as they crossed his body, "Elder, Elder!" when two of his former company lifted him up and carried him into Badajoz.'[46] A day later Surgeon Charles Forbes was taken to the house where Lieutenant Colonel Elder laid and found him with 'severe and dangerous wounds. Whilst apparently doing well, he was seized with locked jaw, which placed him in imminent danger. Contrary to all expectation [*sic*], he recovered. But he has ever since been subject to severe spasms, not only extremely distressing, but very alarming whilst they continue.'[47] He likely went to England in June and did not come back to the Peninsula until November 1813.

Major Manuel Pinto da Silveira
Silveira was severely wounded in the assault.

---

its two subalterns, Lieutenant João Crisóstomo Correia and Ensign José Joaquim Teixeira Pinto, were severely wounded.

46. *Memoirs of General and Flag-Officers Recently Deceased: Major General Sir George Elder. United Services Journal*, pp.236–237.
47. Forbes, Charles, 'Table Talk of an Old Campaigner', *United Services Journal*, p.54.

Captain Joaquim Inácio de Araújo
Araújo of the 4th Company, was severely wounded in the assault.

Captain William Dobbin
Dobbin of the 5th Company was severely wounded and received a temporary pension of £100 per year.

Captain Powell Morphew
Morphew of the 1st Company was killed during the assault.

Lieutenant João Crisóstomo Correia
Correia of the 1st Company was severely wounded in the assault.

Lieutenant Martinho de Magalhães Peixoto
Peixoto of the 6th Company was severely wounded in the assault.

Ensign José Joaquim Teixeira Pinto
Pinto of the 1st Company was severely wounded in the assault.

Chapter 12

The Return to Ciudad Rodrigo 9 April–30 April 1812

For several days after the fall of Badajoz, soldiers returned to their bivouacs. Many brazenly carried their loot as if they had not a care in the world. The soldier who was Lieutenant Kincaid's servant had been missing since the assault and Lieutenant Kincaid had thought he was dead. On 9 April,

> he turned up this morning, with a tremendous gash on his head, and mounted on the top of a horse nearly twenty feet high, carrying under his arm one of those glass cases which usually stand on the counters of jewellers' shops, filled with all manner of trinkets. He looked exactly like the ghost of a horse peddler.[1]

While the soldiers were sacking the city word had reached Wellington, that Marshal Marmont, the commander of the French forces closest to Ciudad Rodrigo, had marched from Salamanca and was moving south to compel the Allies to lift the Siege of Badajoz. Wellington had no option but to move his army north as soon as it was capable of marching. A warning order went out on 8 April to be ready to march, but considering that so many men were still plundering Badajoz, there was no expectation that they would move soon.

The Light Division began its march on 11 April, and it was quite a sight.

> The march of the troops presented the most warlike appearance. Many of the soldiers' blood-stained and torn uniforms were discoloured from explosions; numbers of the soldiers held their arms in slings, and carried their firelocks and caps slung on their knapsacks; whilst others were seen with bandaged heads, or lame from contusions through wounds inflicted by the iron-crows' feet with which the enemy had strewed the ditch of Badajoz.[2]

Captain Harry Smith, the brigade major of the 2nd Brigade, said that the division was so disorganised that 'it became the duty of every officer to exert

1. Kincaid, John, *Adventures in the Rifle Brigade in the Peninsula, France, and the Netherlands from 1809–1815*, p.141.
2. Cooke, John, *A True Soldier Gentleman: The Memoirs of Lt. John Cooke 1791–1813*, p.129.

himself, and nobly did Colonel Barnard set about the task, and ably supported was he by every officer in the Division. We had not marched for the north two days when our soldiers were, like Richard, themselves again.'[3]

The route north was very familiar to the men. It was the fourth time in ten months that they had taken it.

Table 12.1: The March North 11 April–26 April 1812[4]

Date	Stopping Point	Distance Travelled
11 April	Campo Maior	25km
12 April	Arronches	25km
13 April	Portalegre	25km
14 April	Nisa	35km
15 April	Vila Velha to Retaxo	40km
16 April	Castelo Branco	15km
17 April	Halt	
18 April	Escalos de Baixo via Lousã	15km
19 April	Halt	
20 April	São Miguel de Acha	20km
21 April	Penamacor	25km
22 April	Sabugal	35km
23 April	Alfaiates via Aldeia Velha	25km
24 April	Fuenteguinaldo	25km
25 April	Halt	
26 April	El Bodón	12km

The march was at a fairly leisurely pace, averaging about 20km per day with a halt every seventh day. Wellington wanted to pressure the French to return to Salamanca but needed to do so without committing his weakened army to a fight. Major John Hunt described the march.

> This movement was made in consequence of Marmont entering Portugal & ravaging the whole country in the direction of [blank] & as far as Castelo Branco [*sic*], where I am sorry to say, he found a considerable supply of provisions. Luckily the bridge over the Tagus at Vila Velha was removed in

3. Smith, Harry, *The Autobiography of Sir Harry Smith*, pp.72–73. 'Richard himself again' is a misquote from Shakespeare's play *Richard III*. It means that the individual has returned to normal.
4. Hunt, John, 'Peninsular War Diary', *Redcoats of Wellington's Light Division: Unpublished & Rare Memoirs of the 52nd (Oxfordshire) Regiment of Foot*, pp.36–37.

> time, therefore no time was lost in reconstructing it when we arrived at Nisa. The enemy retired before us and I understand that as soon as Marmont, who had proceeded towards Celerico [*sic*]where we had a magazine, heard [that] the Light Division had crossed, he faced about & retired with the utmost celerity. The whole of their track was marked with devastation and even in Spain (particularly at El Bodon) they behaved in an unprecedented cruel manner to the inhabitants.[5]

Quartermaster William Surtees, 3rd Battalion, 95th Rifles, had not served with Wellington's Army before, and had never seen the destruction a French foraging party caused. He was shocked by what he witnessed.

> The utter desolation of Sabugal was beyond conception; filth and misery presented themselves in every direction. It had been made a depot for provisions by the French, I imagine, for on all sides the entrails and other offal of bullocks and sheep polluted the atmosphere by the abominable stench they caused, and had attracted multitudes of vultures and other birds of prey, who had by this time become horribly tame and familiar: one vulture sat so long upon a dead horse as I was riding along the road, that he allowed me to come near enough to make a cut at him with my sword, as he stretched his enormous wings to mount up from his prey.[6]

After marching two weeks, the division was in its cantonments close to where it had stayed in the autumn of 1811. It would spend the next six weeks resting and rebuilding its strength in the vicinity of La Encina.

Table 12.2: Organisation of the Light Division 30 April 1812

Unit	Personnel	Position
Division HQ	LTC Andrew Barnard	Acting Commander
	LT James Shaw 43rd Foot	ADC
	LT William Armstrong 19th Light Dragoons	ADC
	LT John Bell 52nd Foot	DAQMG
	Maj Charles Rowan 52nd Foot	AAG
	Charles Purcell	ACG
	Wentworth Parker	CH
1st Brigade	Bvt Maj William Napier[7]	Acting Commander
	Cpt Charles Beckwith 95th Rifles	Brigade Maj

5. Ibid, p.37.
6. Surtees, William, *Twenty-Five Years in the Rifle Brigade*, p.154.
7. Brevet Major Napier rejoined the regiment on 24 April 1812.

Unit	Personnel	Position
1st Bn 43rd Foot	Cpt John Duffy	Acting Commander
RW 1st Bn 95th Rifles	Cpt John McDiarmid	Acting Commander
2nd Bn 95th Rifles	LT Edward Coxen	Acting Commander
2nd Bn 95th Rifles	Cpt John Hart	Commander
3rd Bn 95th Rifles	Cpt William Percival	Commander
3rd Caç Bn	Maj Agregado Charles F.W. Maclean	Acting Commander
2nd Brigade	Bvt LTC John Hunt, 52nd Foot	Acting Commander
	Cpt Harry Smith 95th Rifles	Brigade Maj
1st Bn 52nd Foot	Cpt John Douglas	Acting Commander
LW 1st Bn 95th Rifles	Bvt Maj Alexander Cameron	Commander
1st Caç Bn	Maj António Lobo Teixeira de Barros	Acting Commander

The Light Division started the year with about 4,400 men with the colours. On 25 April, it reported to HQ that it had about 3,100 men, a decrease of 1,300 or 30 per cent of its strength in four months.

Table 12.3: Strength of the Light Division 25 April 1812 Based on Theatre Returns

Unit	Officers						NCOs	MUS	Other Ranks	
	LTC	Maj	Cpt	LT	Ens	Adj	Sgt	MUS	Fit for Duty	Total
Staff	1	1	2	3	-	-	-	-	-	7
43rd Foot	-	1	8	22	3	-	63	23	529	**649**
52nd Foot	-	2	5	16	10	1	69	26	534	**663**
1st Bn 95th	-	-	7	17	8	1	52	20	420	**525**
2nd Bn 95th	-	-	1	2	1	-	10	2	95	**111**
3rd Bn 95th	-	-	4	7	4	-	26	9	178	**228**
1st Caç	1	1	5	6	5	1	36	12	371	**438**
3rd Caç	1	1	5	6	5	1	34	11	423	**487**
Total	**3**	**6**	**37**	**79**	**36**	**4**	**290**	**103**	**2,550**	**3,108**

However, these numbers are misleading. The theatre returns (which can be found in Appendix I) show every officer who was alive, but does not differentiate between those who were hospitalised and those who were fit for duty. For example, according to the theatre returns the 43rd Foot had thirty-four officers, yet fails to mention that eighteen of them were hospitalised due to wounds and many of them would be sent to England to recover. The 52nd Foot also lists thirty-four officers available, yet only fifteen were with the colours.

The problem was just not with the officers. The number of sergeants and musicians was also over-reported. Like officers, all sergeants and musicians were counted even if they were hospitalised or on command. The theatre returns reported 220 British sergeants with the colours, but an examination of the monthly payrolls, which gives the status of each sergeant, there were only 132, a 40 per cent difference in the numbers. Of the 95th Rifles, its 1st Battalion was missing half of their sergeants while its 3rd Battalion was missing 46 per cent of them. There were seventeen musicians in the British battalions, who were hospitalised, such as Bugler William Green. Yet they were listed as available for duty.

The one number in the returns that is fairly accurate is that for corporals and privates / riflemen. They are listed as either present and fit for duty, sick, or on command, which means they were on duty at a different location.

Another major issue are the returns for the 1st and 3rd Caçadores. Their returns, which can be found in Appendix II, show every officer assigned to the battalion from the previous month. Yet they had two captains and a lieutenant killed, and another eight officers severely wounded, including both commanders. The returns of 18 April 1812 also show officers who were no longer with the battalion, such as Lieutenant Colonel Jorge de Avilez, the commander of the 1st Caçadores in 1811. He left the battalion in October 1811 and was promoted to colonel in February 1812 and given command of the 2nd Infantry Regiment.

The numbers for the sergeants, musicians, and other ranks are also a problem. The returns for April list more sergeants with the two battalions than there were the previous month, despite having one killed and four wounded. This could be accounted for by promotion from the ranks, but since no monthly payrolls could be found, it is hard to say if that was what occurred. The other ranks also have discrepancies. The 1st Caçadores only show a decrease of two soldiers in the total number of soldiers with the colours, while the 3rd Caçadores show an increase of nine soldiers. The number of men hospitalised also shows a discrepancy, for the 3rd Caçadores. The battalion had forty-one men wounded during the siege and this should have been reflected in the number of men hospitalised in the monthly returns. Instead of seeing an increased there was a decreased of ten men hospitalised from the previous months. The number of reported dead is also a problem. The returns for the 1st and 3rd Caçadores show five dead and two dead for the two battalions respectively. Yet according to the official casualty returns for the siege eleven men were killed or died of wounds in the 1st Caçadores and forty-nine in the 3rd Caçadores.

When the figures are adjusted to include only the officers that were reported with the battalion and combined with the number of sergeants and musicians listed in the British payrolls as being present for duty, the number is even smaller.

Table 12.4: Strength of the Light Division 25 April 1812 Based on Payrolls and Officer Casualties

Unit	Officers								Other Ranks	
	LTC	Maj	Cpt	LT	Ens	Adj	Sgt	MUS	Fit for Duty	Total
Staff	1	1	2	3	-	-	-	-	-	7
43rd Foot	-	-	6	7	1	1	41	19	529	**604**
52nd Foot	-	1	2	6	5	1	45	19	534	**613**
1st Bn 95th	-	-	2	9	6	1	26	18	420	**482**
2nd Bn 95th	-	-	1	1	-	-	7	2	95	**106**
3rd Bn 95th	-	-	4	4	2	-	14	5	178	**207**
1st Caç	-	1	5	4	4	-	36	12	371	**433**
3rd Caç	-		4	1	3	-	34	11	423	**476**
Total	**1**	**3**	**26**	**35**	**21**	**3**	**203**	**86**	**2,550**	**2,928**

Due to the incomplete data for the Portuguese, it is possible that they were reporting 50–100 more than there were actually present. If the division was ordered to undertake combat operations it probably could only field between 2,500 and 3,000 troops.

Experience of the Troops

On paper, the Light Division was one of the most experienced divisions in Wellington's Army. But was it in reality? In July 1811, the 43rd Foot received a large number of replacements which increased their number of other ranks by 33 per cent. Over the next five months the battalion saw no combat and were in cantonments, so they would not have the chance to become hardened campaigners. The 52nd Foot was in a similar situation. In February the remnants of its 2nd Battalion were sent home after exchanging its healthiest soldiers for the unfit soldiers in the 1st Battalion. This increased the 1st Battalion's strength by 36 per cent, but after Badajoz it had more soldiers hospitalised than it did fit for duty.

The riflemen of the 1st Battalion 95th Foot was the most experienced of any battalion in the division, if not in the army. Since the formation of the division in February 1810 it had received a total of seventy-two replacements, sixty-five of them had arrived in February 1812. This was the equivalent to 10 per cent of the battalion's strength. In terms of experience, this meant that 90 per cent of the soldiers had been in country since July 1809. They were hardened veterans whose record was second to none. They knew how to survive on campaign and fight. The two companies of the 2nd Battalion 95th Foot, were similar in experience, but had only been in country for about twenty months. The 3rd

Battalion 95th Foot had been in the Peninsula almost as long as the 1st Battalion, however much of that time it was in the garrison at Cádiz. It had only joined the division in August 1811 and had never been campaigning with it.

Little data is available to assess the combat effectiveness of the 1st and 3rd Caçadores. They fought well since joining the Light Division, but even as late as January 1812 they did not appear to be the first unit selected by the division for an operation. Things change at Ciudad Rodrigo, when Lieutenant Colonel Elder insisted that the 3rd Caçadores be part of the attack on the Renaud Redoubt. At Badajoz they were relegated to the reserve, but it was quickly committed, and they fought as hard as the British.

Leadership Problems

The real issue facing the division at the end of April was leadership. The division had a well-deserved reputation of its leaders leading from the front and sharing the dangers of its men. Of the 239 corporals assigned to the division on 25 April only 119 were with the colours. Twenty were killed in action or died of their wounds during the siege, while another ninety-nine were hospitalised. The sergeants, as shown previously, also took heavy casualties; only 133 British sergeants were present. Of them just fifty (38 per cent) had been sergeants when the division was formed in February 1810.

Experience of the Officers

The units that formed the Light Division were authorised 205 officers plus those on the staff. In late April it had seventy-eight with the colours, plus seven serving on the brigade and division staff. It was missing 62 per cent of its officers.

Although numbers make a difference, the experience of the officers was equally important. Experience was gained by performing the job under a variety of conditions. Commanding a company on campaign required different skills than commanding one in the garrison. The longer the individual held the position the more experience he had. The Light Division's problem was there were so many vacancies in the command structure that to fill those holes, the senior officers in the next lower grade were given temporary command. A lieutenant colonel was commanding the division, and two of its four majors were commanding its brigades. Of its six battalions, four were commanded by captains. Of its forty-seven companies, fifteen were commanded by lieutenants, and two by ensigns!

The 43rd Foot had the most experienced officers. Its acting commander, Brevet Major William Napier, went to England the previous August to recover from his wounds, but had been with the division since its formation in February 1810.

Table 12.5: Number of Officers Authorised Versus Number Present for Duty (PFD) 25 April 1812

Unit	LTC		Maj		Cpt		LT		Ens/2LT		Total with the Colours
	Auth	**PFD**	**Auth**	**PFD**	**Auth**	**PFD**	**Auth**	**PFD**	**Auth**	**PFD**	
1st Bn 43rd Foot	1	-	2	1	10	5	22	7	8	-	13 (30%)
1st Bn 52nd Foot	1	-	2	1	10	2	22	6	8	5	14 (33%)
1st Bn 95th Foot (8 Companies)	1	-	2	1	8	1	20	9	8	6	17 (47%)
2nd Bn 95th Foot (2 Companies)	-	-	-	-	2	1	4	1	2	-	2 (20%)
3rd Bn 95th Foot (5 Companies)	1	-	1	-	5	4	11	4	4	2	10 (45%)
1st Caç Bn	1	-	1	1	6	4	6	4	12	4	13 (50%)
3rd Caç Bn	1	-	1	-	6	4	6	1	12	3	8 (31%)
Total	**6**	-	**9**	**4**	**47**	**21**	**91**	**32**	**54**	**20**	77 (38%)

He returned in late April. Its captains had been in command for an average of four and a half years. The two senior captains would temporarily serve as the battalion's majors. Of its ten companies, three were commanded by captains; the other seven companies were commanded by lieutenants. Three officers, Captains George Johnston and John Hopkins, and Lieutenant Philip McPherson, had been with the battalion since it landed in Portugal in July 1809. Its real weakness was that should the battalion be sent on campaign it had only one officer per company, and he would be totally reliant on his sergeants and corporals.

Table 12.6: Officer Experience in the 43rd Foot 25 April 1812

Rank	Number of Officers	Time in Grade	Time With Division	Average Age
Brevet Major	1	8 Months	25 Months	26
Captains	5	43 Months	20 Months	34
Lieutenants	7	18 Months	15 Months	23

The 52nd Foot was in as bad of shape as the 43rd Foot. Its acting commander was Major John Philip Hunt, who had served during the 1811 campaign but went home in November 1811. He returned from England in time to for the assault on Badajoz. Two of its captains had over six years in command, but were the battalion's acting majors. Six of the companies were commanded by lieutenants and four by ensigns. Only one company would have more than one officer. One of its strengths was its adjutant, Lieutenant John Winterbottom, a former sergeant major. He had been with the battalion since its arrival in Portugal in July 1809. Lieutenants William Rintoul and Augustus Harvest had also been with the battalion since its arrival in Portugal.

Table 12.7: Officer Experience in the 52nd Foot 25 April 1812

Rank	Number of Officers	Time in Grade	Time With Division	Age
Major	1	41 Months	9 Months	31
Captains	2	77 Months	16 Months	34
Lieutenants	6	18 Months	19 Months	23
Ensigns	5	12 Months	7 Months	20

Forty per cent of the officers with the division were with the 1st Battalion 95th Rifles. On the surface this was a good thing, but fifteen of the seventeen officers were first and second lieutenants. The average length of time for the 2nd lieutenants being with the battalion was seven months. However, 2nd Lieutenant William Haggup had been with the battalion for nineteen months. If you remove him from the equation, the average length of time drops to five months. None of these five had been on a campaign. Two had not arrived until January 1812. Counter-balancing the relative inexperience of the second lieutenants were the six officers who had been with the battalion since it arrived in Portugal in July 1809. Among them were the four senior officers Brevet Major Alexander Cameron, Captain John McDiarmid, and First Lieutenants Thomas M'Namara and John Layton. Additionally, First Lieutenants George Simmons and Charles Traile had also been with the battalion since July 1809. On the whole, the 1st Battalion's lieutenants were very experienced. Seven of the nine lieutenants had been with the division since 1810. The battalion operated in two wings with Brevet Major Cameron commanding one and Captain McDiarmid the other. All eight companies would be commanded by first lieutenants and unlike the other battalions, every company except one would have a second officer.

Table 12.8: Officer Experience in the 1st Battalion 95th Rifles 25 April 1812

Rank	Number of Officers	Time in Grade	Time With Division	Age
Brevet Major	1	11 Months	26 Months	31
Captains	1	67 Months	26 Months	34
Lieutenants	9	23 Months	19 Months	24
Second Lieutenants	6	10 Months	7 Months	22

The two companies of the 2nd Battalion 95th Rifles had only a captain and a lieutenant between them. While in the garrison, they likely combined the two companies into one.

The 3rd Battalion 95th Rifles officers were the most junior officers in the 95th Rifles. The captains had been in command for three years but only with the division for less than a year. None had any recent campaign experience.

Table 12.9: Officer Experience in the 3rd Battalion 95th Rifles 25 April 1812

Rank	Number of Officers	Time in Grade	Time With Division	Age
Captains	4	35 Months	11 Months	28
Lieutenants	4	25 Months	9 Months	23
Second Lieutenants	2	7 Months	5 Months	20

Little data is available about the officers of 1st and 3rd Caçadores, except for their time of service with the Light Division. Almost every officer in both battalions had been with their battalion since it joined the division in 1810. Most of the captains had been in command of their companies since 1809, while the lieutenants had been commissioned for at least two years. Even the ensigns had at least seventeen months with the division. The one exception was

Major Agregado Charles Maclean, the acting commander of the 1st Caçadores. He was a British officer who had only been in country for six months. The real weakness of the caçadores was the lack of officers. The 1st Caçadores had thirteen officers present for duty, while the 3rd Caçadores had only eight.

Table 12.10: Officer Experience in the 1st and 3rd Caçadores 25 April 1812

1st Caçadores		
Rank	**Number of Officers**	**Time With Division**
Major Agregado	1	6 Months
Captains	4	26 Months
Lieutenants	4	26 Months
Ensigns	4	23 Months
3rd Caçadores		
Rank	**Number of Officers**	**Time With Division**
Captains	4	25 Months
Lieutenants	1	25 Months
Ensigns	3	17 Months

Wellington was well aware of the shortage of officers and men in his divisions. Part of the problem was that an officer could be recalled back to Great Britain by his regiment. If an officer was promoted or transferred to another battalion in his regiment, he was authorised to join his new battalion, even if it meant the losing unit was on active operations. In many cases, this meant the officer would return to Great Britain and eventually be replaced by someone who was junior to him and likely less experienced. Wellington could not prevent an officer from leaving but by mid-April he could force the officer to remain with his battalion until his replacement arrived.

On 22 April 1812, he wrote to Lieutenant General Thomas Graham about the problem.

> I have received your letter of the 18th, regarding Lieut. of the ___ th regiment. There are…six subalterns less than I have endeavored to keep with every battalion in the army; and Lieut…is now the third lieutenant in the second battalion. He has omitted to inform you, however, that there are three subalterns belonging to the first battalion, now doing duty in the second battalion; and, under the King's order, I must detain them till they shall be relieved. I should in like manner be obliged to detain him, even after he should become effective in the first battalion; and of course cannot allow him to go to that battalion before his seniors, and before he shall belong to it. I always feel much concern in being obliged to refuse officers who

> wish to quit the army; indeed it is the most painful duty I have to perform. But it must be performed; otherwise, between those absent on account of wounds and sickness, and those absent on account of business or pleasure, I should have no officers left.[8]

This stopped the hemorrhaging of officers from Wellington's Army, but there was little he could do about getting replacements for them or the other ranks. Great Britain was over extended and was having trouble finding recruits to fill all its shortages throughout the world.

Breakdown in Discipline

Another problem the surviving officers were faced with was the complete breakdown in discipline during the three days that Badajoz was sacked. The division's officers were ignored by the soldiers and there was little they could do to restore discipline. At best they were disrespected. At worse they were threatened by their soldiers who used chaos to remain anonymous. This attitude towards the chain of command was still there at the end of April. Brevet Major William Napier, who only rejoined the division on 24 April, after a seven-month absence, wrote to his wife a few days later that

> I have 520 or more men left in the regiment, but the plundering after the town was taken, and the death or wounds of almost all their officers (only 7 being with the regiment fit for duty), has so disorganised them for a time, that I have been forced the two first days of my command to punish three of them by that most infamous manner of flogging, which is now doubly so from the gallantry of their conduct at the storm; but robbery and insolence to their officers are crimes not possible to be forgiven.[9]

These problems continued well into May. It had a profound effect on Major Napier, who had been with the division for nineteen months in 1810 and 1811. He was so disillusioned with his troops he was considering leaving the army. On 26 May he wrote to his wife that

> if the Duke would allow me to sell my commission I should go…you will easily understand this when I tell you that the barbarity of our soldiers extended to that pitch that they would not for two days carry off the wounded men at the foot of the walls, our *own men*!!! They also stripped them naked, the officers as well as the men who were wounded; I do not

8. *W.D.* (enlarged ed.), Vol. 9, 1836, p.176.
9. Napier, William, *At War With Wellington: The Peninsular War Letters of William, George and Charles Napier*, p.123.

> mean our regiment in particular, the 95th were the worst. The town was dreadfully plundered and the inhabitants murdered of all ages and sexes. The French were the only people to whom they gave quarter, out of a spirit of honour not humanity. They even killed one another.[10]

Conclusion

The Light Division that marched north from Badajoz in April 1812 was a far cry from that which earned its reputation manning the outposts in 1810. The twin sieges of Ciudad Rodrigo and Badajoz had broken it. In the space of three months the division lost 35 per cent of its strength and it would be many months before the fallen could be replaced. Its leadership was gutted with huge losses from among the non-commissioned officers and the virtual destruction of its officers' corps. NCOs could be promoted from the ranks, however officers had to come from England. On 1 January 1812, the division had 185 officers[11] assigned to it. By 25 April the division lost 107 of them (60 per cent). The losses included two major generals, its only colonel, three lieutenant colonels, five majors, forty-seven lieutenants, and six ensigns. Particularly hard hit were the captains who commanded companies. Forty of forty-seven company commanders were casualties.

Table 12.11: Officer Losses From 1 January 1812–25 April 1812

	Maj Gen	Colonel	LTC	Maj	Cpt	LT	Ens/2LT	Total
Division & Brigade Staffs	2	1	-	-	-	-	-	3
1st Bn 43rd Foot	-	-	1	2	11	18	-	32
1st Bn 52nd Foot	-	-	1	2	10	14	3	30
1st Bn 95th Foot (8 Companies)	-	-	-	1	5	8	1	15
2nd Bn 95th Foot (2 Companies)	-	-	-	-	2	2	-	4
3rd Bn 95th Foot (5 Companies)	-	-	-	1	9	1	-	11
1st Caç Bn	-	-	-	1	1	1	1	4
3rd Caç Bn	-	-	1	1	2	3	1	8
Total	2	1	3	8	40	47	6	107

10. Ibid, p.125.
11. This does not include the staff officers assigned to the battalions, such as the quartermaster or surgeon.

This loss of leadership was unsustainable. Replacements could be brought from England, but it would take a long time to replace their experience. Wellington realised this and it would affect how he used the division in the coming year. He also took drastic steps to address the shortage of men, by authorising the recruitment of Spaniards into British regiments, but it would take months to rebuild the officer corps.

During the upcoming campaign, the division would be relegated to a supporting role, instead of leading the army. After the Battle of Salamanca in July 1812, the division would stay in the rear as part of the garrison of Madrid, while much of the army moved north. Another issue that could not be ignored was the breakdown in discipline. How it was handled and the performance of the division in the 1812 campaign is a story for another book.

Chapter 13

What Happened to Them

We are always curious about what happened to the officers and men of the Light Division who are featured so prominently in this book. Most of the officers and men continued to fight with their regiments over the next forty months. Some were killed and many were seriously wounded. Many of those who survived went on to attain superior rank in the British Army.

Note: the spelling of the battles for which the medals were awarded is how it appeared on the medals and clasps.

Division Staff

Andrew Francis Barnard
Barnard continued to temporarily command the 1st Brigade until May 1813. After General Craufurd died on 24 January 1812, Barnard temporarily commanded the Light Division until May 1812. He fought at Waterloo and was appointed British Commandant of Paris in 1815. He was promoted to brevet colonel in 1813, major general in 1819, lieutenant general in 1837 and full general in 1851. In 1849 he was appointed Lieutenant Governor of the Royal Hospital, Chelsea. He died on 17 January 1855. He was awarded the AGC with four clasps[1] and the Waterloo Medal. He was created a KCB in 1815 and a GCB in 1840.

Robert Craufurd
Craufurd was posthumously awarded the AGM with a clasp for Bussaco and Ciudad Rodrigo.

John Ormsby Vandeleur
Vandeleur returned to the division in May 1812. In July 1813 he left the Light Division to take command of a light cavalry brigade and led it to the end of the war. He commanded the 4th Cavalry Brigade at Waterloo. He was promoted

1. Barrosa, Ciudad Rodrigo, Badajoz, Salamanca, Vittoria, Nivelle, Orthes, and Toulouse.

to lieutenant general in 1821 and general in 1838. He died in Dublin on 1 November 1849. He was created a KCB in 1815 and a GCB in 1833. He was awarded the AGC for Ciudad Rodrigo, Salamanca, Vittoria and Nive, and the Waterloo Medal.

The 43rd Foot

John Henry Cooke

Cooke was wounded at Vitoria in 1813. He continued to serve with his battalion until the peace in 1814. He fought in the War of 1812, and served in France after Waterloo until 1818. He was promoted to captain in 1823, brevet major in 1838, exchanged into the 25th Foot in 1838 and into the 21st Foot in 1855. He was promoted to brevet lieutenant colonel in 1855, backdated to 1851. He retired as a captain and brevet lieutenant colonel in 1855. He was a Yeoman of the Guard in 1862 and knighted in 1867. He died on 13 January 1870. He received the MGSM with eight clasps.[2]

John Duffy

Duffy went to England in May 1812 and returned to the Peninsula in February 1813. He was promoted to major in 1813. He was slightly wounded at Vitoria. He was promoted to lieutenant colonel in 1813. He returned to England in January 1814. He became lieutenant colonel in the 95th Foot in 1815 and 8th Foot in 1819. He was promoted to brevet colonel in 1830, major general in 1841 and lieutenant general in 1851. He was awarded a CB in 1831. He received the AGM for Badajoz. He received the MGSM with seven clasps.[3] He died in 1855.

James Fergusson

Fergusson received a temporary pension of £300 per annum for his Ciudad Rodrigo wounds. He was promoted to major in the 79th Foot in December 1812. A month later he exchanged into the 85th Foot and remained in the Peninsula until the end of the war in April 1814. He became lieutenant colonel in the 88th Foot in 1819 and 52nd Foot in 1825. He was promoted brevet colonel and appointed ADC to the king in 1830. He was promoted to major general in 1841, lieutenant general in 1851 and full general in 1860. He commanded on Malta and Gibraltar in the 1850s. He died in 1865. He was made a CB in 1831, KCB in 1855 and GCB in 1860. He received the MGSM with seven clasps.[4]

---

2. Ciudad Rodrigo, Badajoz, Salamanca, Vittoria, Pyrenees, Nivelle, Nive and Toulouse.
3. Fuentes d'Onor, Ciudad Rodrigo, Vittoria, Pyrenees, Nivelle, Nive and Egypt.
4. Vimiera, Corunna, Bussaco, Fuentes d'Onor, Ciudad Rodrigo, Salamanca, and Nive.

William Freer

Freer returned to the Peninsula in February 1813. He was wounded at Nivelle in November 1813 and promoted to captain on 1 December 1813. William was eventually promoted in May 1833 to lieutenant colonel in the 10th Foot. He was in command of the 10th Foot on Corfu when he died on 2 August 1836.

Thomas Garretty

Garretty returned to England in 1813. He was medically retired in 1817. He was recalled to duty in 1819 and found fit for service in a veteran's battalion. He retired in 1823 after seventeen years of service. His date of death is unknown; however, he was still alive in 1848 and received the MGSM with four clasps.[5]

Charles McLeod

McLeod posthumously received the AGM and clasp for Ciudad Rodrigo and Badajoz.

Henry Oglander

Oglander returned to the Peninsula as a captain in the 47th Foot in February 1813. He was seriously wounded at San Sebastian in 1813, where he was shot in the body and lost the index finger on his right hand. Due to his wounds, he received a £450 per year pension. He stayed in the army and was promoted to brevet major in 1813, major in the 40th Foot in 1815, lieutenant colonel in the Watteville Regiment in 1815 and brevet colonel in 1837. He commanded the 26th Foot from 1817 until his death at sea in June 1840 off the coast of China. He was made a CB in 1838. He served in India from 1828 finally commanding as major general in the Cawnpore Division in the Bengal Presidency. He resigned his rank and command, as well as cancelling his furlough for health reasons in order to accompany his regiment on active service in China. He was awarded the AGM for St Sebastian.

The 52nd Foot

George Ulrick Barlow

Barlow went back to Portugal in the spring of 1813 and was severely wounded in the foot at the Nivelle. He left the Peninsula in December 1813 and was promoted to captain in the 69th Foot at the end of the year. He fought at Waterloo. He exchanged into the 4th Light Dragoons in 1821 and died in India in 1824. He received the Waterloo Medal.

5. Bussaco, Fuentes d'Onor, Ciudad Rodrigo and Badajoz.

John Colborne

Colborne returned to the 1st Battalion in July 1813 and occasionally temporarily commanded the 2nd Brigade until the peace in 1814. He commanded the battalion, and temporarily a brigade, at Waterloo and served in France until 1818. He was promoted to brevet colonel in 1814, major general in 1825, lieutenant general in 1838, full general in 1854, and to field marshal in 1860. He served as the commander in chief of Canada from 1836–1839 and commander in chief of Ireland from 1855–1860. He died on 17 April 1863. He was awarded the AGC with seven clasps,[6] the MGSM with five clasps, [7] and received the Waterloo Medal. He was created a KCB in 1815, a GCB in 1838, and Baron Seaton in 1839.

Charles Dawson

Dawson returned to Peninsula in November 1813. He was severely wounded in the lung at Waterloo. He died from complications of his wound in France on 3 June 1817. He was awarded the Waterloo Medal.

Henry Dawson

Dawson was promoted to captain in 1812 and was killed by a musket ball to the chest at San Munoz on 17 November 1812.

John Dobbs

Dobbs served with the regiment until 1813 when he was seconded to the 5th Caçadores and promoted to captain in the Portuguese Army. He was severely wounded at Bayonne in April 1814 and returned to the 52nd Foot on 13 October 1814. He was promoted to captain in 1815, but it was backdated to 1814. He went on half-pay in 1816 and exchanged into the 6th Foot in 1835. He retired in 1835 and died on 23 August 1880. He received the MGSM with ten clasps.[8]

John Frederick Ewart

Ewart recovered from his wound and fought with the regiment throughout the campaign of 1812 but returned to England in December 1812 after being promoted to major in the Royal York Rangers. He stayed in the army and was promoted lieutenant colonel in the York Chasseurs in 1814 and in the 67th Foot in 1818, brevet colonel in 1837, major general in 1846, and lieutenant general in

6. Corunna, Albuhera, Ciudad Rodrigo, Nivelle, Nive, Orthes, and Toulouse.
7. Maida, Benevente, Bussaco, Pyrenees, and Egypt.
8. Corunna, Fuentes d'Onor, Ciudad Rodrigo, Badajoz, Salamanca, Vittoria, Pyrenees, San Sebastian, Nivelle, and Nive.

1854. He was appointed an Inspecting Field Officer of a Recruiting District in 1826. He died on 23 October 1854. He received the MGSM with five clasps.[9]

Charles Kinloch

Kinloch was seriously wounded in the back at Badajoz. He returned home to recuperate in May. His wound never healed properly, and he would be plagued by pain from it for the rest of his life. He was promoted to captain in the 99th Foot in 1813 and exchanged into the 52nd Foot in 1813. He rejoined Wellington's Army in southern France in December 1813 as an ADC to Lieutenant General Sir John Hope and served in that position until the end of the war. He missed Waterloo but joined the 52nd Foot in Paris in July 1815. He went on half-pay in July 1816. He died on 22 October 1828.

George Napier

Napier spent the next two years recovering. He returned to his battalion in the Peninsula in January 1814. He was promoted brevet lieutenant colonel in 1812, became lieutenant colonel in the 71st Foot in 1814, captain and lieutenant colonel in the 3rd Foot Guards in 1814, and in the 44th Foot in 1814. He was created a CB in 1815 and a KCB in 1838. He was promoted to brevet colonel in 1825, major general in 1837, lieutenant general in 1846, and general in 1854. He died on 16 September 1855. He was appointed an ADC to the king in 1825. He received the AGM for Ciudad Rodrigo and the MGSM with four clasps.[10]

The 95th Rifles

Thomas Sydney Beckwith

Beckwith became the AQMG of the British forces in Canada later in 1812. He commanded a brigade in the 1813 Chesapeake campaign. He was promoted to major general in 1814 and appointed the quartermaster general of the British forces in Canada. In 1829, he became the commander of the East India Company's Bombay Army, and in 1830 was promoted to lieutenant general. He died of a fever in 1831. He was knighted in 1812 and created a KCB in 1815. He received the AGM with clasps for Vimiera, Corunna and Bussaco.

Alexander Cameron

Cameron returned to England in August 1813. He was promoted to brevet lieutenant colonel in April 1812 and substantive major in May 1812. He was

9. Vimiera, Fuentes d'Onor, Ciudad Rodrigo, Badajoz, and Salamanca.
10. Corunna, Bussaco, Orthes, Toulouse.

severely wounded at Vittoria in June 1813 and at Waterloo. He exchanged to half-pay in 1817. He was made deputy governor of St Mawes in 1828. He was promoted to brevet colonel in 1830 and major general in 1838. He was created a CB in 1815 and a KCB in 1838. He received the AGM with clasps for Ciudad Rodrigo, Badajoz and Salamanca. He was awarded the Waterloo Medal and the MGSM with five clasps.[11] He died in July 1850.

Edward Costello

Costello fought with the 1st Battalion in the Peninsula until April 1814 when peace was declared. He ended the war as a sergeant. His trigger finger was shot off at Quatre Bras and he was pensioned out of the army in 1818. In 1835 he was commissioned as a captain in the British Legion and fought in Spain during the Carlist War. He returned to England in 1838 and was appointed a Yeoman Warder of the Tower of London. He died in 1869 at the age of 81. He was one of the most decorated soldiers in the 95th Rifles. He was awarded the Waterloo Medal and the MGSM with eleven clasps.[12]

John Cox

Cox returned to the Peninsula in January 1813 and served with the 1st Battalion until the war ended in April 1814. He was severely wounded at Tarbes in March 1814 when his left leg was broken by a musket ball. In 1818 he received a temporary pension of £70 per annum for his wounds. He fought at Waterloo. He was promoted to captain in 1819, major in 1828, lieutenant colonel in 1837, brevet colonel in 1851, and major general in 1855. He died on 7 February 1863. He was awarded the Waterloo Medal and the MGSM with ten clasps.[13]

William Green

Green was eventually sent to Chelsea Hospital in England, where he was discharged from the army with a pension of 9d per day.

John Kincaid

Kincaid served with the 1st Battalion throughout the rest of the Peninsular War and was its adjutant at Waterloo. He was promoted to captain in 1826 and retired in 1831. For his service he was appointed Exon of the Yeomen of

11. Vimiera, Corunna, Bussaco, Fuentes d'Onor and Vittoria.
12. Bussaco, Fuentes d'Onor, Ciudad Rodrigo, Badajoz, Salamanca, Vittoria, Pyrenees, Nivelle, Nive, Orthes, and Toulouse.
13. Roleia, Vimiera, Bussaco, Fuentes d'Onor, Ciudad Rodrigo, Vittoria, Pyrenees, Nive, Orthes, and Toulouse.

the Guard in 1844. He was knighted in 1852. He died on 22 April 1862. He received the MGSM with nine Clasps[14] and the Waterloo Medal.

Jonathan Leach

Leach commanded his company until the end of the Peninsular War 1814. He was wounded at Waterloo. He was promoted to brevet major in 1813 and brevet lieutenant colonel in 1815. He was promoted to major in the Rifle Brigade in 1819 and retired in 1821. He was created a CB in 1815. He received the MGSM with twelve clasps[15] and the Waterloo Medal. He died on 14 January 1855.

Peter O'Hare

O'Hare was posthumously awarded the AGM with clasps for Fuentes d'Onor, Ciudad Rodrigo and Badajoz.

George Simmons

Simmons was with the battalion until the end of the war in 1814. He was severely wounded at Waterloo. He was promoted to captain in 1828, major in 1838, and retired in 1845. He died in 1858. He received the MGSM with eight clasps[16] and the Waterloo Medal.

Harry Smith

Smith was appointed brigade major of the 2nd Brigade of the Light Division in March 1811 and served in that position until the end of the war in April 1814. He was promoted to captain in 1812. After the Peninsular War was over, he went to North America and served on the staff during the Chesapeake and New Orleans campaigns. He returned to Europe in time to participate in the Waterloo campaign. He was promoted brevet major in 1814 and brevet lieutenant colonel in 1815. He was promoted to major in 1826 and lieutenant colonel in 1830. From 1828 to 1840 he served in South Africa and fought in the Kaffir War. He was sent to India in 1840, where he served as the adjutant general. He fought in the Gwalior campaign of 1843, commanded a division in the 1st Sikh War and won the battle of Aliwal on 28 January 1846. He was promoted to major general in 1846 and returned to South Africa in 1847, where he was appointed governor of the Cape of Good Hope. He served in that position until 1852. During that time he led the British forces in the 7th and 8th Kaffir

14. Fuentes d'Onor, Ciudad Rodrigo, Badajoz, Salamanca, Vittoria, Pyrenees, Nivelle, Nive, and Toulouse.
15. Roleia, Vimiera, Bussaco, Fuentes d'Onor, Ciudad Rodrigo, Badajoz, Salamanca, Vittoria, Pyrenees, Nivelle, Nive, and Toulouse.
16. Fuentes d'Onor, Ciudad Rodrigo, Badajoz, Salamanca, Vittoria, Pyrenees, Nivelle, and Toulouse.

Wars between 1847 and 1851. He returned to Britain and served on the Home Staff, and was promoted to lieutenant general in 1854. He retired in 1859 and died on 12 October 1860. For his service he was made a CB in 1815, a KCB in 1844 and a GCB in 1846. In July 1846 he was created a baronet. He received the MGSM with twelve clasps[17] and the Waterloo Medal.

17. Corunna, Bussaco, Fuentes d'Onor, Ciudad Rodrigo, Badajoz, Salamanca, Vittoria, Pyrenees, Nivelle, Nive, Orthes and Toulouse.

Appendix I

Strength of the Light Division's British Units January–April 1812[1]

Every infantry battalion and cavalry regiment in the British Army was required to submit a report to the Horse Guards of its strength on the twenty-fifth day of each month. For those battalions in Great Britain, the strength return was submitted by the regiment. For battalions on active service, the return was sent up through its chain of command to the headquarters of the theatre where the battalion was assigned. A return was also sent to its regiment in Great Britain. The regimental returns usually did not contain as much information as those from the theatre headquarters. Furthermore, because of the delay in receiving the returns from the theatre, the information in the regimental returns could be one or two months out-of-date.

The returns are divided into four separate categories:

Officers Present

This reflected the officers who were present for duty with the battalion, regardless of their status. It includes those hospitalised or on convalescent leave.

Staff Officers

Like Officers Present, this section only included the officers who were present for duty with the battalion and not those who were performing temporary duty on the staff of the army.

NCOs

This included sergeants, but not corporals. Additionally musicians, such as drummers, buglers, and trumpeters were also included in this section.

Rank and File

This section included all soldiers who were not officers, sergeants, or musicians. It did not differentiate by rank.

---

1. WO 17/2469

- Fit for Duty: the total number of soldiers who were available to perform their duty. Some returns have this category as Present or Present Fit for Duty. This number was known as the effectives.
- Sick: the number of soldiers who were incapacitated due to injury, illness, or wounds. The returns did not break the numbers down by why the soldiers were incapacitated. In some returns it was further divided by those who were sick in their quarters and those who were hospitalised.
- On Command: the number of soldiers who were assigned to the battalion but were detached for duty in another location.
- Total: the total of rank and file soldiers assigned to the battalion, regardless of their status.
- Dead: the number of soldiers who died from disease, injury, or combat since the previous return.
- Deserters: this section shows the number of deserters since the previous month. It also listed those soldiers thought to have been taken prisoner.
- Sent Home: the number of other ranks who were sent home, usually due to poor health.

Table AI.1: 1st Battalion 43rd Foot January–April 1812

Date	Officers Present					Staff Officers					NCOs		Rank and File							
	LTC	Maj	Cpt	LT	Ens	Pay	Adj	QM	Surgeon	Assistant Surgeon	Sgt	Dr	Fit for Duty	Sick	On Command	Total	Joined	Dead	Deserted	Sent Home
Jan	1	2	8	24	3	-	-	1	1	2	64	23	854	246	51	**1,151**	-	4	1	6
Feb	1	2	8	24	3	-	-	1	1	2	66	23	863	222	45	**1,130**	-	10	2	-
Mar	1	2	8	24	3	-	-	1	1	2	63	23	844	237	34	**1,115**	-	1	1	-
Apr	-	1	8	22	3	-	-	1	-	1	63	23	529	446	48	**1,023**	1	95	-	-

Table AI.2: 1st Battalion 52nd Foot January–April 1812

Date	Officers Present					Staff Officers					NCOs		Rank and File							
	LTC	Maj	Cpt	LT	Ens	Pay	Adj	QM	Surgeon	Assistant Surgeon	Sgt	Dr	Fit for Duty	Sick	On Command	Total	Joined	Dead	Deserted	Sent Home
Jan	1	1	3	17	6	1	1	1	1	2	66	22	578	191	51	**820**	1	13	1	15
Feb	-	1	9	17	11	1	1	1	1	1	69	26	905	333	42	**1,280**	-	1	-	1
Mar	-	1	8	16	10	1	1	1	1	2	69	26	895	324	49	**1,268**	8	11	-	-
Apr	-	2	5	16	10	-	1	1	1	2	69	26	534	557	57	**1,148**	1	98	-	-

Table AI.3: 2nd Battalion 52nd Foot January–February 1812

Date	Officers Present					Staff Officers					NCOs		Rank and File							
	LTC	Maj	Cpt	LT	Ens	Pay	Adj	QM	Surgeon	Assistant Surgeon	Sgt	Dr	Fit for Duty	Sick	On Command	Total	Joined	Dead	Deserted	Sent Home
Jan	1	1	7	16	1	-	1	1	1	1	47	17	269	275	10	**554**	28	20	-	9
Feb	1	1	6	5	2	-	1	1	1	1	42	13	51	17	-	**68**	3	12	9	153

Table AI.4: 1st Battalion 95th Rifles January–April 1812

Date	Officers Present					Staff Officers					NCOs		Rank and File							
	LTC	Maj	Cpt	1LT	2LT	Pay	Adj	QM	Surgeon	Assistant Surgeon	Sgt	Bu	Fit for Duty	Sick	On Command	Total	Joined	Dead	Deserted	Sent Home
Jan	-	1	8	16	8	-	1	1	1	1	49	17	567	114	13	**694**	2	9	-	
Feb	-	1	6	19	8	-	1	1	1	1	53	20	621	95	28	**744**	65	6	-	7
Mar	-	1	7	19	8	-	1	1	1	1	53	20	569	143	21	**733**	1	11	-	1
Apr	-	-	7	17	8	-	1	1	1	2	52	20	420	246	32	**698**	-	34	-	2

Table AI.5: 2nd Battalion 95th Rifles January–April 1812

Date	Officers Present					Staff Officers					NCOs		Rank and File							
	LTC	Maj	Cpt	1LT	2LT	Pay	Adj	QM	Surgeon	Assistant Surgeon	Sgt	Bu	Fit for Duty	Sick	On Command	Total	Joined	Dead	Deserted	Sent Home
Jan	-	-	2	4	1	-	-	-	-	-	10	2	142	38	1	181	-	4	-	-
Feb	-	-	2	3	1	-	-	-	-	-	10	2	149	25	-	174	-	5	-	3
Mar	-	-	2	3	1	-	-	-	-	-	10	2	139	33	1	173	-	1	-	1
Apr	-	-	1	2	1	-	-	-	-	-	10	2	95	59	3	157	-	16	-	-

Table AI.6: Right Wing 3rd Battalion 95th Rifles January–April 1812[1]

Date	Officers Present					Staff Officers					NCOs		Rank and File							
	LTC	Maj	Cpt	1LT	2LT	Pay	Adj	QM	Surgeon	Assistant Surgeon	Sgt	Bu	Fit for Duty	Sick	On Command	Total	Joined	Dead	Deserted	Sent Home
Jan	1	-	5	11	2	-	-	-	1	1	26	10	221	135	7	**363**	-	7	-	-
Feb	1	-	4	11	2	-	-	1	1	1	26	10	242	107	7	**356**	1	4	-	-
Mar	1	-	4	11	3	-	-	1	1	1	25	9	232	113	7	**352**	1	7	-	-
Apr	1	-	4	7	4	-	-	1	1	1	26	9	178	134	12	**324**	-	26	-	-

1. Five Companies.

Appendix II

Strength of the 1st and 3rd Caçadores January–April 1812

Every infantry regiment, caçadores battalion, and cavalry regiment in the Portuguese Army was required to submit a report to the army HQ of its strength on the twenty-fifth day of each month. The below returns were found in The National Archives at Kew and are in WO 17/2466 (Portugal, 1810–1812).[1]

The returns are divided into five separate categories:

Staff

The officers, sergeants, and specialists who were present for duty with the battalion.

NCOs

This included the sergeants, but not corporals. Buglers were also included in this section.

Rank and File

This section included all soldiers who were not officers, sergeants, or musicians. It did not differentiate by rank.

- Present: the total number of soldiers who were available to perform their duty. This is the same as the British effectives.
- Sick: the number of soldiers who were incapacitated due to injury, illness, or wounds. Most were sent to higher level hospitals.
- Detached and On Command: the number of soldiers who were assigned to the battalion but were detached for duty in another location.
- Changes From Previous Month: Former Deserters: from time to time the government issued an amnesty decree as an incentive to deserters to

1. Unfortunately, the archives were missing the returns for March 1812.

return to their units. Most deserters were soldiers returning home. Many times they remained hidden by their families. If they were arrested they were returned to the unit without further punishment unless they were NCOs or corporals who were demoted to privates. Initially Beresford court martialed and shot some deserters to make an example but soon give up because it did not deter the men, so he began asking the government to pressure the local magistrates to be more active in tracking and arresting the deserters and returning them to their units.

- Changes From Previous Month: From Punishment: men that were court martialed and punished with some sentence that took them out of the unit, such as forced labour. Once they completed their sentence they were returned to their unit.

At the end of the NCOs and Other Ranks section is Total. This is the total of all officers, NCOs, and other ranks assigned to the battalion, regardless of their status.

Table AII.1: 1st Caçadores January–April 1812

Month	Staff														Company Officers		
	LTC	Maj	Adj	Pay	QM	Adj Sgt	QMS	CH	Sur	AS	Cor	Esp	BD	Mus	BM	Cpt	LT	Ens
Jan	1	1	1	1	1	1	1	1	1	2	1	-	1	7	1	5	6	5
Feb	1	1	1	1	1	1	1	-	1	2	1	1	1	7	1	5	6	5
Apr	1	1	1	1	1	1	1	1	1	2	1	-	1	8	1	5	6	5

Month	NCOS and Buglers			Rank and File										
	Sgt	Fur	Bu	Present	Det	On Command	Arrested	Sick		Absent		Recruits	Boys	Total
								Hos	BH	Leave	AWOL			
Jan	28	3	12	373	46	45	-	66	6	-	-	64	-	680
Feb	28	3	12	373	46	45	-	64	6	-	-	64	-	680
Apr	30	6	12	371	46	49	-	103	10	-	-	30	-	695

Changes From Previous Month								
Month	New Soldiers		Returnees		Discharges		Deserters	Dead
	Volunteers	Conscripts	Former Deserters	From Punishment	Unfit for Duty	Bad Conduct		
Jan	2	39	-	-	-	-	2	6
Feb	2	39	-	-	-	-	2	6
Apr	80	-	-	-	-	-	3	5

Table AII.2: 3rd Caçadores January–April 1812

Month	Staff															Company Officers		
	LTC	Maj	Adj	Pay	QM	Adj Sgt	QMS	CH	Sur	AS	Cor	Esp	BD	Mus	BM	Cpt	LT	Ens
Jan	1	1	1	1	-	1	1	1	1	1	1	1	1	8	1	5	6	5
Feb	1	1	1	1	-	1	1	-	1	1	1	1	1	8	1	5	6	5
Apr	1	1	1	1	-	1	1	1	1	1	1	1	1	8	1	5	6	5

Month	NCOS and Buglers			Rank and File										
	Sgt	Fur	Bu	Present	Det	On Command	Arrested	Sick		Absent		Recruits	Boys	Total
								Hos	BH	Leave	AWOL			
Jan	26	6	12	444	-	14	-	76	-	-	-	66	-	681
Feb	25	6	12	414	-	18	3	89	-	-	-	76	-	680
Apr	29	5	11	423	-	12	6	77	-	-	-	79	-	679

Changes From Previous Month								
Month	New Soldiers		Returnees		Discharges		Deserters	Dead
	Volunteers	Conscripts	Former Deserters	From Punishment	Unfit for Duty	Bad Conduct		
Jan	-	-	-	-	-	-	1	5
Feb	-	1	-	-	-	-	2	8
Apr	3	-	2	1	2	-	2	2

Appendix III

Major General Craufurd's Funeral

> Alas! My dear friend, of our small party of five who were headed by you, and first knew each other in '96, how many are gone, and how cruelly have others suffered, poor Anstruther, and Robert, and Yourself, who have gone through so much! Proby and myself alone remain; and while we lament over our two invaluable lost friends, the conviction of their merits and the force of their example should never be absent from our thoughts.
>
> General Charles Stewart, Marquis of Londonderry[1]

General Craufurd's funeral began at noon on 25 January 1812. The procession was led by Lieutenant Colonel McLeod, 43rd Foot, and followed by 100 men from the 43rd Foot, then 100 men from the 1st Battalion 52nd Foot, and 100 men from the 2nd Battalion 52nd Foot. The 100 men from each of these battalions were led by 1 captain and 3 subalterns. Next came the band of the 1st Battalion 95th Rifles, followed by fifty men from each of the three rifle battalions. The final formation in the procession were 100 men from the 3rd Caçadores. The 1st Caçadores were not present because they were escorting French prisoners to Lisbon.[2]

Next came the coffin, carried by the sergeant majors of the five British battalions and the senior sergeant of the 3rd Caçadores: Sergeant Majors Thomas Russell 1st Battalion 43rd Foot, Samuel M'Cann 1st Battalion 52nd Foot, John Smith 2nd Battalion 52nd Foot, William Fry 1st Battalion 95th Rifle, and John Garrett 3rd Battalion 95th Rifles. Although none of the British sources mention a Portuguese soldier with the British sergeant majors, it is very likely that a senior sergeant from the 3rd Caçadores was included in the party carrying the coffin. The Portuguese Army at this time did not have the rank of sergeant major. The senior sergeant on the battalion staff of the 3rd Caçadores was Adjutant Sergeant Manuel Martins Taveira and was probably the sergeant chosen to represent the battalion.[3]

---

1. Stewart, Charles, *Riflemen of Wellington's Light Division in the Peninsular War 1808–14*, p.169.
2. Oglander, Henry, *The Journals of Captain Henry Oglander of the 43rd & 47th Foot*, pp.119–120.
3. Email from Moisés Gaudêncio, dated 25 September 2024.

Following the coffin were six pall bearers, who were the surviving field officers of the Light Division. They were Lieutenant Colonel George Elder 3rd Caçadores, Major Daniel Hearn 1st Battalion 43rd Foot, Major Joseph Wells 1st Battalion 43rd Foot, Major Edward Gibbs 1st Battalion 52nd Foot, Major Peter O'Hare and Brevet Major Alexander Cameron 1st Battalion 95th Rifles. They were followed by the chief mourners: Major General Charles Stewart, Wellington's adjutant general, and Craufurd's two aides-de-camp, Lieutenants Charles Wood 52nd Foot and James Shaw 43rd Foot, his former DAQMG Captain William Campbell 23rd Foot, and the rest of the staff of the Light Division: AAG Major Charles Rowan 52nd Foot, DAQMG Lieutenant John Bell 52nd Foot, ACG Charles Purcell, and Chaplain Wentworth Parker. Then came Lord Wellington, Marshal William Beresford, Lieutenant General Thomas Graham, General Francisco Castanos, and officers from the divisions in the area.[4] Major General Vandeleur was still recovering from his wounds and did not go to the funeral. It is unclear where Lieutenant Colonel Andrew Barnard was. However, as the senior officer from the Light Division, he was likely with the division commanders. Behind them were most of the officers from the Light Division. Lieutenant Henry Oglander, despite having a very contentious relationship with Craufurd, was one of them. Notably many officers from the 1st King's German Legion Light Dragoons also joined the procession, to pay their respect to the general who commanded the outposts in 1810.[5]

The funeral procession wound its way down the road from the house where he died, near the Convent of San Francisco, to the Lesser Breach. The road was lined on both sides by soldiers from the 5th Division, with their muskets reversed – the barrel of the musket on the ground and their hands folded on its butt.

Upon arrival at the foot of the Lesser Breach, the 100 men from each of the Light Division's battalions formed around the grave the best they could. Then the sergeants carrying the coffin moved forward, led by Chaplain Wentworth.

> At this moment the military music ceased, and no sound could be heard except the voice of the clergyman, who faltered forth, rather than read, the solemn declaration, 'I am the resurrection and the life.' Arrived at the brink of the sepulchre the procession paused, and the shell was rested upon the ground; and then I could distinctly perceive, that among the six rugged veterans who had borne it, there was not a dry eye, and that even of the privates who looked on, there were few who manifested not signs

4. Stewart, Charles, *Riflemen of Wellington's Light Division in the Peninsular War 1808–14*, p.168.
5. Ewart, John, *Peninsular War Diary of Captain John Frederick Ewart, 52nd Light Infantry, 1811–1812*, p.13.

> of sorrow, such as men are accustomed to exhibit only when they lose a parent or a child.
>
> The few striking sentences having been read, which that most affecting of all rituals, the Funeral Service of the Church of England requires, the body was lowered into the grave, and 'dust' was committed to dust, and 'ashes to ashes.' This part of the ceremony being concluded; there followed that salute, both of artillery and musketry, which the rank of the deceased required; and then, the corps being once more formed into marching order, filed back to their several cantonments.[6]

Tradition has it that while the Light Division was marching back to its cantonments after the funeral

> their route traversed some deep muddy ground interspersed with pools of water, such as is so commonly seen where siege operations have been carried on in wet weather. Not a word was spoken, the deepest depression pervaded all ranks, the men moving along in gloomy silence. As they approached the wet piece of ground they suddenly closed up their ranks and in perfect formation, as if passing a reviewing general, splashed their way doggedly through the deep mire. Not another sound was heard! But its meaning none could fail to understand. It was the last voiceless tribute of these gallant fellows to the memory of their lost Chief who, although many feared him, had earned the admiration and absolute confidence of both officers and men who long since had realized that it was due to his draconic discipline and admirable thought for the welfare of his men that the Light Division had become 'the admiration and the envy of the whole Army.'[7]

6. Anonymous, pp.27–28.
7. Verner, Willoughby, 'Ciudad Rodrigo 19 January 1812', *Saturday Review*, p.80. This anecdote was told to Mr. Verner about 1882 by an old officer of the Rifle Brigade, General Sir Martin Dillon, who heard it from Thomas Smith, who was in the 1st Battalion 95th Rifles and present at the Siege of Ciudad Rodrigo.

Bibliography

The National Archives, Kew

WO 17/2466 (Portugal, 1810–1812) Theatre Returns
WO 17/2469 (Jan–June 1812) Theatre Returns
WO 17/2470 (July–Dec 1812) Theatre Returns
WO 12/5574 Quarterly Pay Returns 43rd Foot 1st Battalion 1812–1813
WO 12/6251 Quarterly Pay Returns 52nd Foot 1st Battalion 1811–1812
WO 12/6314 Quarterly Pay Returns 52nd Foot 2nd Battalion 1812–1813
WO 12/9523 Quarterly Pay Returns 95th Foot 1810–1812
WO 12/9583 Quarterly Pay Returns 95th Foot 2nd Battalion 1812
WO 12/9587 Quarterly Pay Returns 95th Foot 3rd Battalion 1811–1812

Arquivo Histórico Militar (AHM) (Portuguese Military Archives)

AHM 1-14-256-04 M-13 to AHM 1-14-256-04 M-17
AHM 1-14-256-04 M-20 to AHM 1-14-256-04 M-23
AHM-DIV-1-14-320-26 M0005
PT-AHM-DIV-1-14-057-04
PT-AHM-DIV-1-14-057-05
PT-AHM-FE-010-A07-MD-08
PT-AHM-G-LM-C-03-01

Print and Internet Sources

Anonymous, 'The Funeral of General Craufurd', *Memoir of the Late Major-General Robert Craufurd*, London: Private Impression, 1842, pp.22–30

Barlow, George Ulrich, *A Light Infantryman With Wellington: The Letters of Captain George Ulrich Barlow, 52nd and 69th Foot, 1808–1815,* Solihull (UK): Helion, 2018

Barnard, Andrew, *Riflemen of Wellington's Light Division in the Peninsular War 1808–14,* Barnsley: Frontline 2023, pp.6–20

Bell, John, 'Letter dated 7 April 1812' in Kinloch, Charles, *A Hellish Business: The Letters of Captain Charles Kinloch 52nd Light Infantry 1806–1816*, Godmanchester: Ken Trotman, 2007, pp.94–95

Belmas, J, *Journaux des sièges dans la péninsule de 1807 à 1814*, 4 volumes, Paris: Chez Firmin Didot, 1837

Booth, Charles, *Redcoats of Wellington's Light Division: Unpublished & Rare Memoirs of the 52nd (Oxfordshire) Regiment of Foot*, Barnsley: Frontline, 2022, pp.114–115

Boyle, Gerald, *Rifle Brigade Century: An Alphabetical List of the Officers of the Rifle Brigade (The Prince Consort's Own) (Regular Battalions) from 1800 to 1905*, London: William Clowes, 1901

Burgoyne, John, *Life and Correspondence of Field Marshal Sir John Burgoyne*, 2 volumes, Wrottesley, George (ed.), London: Richard Bentley, 1873

Caldwell, George, and Cooper, Robert, *Rifle Green in the Peninsula*, 4 volumes, Leicester: Bugle Horn, 1998

Cameron, Alexander, *Riflemen of Wellington's Light Division in the Peninsular War 1808–14,* Barnsley: Frontline, 2023, pp.42–61

Colborne, John, 'Letter Describing Attack on the Upper Teson Redoubt, 1812', *Redcoats of Wellington's Light Division: Unpublished & Rare Memoirs of the 52nd (Oxfordshire) Regiment of Foot*, Barnsley: Frontline, 2022, pp.33–35

Cooke, John, *A True Soldier Gentleman: The Memoirs of Lt. John Cooke 1791–1813*, Swanage: Shinglepicker, 2000

Cooke, John, 'The Storming of Badajoz', *Stories of the Peninsular War*, London: George Routledge, 1870, pp.138–150

Cope, William, *The History of the Rifle Brigade (The Prince Consort's Own) Formerly the 95th*, London: Chatto and Windus, 1877

Costello, Edward, *Adventures of a Soldier,* London: Henry Colburn, 1841

Cox, John, *Riflemen of Wellington's Light Division in the Peninsular War 1808–14,* Barnsley: Frontline, 2023, pp.92–121

Crumplin, Michael, *Guthrie's War: A Surgeon of the Peninsula & Waterloo*, Barnsley: Pen & Sword, 2010

C.W.N., *George Gawler, K.H., 52nd Light Infantry: A Life Sketch*, London: Bemrose, 1900

Davies, Francis, *Redcoats of Wellington's Light Division: Unpublished & Rare Memoirs of the 52nd (Oxfordshire) Regiment of Foot*, Barnsley: Frontline, 2022, pp.168–170

Dawson, Charles, *Redcoats of Wellington's Light Division: Unpublished & Rare Memoirs of the 52nd (Oxfordshire) Regiment of Foot*, Barnsley: Frontline, 2022, pp.156–165.

Dawson, Henry, *Redcoats of Wellington's Light Division: Unpublished & Rare Memoirs of the 52nd (Oxfordshire) Regiment of Foot*, Barnsley: Frontline, 2022, pp.140–148

Dobbs, John, *Recollections of an Old 52nd Man,* Staplehurst: Spellmount, 2000

Duffy, John, *Journals of Majors John Duffy and John Maxwell Tylden of the 43rd Foot*, Godmanchester: Ken Trotman, 2023

Elder, George, 'Memorandum of the Siege and the Assault of Badajoz on the Evening of the 6th of April, 1812', *United Services Journal*, Part III, London: Henry Colburn, 1834, pp.54–56

Ewart, John, 'Letter Describing the Storming of Ciudad Rodrigo', *Redcoats of Wellington's Light Division: Unpublished & Rare Memoirs of the 52nd (Oxfordshire) Regiment of Foot*, Barnsley: Frontline, 2022, pp.92–94

Ewart, John, *Peninsular War Diary of Captain John Frederick Ewart, 52nd Light Infantry, 1811–1812*, Gareth Glover (ed.), Godmanchester: Ken Trotman, 2010

Fergusson, James, *Men of Wellington's Light Division: Unpublished Memoirs of the 43rd (Monmouthshire) Regiment in the Peninsular War*, Barnsley: Frontline, 2022, pp.53–89

Fitzmaurice, John, *A Biographical Sketch of Major General John Fitzmaurice,* Anghiari: Tiber, 1908

Forbes, Charles, 'Table Talk of an Old Campaigner', *United Services Journal*, Part III, 1834, pp.54–57

Freer, Edward, *With the 43rd in the Peninsula: The Letters of William Freer, Edward Freer and Daniel Gardner of the 43rd Foot (1808–15)*, Godmanchester: Ken Trotman, 2022

Freer, William, *With the 43rd in the Peninsula: The Letters of William Freer, Edward Freer and Daniel Gardner of the 43rd Foot (1808–15)*, Godmanchester: Ken Trotman, 2022

Gairdner, James, *The American Sharpe: The Adventures of an American Officer of the 95th Rifles in the Peninsula & Waterloo Campaigns*, Barnsley: Frontline, 2017

Garretty, Thomas, *Memoirs of a Sergeant Late in the Forty-Third Light Infantry Regiment*, Cambridge: Ken Trotman, 1998

Gaudêncio, Moisés, and Burham, Robert, *In the Words of Wellington's Fighting Cocks*, Barnsley: Pen & Sword, 2021

General Orders: Spain and Portugal, Vol. 4, London: Egerton Military Library, 1812

Green, William, *Where Duty Calls Me: The Experiences of William Green of Lutterworth in the Napoleonic Wars*, Teague, John, and Teague, Dorothea, (ed.), West Wickham: Synjon Books, 1975

Hall, John, *Biographical Dictionary of British Officers Killed and Wounded, 1808–1814*, London: Greenhill, 1998

Hamilton, Anthony, *Hamilton's Campaign With Moore and Wellington During the Peninsular War*, Staplehurst: Spellmount, 1998

Hamilton, William, *Riflemen of Wellington's Light Division in the Peninsular War 1808–14*, Barnsley: Frontline, 2023, pp.125–126

Hunt, John, 'Peninsular War Diary', *Redcoats of Wellington's Light Division: Unpublished & Rare Memoirs of the 52nd (Oxfordshire) Regiment of Foot*, Barnsley: Frontline, 2022, pp.36–64

Jones, John, *Journal of the Sieges Carried on by the Army Under the Duke of Wellington Between the Years 1811 & 1814*, 3 volumes, Cambridge: Ken Trotman, 1998

Jones, John, Unpublished Journal

Jones, Rice, *An Engineer Officer Under Wellington in the Peninsula*, Cambridge: Ken Trotman, 1986

Keim, A., *Geschichte des 4, Großherzoglich Hessischen Infanterie-Regiments (Prinz Karl) Nr. 118*, Berlin: Mittler, 1879

Kincaid, John, *Adventures in the Rifle Brigade in the Peninsula, France, and the Netherlands from 1809–1815,* Staplehurst: Spellmount, 1998

Kincaid, John, *Random Shots from a Rifleman*, Philadelphia: Carey & Hart, 1835

Kinloch, Charles, *A Hellish Business: The Letters of Captain Charles Kinloch 52nd Light Infantry 1806–1816*, Godmanchester: Ken Trotman, 2007

Lamare, Jean, *An Account of the Second Defense of the Fortress of Badajoz by the French in 1812*, Cambridge: Ken Trotman, 2003

Leach, Jonathan, *Rough Sketches of the Life of an Old Soldier*, Cambridge: Ken Trotman, 1986

Levinge, Richard, *Historical Records of the Forty-Third Regiment Monmouthshire Light Infantry 1739 to 1867*, Uckfield: Naval & Military, 2014

Macleod, Charles, *Men of Wellington's Light Division: Unpublished Memoirs of the 43rd (Monmouthshire) Regiment in the Peninsular War*, Barnsley: Frontline, 2022, pp.11–22

Madden, Wyndham, *Men of Wellington's Light Division: Unpublished Memoirs of the 43rd (Monmouthshire) Regiment in the Peninsular War*, Barnsley: Frontline, 2022, pp.173–189

Martinien, Aristide, *Tableaux par Corps et par Batailles des Officiers Tués et Blessés pendant les Guerres de l'Empire (1805–1815)*, Paris: Éditions Militaires, ND

McGuigan, Ron, and Burham, Robert, *Wellington's Brigade Commanders*, Barnsley: Pen & Sword, 2017

Memoir of the Late Major-General Robert Craufurd, London: Private Impression, 1842

Memoirs of General and Flag-Officers Recently Deceased: Major General Sir George Elder, United Services Journal, Part II, 1837, pp.233–239

Moore Smith, George, *The Life of John Colborne*, London: J. Murray, 1903

Moorsom, William, *Historical Record of the Fifty-Second Regiment*, London: Richard Bentley, 1860

Napier, George, *At War With Wellington: The Peninsular War Letters of William, George and Charles Napier*, Barnsley: Frontline, 2024

Napier, William, *At War With Wellington: The Peninsular War Letters of William, George and Charles Napier*, Barnsley: Frontline, 2024

Oglander, Henry, *The Journals of Captain Henry Oglander of the 43rd & 47th Foot*, Godmanchester: Ken Trotman, 2023

Oman, Charles, *A History of the Peninsular War*, 7 volumes, Oxford: AMS, 1980

Ortiz, Fernando, 'Civilian Casualties During the Sack of Badajoz 1812', *The Napoleon Series Online*, 21 October 2024

Rowan, Charles, 'Letter Regarding Wounding of Major George Napier at Ciudad Rodrigo', *Redcoats of Wellington's Light Division: Unpublished & Rare Memoirs of the 52nd (Oxfordshire) Regiment of Foot*, Barnsley: Frontline, 2022, pp.90–91

Shaw, James, *Riflemen of Wellington's Light Division in the Peninsular War 1808–14,* Barnsley: Frontline, 2023, pp.171–173

Simmons, George, *A British Rifleman: Journals and Correspondence During the Peninsular War and the Campaign of Wellington*, London: Greenhill, 1986

Smith, Harry, *The Autobiography of Sir Harry Smith*, London: John Murray, 1901

Stewart, Charles, *Riflemen of Wellington's Light Division in the Peninsular War 1808–14,* Barnsley: Frontline, 2023, pp.66–71

Surtees, William, *Twenty-Five Years in the Rifle Brigade*, London: Greenhill, 1996

Thompson, Mark, *Wellington's Favourite Engineer John Fox Burgoyne: Operations, Engineering, and the Making of a Field Marshal*, Warwick: Helion, 2020

Verner, Willoughby, *History & Campaigns of the Rifle Brigade: 1800–1813*, 2 volumes, London: Buckland and Brown, 1995

Verner, Willoughby, 'Ciudad Rodrigo 19 January 1812', *Saturday Review*, 20 January 1912, p.80

Wellington, Duke of, *The Dispatches of Field Marshal the Duke of Wellington, During His Various Campaigns in India Denmark, Portugal, Spain, the Low Countries, and France, from 1799 to 1818,* Gurwood, Lieutenant Colonel John, (ed.), London: John Murray, 1834–1839, [Referenced as *W.D.*]

——. *Dispatches of Field Marshal the Duke of Wellington, During His Various Campaigns in India Denmark, Portugal, Spain, the Low Countries, and France,* Gurwood, Lieutenant Colonel John (ed.), London: Parker, Furnivall and Parker, 1844–1847, [Referenced as *W.D.* (enlarged ed.)]

Index

Name Index

Algeo, John, 15, 19, 81, 93, 180
Allix, William, 177
Allman, Joseph, 96, 97
Alten, Charles, 82
Antoins, John, 117
Araújo, Joaquim, 181
Arbuthnott, Hugh, 12
Armstrong, William, 19, 46, 80, 92, 132, 184

Baillie, Mackay, 166
Balvaird, William, 108, 175
Barbot, Elie, 126
Barclay, Robert, 3
Barlow, George, 29, 31, 40, 59, 61, 81, 87, 106, 109, 124, 140, 143, 170, 171, 198
Barnard, Andrew, 4, 9, 14, 19, 41, 63, 64, 80, 92, 123, 131, 136, 137, 142, 144, 145, 147, 150, 161, 183, 184, 196, 214
Barrié, Jean, 47, 57, 68
Beckwith, Charles, 19, 80, 92, 184
Beckwith, Thomas, 3, 4, 87, 92, 95, 98, 200
Bedell, Walter, 78, 131
Bell, John, 19, 80, 92, 132, 140, 184, 214
Beresford, William, 43, 210, 214
Blackwood, Robert, 120, 171
Booth, Charles, 106, 131, 171
Botelho, Afonso, 16
Botelho, Damião, 16
Bowley, Joseph, 45
Bramwell, John, 44, 74
Broke, Charles, 143
Brooks, James, 110
Brotherwood, William, 115
Burns, Thomas, 117

Cameron, Alexander, 19, 36, 45, 63, 81, 93, 130, 136, 137, 146-8, 150, 151, 185, 191, 200, 214
Cameron, George, 85
Campbell, Colin, 146
Campbell, Robert, 46, 81, 93, 162, 169
Campbell, William, 214
Capel, Thomas, 166
Carey, Arthur, 133, 177
Castanos, Francisco, 214
Castles, Johnny, 152
Cathala, Jean-Pierre, 47
Chalmers, William, 87
Charpentier, 100
Clinton, Henry, 82
Colborne, John, 12, 19, 27-32, 44, 46, 49, 56, 74, 75, 77, 78, 199
Comarford, Patrick, 45
Considine, James, 166
Cooke, John, 22, 34, 54, 62, 69, 70, 107, 108, 111, 132, 153, 162, 166, 167, 197
Correia, João, 181
Costello, Edward, 26, 33, 49, 51, 56, 59, 61, 69, 70, 85, 97, 110, 120, 131, 134, 137, 142, 148, 152, 165, 201
Coupin, L., 101
Cox, John, 78, 201
Coxen, Edward, 131, 185
Crampton, Jeremiah, 28, 131, 175
Craufurd, Robert, 3, 8, 19, 23, 27, 33, 40-3, 45, 46, 50, 53, 54, 72, 73, 75, 77, 81, 87, 196, 213, 214
Croudace, Christopher, 133, 178
Cummings, James, 84, 85
Cuthbert, Robert, 109

D'Andre-Saint-Victor, 101
Da Cunha, Joaquim, 15
Da Fonseca, Joaquim, 15
Da Rosa, José, 15
Da Silveira, Manuel, 16, 180
Davies, Francis, 171
Davis, Edward, 117
Dawson, Charles, 18, 87, 114, 115, 172, 199
Dawson, Henry, 58, 172, 199
De Avilez, Jorge, 15, 186
De Bruenig, Anthony, 16
De Figueiredo, Luis, 16
De Grasse, M., 100
De León, Juana, 153
De Mesquita, Miguel, 16
De Mesquita, Vicente, 16
De Salaberry, Edward, 132
Demeuve, 100
Denisot, 10
Dennis, Kelly, 131
Derby, Luke, 45
Diggle, Thomas, 131, 177
Dobbin, William, 16, 181
Dobbs, John, 26, 133, 160, 199
Dobbs, Joseph, 28, 46, 70, 75, 76
Douglas, John, 185
Drummond, George, 4
Duffy, John, 28, 30,46, 54, 56, 61, 87, 96, 109, 111, 185, 197
Duhamel, 100

Ecke, George, 45
Eeles, Charles, 119, 131
Elder, George, 16, 19, 27, 50, 81, 92, 132, 133, 143, 180, 188, 214
Ellicombe, Charles, 41, 50
Ennis, Joseph, 118
Evans, Edward, 117
Ewart, John, 31, 46, 60, 64, 65, 110, 114, 115, 117

Fairfoot, Robert, 45, 79, 139,
Fergusson, James, 28, 29, 31, 42, 44, 45, 51, 74, 111, 131, 165, 197
Firman, Walter, 178
Fishlock, Roger, 117
Fitzmaurice, John, 36, 49, 50, 67, 176
Fleming, Patrick, 131, 134
Fletcher, Richard, 123,
Forbes, Charles, 180
Forster, Jonathan, 162, 175
Fourtines, Pierre, 57
Freer, Edward, 166
Freer, Richard, 109, 162, 175
Freer, William, 166, 198
Fry, William, 213
Fuller, Robert, 84

Gairdner, James, 96, 98, 132, 175, 176
Garrett, John, 213
Garretty, Thomas, 31, 50, 52, 60, 66, 71, 83, 118, 130, 135, 140, 146, 155, 198
Garty, Patrick, 117
Gawler, George, 131, 137, 173, 174
Gibbons, Joseph, 117
Gibbs, Edward, 12, 19, 26, 31, 81, 87, 93, 169, 214
Gibson, John, 118
Goodman, Stephen, 84,
Graham, Thomas, 43, 192, 214
Gran, Wilhelm, 126
Gray, Loftus, 175
Green, William, 55, 107, 123, 131, 132, 138, 156, 186, 201
Grübel, Johann, 126
Guiraud, 101
Gurwood, John, 30, 31, 42, 44, 51, 53-5, 57, 76, 87
Guthrie, George, 73, 77, 167

Haddock, Robert, 16
Haggup, William, 190
Hall, George, 111, 174
Hamilton, Anthony, 137, 165
Hamilton, Douglas, 44, 87
Hamilton, William, 78
Hanlon, Richard, 117
Hart, John, 13, 19, 45, 81, 92, 131, 185
Harvest, Augustus, 190
Harvest, Horatio, 130, 132, 139, 166
Hawksley, Rutherford, 32
Hearn, Daniel, 214
Hodgson, Augustus, 166
Hodgson, Miles, 84, 85
Holloway, William,114
Hopkins, John, 190
Hovenden, Tarleton, 178
Hunt, John, 12, 183-5, 190

Johnston, George, 111, 165, 190
Johnston, William, 44, 130, 176
Jones, John, 99, 109, 112, 116
Jones, Rice, 44, 50, 52
Jones, William, 12, 28, 29, 42, 44, 60, 81, 114, 130, 133, 134, 139, 170
Juzarte, José, 180

Kempt, James, 84, 103, 113, 115, 117
Kenderine, William, 117
Kincaid, John, 35, 36, 44, 51, 63-5, 103, 104, 117, 122, 136, 144, 146, 147, 151-4, 176, 182, 201
Kinloch, Charles, 141, 172, 200
Knox, John, 44

L'Espganol, 101
Lamare, Jean, 100-2, 113, 124, 125
Larkin, David, 45
Lavasey, Peter, 117
Layton, John, 191
Leach, Jonathan, 21, 67, 71, 88, 202
Lee, John, 118
Lefaivre, 101
Leitão, António, 79
Lennox, Charles, 76
Lobo, António, 185
Lobo, Dom, 15
Lurat, Durand, 127

M'Cann, Samuel, 213
M'Namara, Thomas, 28, 191
MacDonald, Donald, 180
MacDonnell, Alexander, 178
Mackie, William, 57
Mackinnon, Henry, 41, 56
Maclean, Charles, 15, 185, 192
Madden, William, 116, 170
Madden, Wyndham, 62, 167
Maillet, 139
Malone, John, 84
Manners, Henry, 131, 177
Marmont, Marshal, 182-4
Marr, Patrick, 156
Massot, 100
McCurry, Hugh, 56
McDiarmid, John, 175, 185, 191
McGregor, Alexander, 79, 131
McInnes, Malcolm, 84
McLeod, Charles, 11, 19, 58, 59, 61, 81, 82, 92, 142, 164, 198, 213
McNair, James, 131, 154, 173
McPherson, Donald, 176
McPherson, Philip, 190
Mein, William, 28, 30-2, 76, 87, 170
Meister, Gottfried, 126
Merry, Augustus, 28, 46, 87, 170
Meynhart, 101
Mills, William, 84
Mitchell, Samuel, 13, 19, 44, 45, 79, 81, 92
Moore, William, 87
Morphew, Powell, 16, 132, 133, 179, 181
Mulcaster, Edmund, 28, 29
Murralls, Francis, 118

Napier, George, 12, 27, 31, 36, 42-5, 49, 50, 52, 58, 75-7, 87, 200
Napier, William, 82, 155, 184, 188, 193
Nesbitt, John, 45
Nixon, William, 114, 117, 174

O'Brian, Martin, 109
O'Brien, Patrick, 148, 149
O'Connell, John, 44, 167
O'Hare, Peter, 13, 19, 81, 92, 130, 133-5, 139, 175, 202, 214
O'Neil, Patrick, 84
Ogilvy, William, 87
Oglander, Henry, 26, 34, 42, 167, 168, 198, 214
Orange, William Prince of, 76

Pack, Denis, 18, 24
Pallentine, William, 109
Parker, Wentworth, 19, 80, 92, 184, 214
Pattenson, Cook Tylden, 74
Pazius, 101
Peixoto, Martinho, 181
Peixoto, Pedro, 16
Percival, William, 14, 19, 81, 133, 154, 185
Pereira, José, 16
Philippon, Armand, 100
Picoteau, 101
Picton, Thomas, 63, 109
Pineau, 100
Pinto, José, 181
Pollock, Samuel, 168
Poole, Clement, 170
Price, Thomas, 84,85
Purcell, Charles, 19, 80, 92, 184, 214

Rebelo, Feliciano, 180
Ridout, George, 168
Rintoul, William, 190
Robinson, William, 84,
Rodrigues, Manuel, 15

Ross, Hew, 23
Rowan, Charles, 19, 80, 92, 132, 184, 214
Royds, William, 173
Royle, Job, 173
Royle, John, 44
Russell, Thomas, 213

Sécio, Manuel, 15
Shaw, James, 19, 40-3, 53, 80, 92, 131, 142, 184, 214
Shea, James, 117,
Simmons, George, 34, 45, 63, 68, 79, 115-7, 119, 175, 191, 202
Smith, Harry, 19, 28, 42, 45, 46, 55. 56, 81, 86, 93, 96, 115, 119, 136, 145, 150, 153, 182, 185, 202
Smith, John, 213
Sobral, Manuel, 15
Somerset, Lord Fitzroy, 76, 145
Spencer, John, 45,
Stanway, Francis, 121
Steele, Lawrence, 44
Stewart, Charles, 81, 82, 213, 214
Stewart, Duncan, 178
Stewart, James, 56, 119
Stokes, James, 114, 115, 176
Strode, Thomas, 165
Surtees, Wiliam, 133, 154, 177, 184

Taggart, Charles, 131, 168
Taveira, Manuel, 213
Thierry, Gaspard, 100, 113
Thomson, Alexander, 28, 30
Toole, John, 117
Tracey, Thomas, 110, 111
Traile, Charles, 191
Travers, James, 28
Truilhier, 101
Tute, Richard, 45
Uniacke, John, 45, 49, 55, 56, 70, 79

Vandeleur, John, 4, 19, 41, 46, 56, 74, 80, 81, 88, 92, 96, 98, 196, 214
Veiland, Michel, 100
Vienné, 101
Von Eugen, Graf, 126

Walker, Thomas, 73, 76, 77
Wallis, Henry, 87
Weber, Christian, 126
Wellington, Duke of, 1, 2, 17, 27, 40, 43, 49, 50, 66, 78, 81, 82, 85, 102, 103, 120, 143-145, 151, 158, 183, 187, 192, 193, 214
Wells, Joseph, 11, 83, 165, 214
West, Henry, 131
Wild, Jonathan, 52
Wilkie, 57, 69, 70
Wilkinson, Thomas, 168
Williams, John, 132
Winterbottom, John, 174, 190
Wood, Charles, 19, 80, 87, 214
Woodgate, John, 32, 78
Worsley, Thomas, 178, 179
Wright, Peter, 41, 50
Wynch, James, 3, 4

Yorke, Charles, 173
Young, George, 44

Place Index

Águeda River, 24, 26, 37, 40, 66
Alcains, 95
Aldeia de Santa Margarida, 94
Aldeia Velha, 183
Alfaiates, 94, 183
Almeida, 2, 82
Alpedrinha, 95
Arronches, 98, 183
Atalaia, 96

Badajoz, 2, 88-91, 93, 99-182, 187-8, 190, 193-4, 196-203
Barrosa, 9, 14, 196
Beira, 10
Bismula, 94
Bussaco, 1, 3, 85, 196-203

Cádiz, 4, 9, 13, 14, 188
Calamon stream, 108
Campillo de Azaba, 83
Campo Maior, 183
Capinha, 95
Casillas de Flores, 94
Casteleiro, 94,
Castelo Branco, 94-5, 165-6, 183
Castelo de Vide, 96

Celerico, 82,
Chelsea Hospital, 196-201
Christoval, 99, 100
Cuidad Rodrigo, 1-3, 18-79, 84-5, 90, 96, 103, 111, 124, 130-1, 133, 146, 165, 170, 194, 196-203
Côa River, 1, 11
Coimbra, 75-6
Copenhagen, 83
Corunna, 11-2, 197, 199-201,203

El Bodón, 22-4, 65-6, 81, 83-4
Elvas, 98, 105, 112-3, 117, 148, 156, 158, 160m, 172, 175-7
Escalos de Baixo, 183
Escalos de Cima, 94
Escarigo, 95
Escusa, 95
Estremores, 156
Estremoz, 156, 166, 168, 179, 172, 175-6

Forcalhos, 94
Fuentes de Onoro, 19, 80, 81, 83, 93, 183
Fuentes d'Onor, 197-203
Fuenteguinaldo, 165

Gallegos, 67, 75-9
Great Teson, 24, 26-7, 29, 32-3, 41-2, 46
Guadiana, 2, 99, 105, 112, 128

Ituero de Azaba, 83, 85

La Caridad Monastery, 24, 37, 40, 42
La Encina, 19, 22, 24, 81, 83, 184
La Trinidad Bastion, 102-3, 24, 126-8, 139, 143
Lardoso, 95
Lisbon, 1, 4, 18, 75, 159, 167, 176, 213
Lousa, 94, 183

Martiago, 19, 23
Meimoa, 94

Nave de Haver, 84-5
Nisa, 95-6, 183-4
Nive, 197, 197, 183-4
Nivelle, 197-9, 201-3

Orthes, 196, 199-201, 203

Pardaleras, 99, 105, 128
Pastores, 19, 22, 24, 81
Pedrógão de São Pedro, 94
Penamacor, 183
Picurina fort, 99, 102-3, 107-8, 110-18
Portalegre, 74, 98, 172, 183
Pueblo d'Azaba, 83, 94
Pyrenees, 197, 199, 200, 202-3

Quinta de Aguila, 94

Renaud Redoubt, 27-32, 76, 78, 188
Rendo, 94
Represa, 95,
Retaxo, 95, 96, 183
Rivilas Stream, 99, 100, 102, 108, 120, 122, 124
Robadillia, 21-2
Roleia, 201-2

Sabugal, 1, 2, 12, 94, 183, 184
Salamanca, 2, 27, 41, 44, 82, 96, 182-3, 195-7, 189, 200-3
San Francisco Convent, 27, 40-3, 49, 73-4, 214
Santa Maria Bastion, 102, 124-6, 128, 132, 137, 139, 143, 173
San Sebastian, 198-9
Santa Eulalia, 98
Sanjuanejo, 24
Santarem, 2
Santo Estevao, 94
Sao Miguel de Acha, 94, 183
Serra da Estrela, 93
Sierra de Gata, 21
Sierra de San Miguel, 107
Sortelha, 94-5

Tagus River, 93-6, 183
Tarbes, 201
Torres Vedras, 1
Toulouse, 196-7, 200-3
Tras-os Montes, 10,16

Val de Lobo, 94
Vila Velha, 93, 95, 183
Vilar Maior, 94
Vimiera, 197, 200-2
Vitoria, 197
Vittoria, 196-7, 199, 201-3
Walcheren, 8, 9, 11